W9-ATT-510

BARRON'S

JUNIOR FACT FINDER

Jean-Paul Dupré

JUNIOR
FACT FINDER

An Illustrated Encyclopedia
for Children

BARRON'S

New York • London • Toronto • Sydney

First English-language edition published 1989 by Barron's
Educational Series, Inc.

© Editions Fernand Nathan, 1987.

All inquiries should be addressed to:
Barron's Educational Series, Inc.
250 Wireless Boulevard
Hauppauge, N.Y. 11788

International Standard Book No. 0-8120-6072-5

Library of Congress Catalog Card No. 89-6454

Library of Congress Cataloging-in-Publication Data

Dupré, Jean-Paul.
   [Visa junior, English]
   Barron's junior fact finder/Jean-Paul Dupré.—1st English
language ed.
     p.   cm.
   Translation of: Visa junior.
   Summary: An illustrated encyclopedia exploring topics in
history, geography, science, English, math, and the arts.
   ISBN 0-8120-6072-5
   1. Children's encyclopedias and dictionaries. [1. Encyclo-
pedias and dictionaries.] I. Title.
AG5.D8713   1989
031'.02—dc19   89-6454
                                                     CIP
                                                     AC

Illustrations

Tudor Banus	Steve Wilson
Christine Michaud	Pascale Wirth
Lorna Tormei	Clarie Witt
André Vial	Miro Zupancic
François Vincent	

Cover Design by Milton Glaser, Inc.

Translation by Marguerite and Albert Carozzi

PRINTED AND BOUND IN HONG KONG

9012   4900   987654321

Contents

LANGUAGE AND ITS USES

MATHEMATICS

PHYSICAL SCIENCE

NATURAL SCIENCE

ENGLISH GRAMMAR

ARITHMETIC

A Few Words
for the Young Reader

Books are very useful. The only problem is: they are not always available.

Of course, you can use your parents' encyclopedia, but it may seem just a little difficult. You can also borrow books at school or at the public library for information on history, stories, or documents.

But you can't be everywhere at the same time.

For this reason we have written this book where you will find everything—or almost everything—that you will want to know.

Think of knowledge as a huge garden. Here is math and there is history; over there are geography and natural science; and right there are physical science and English.

Each subject is shown on illustrated double pages. Pictures help you to understand and memorize better; diagrams replace long explanations; drawings let you imagine specific scenes, and maps provide useful data on location.

Thus, in a single volume, you can find the answers to all your questions—those asked in school . . . or elsewhere. An author, a group of illustrators, and an entire team of experts have worked together to tell you the most important things you want to know . . . and even a little more. This is BARRON'S JUNIOR FACT FINDER!

Early Life on Earth

4.5 Billion Years Ago

The earth was at first a fused mass from which toxic gases escaped. Life did not exist. A long period of cooling began. It rained for millions of years.

3 Billion Years Ago

The first signs of life. The first living cells appeared in the oceans. They resembled *bacteria*.

Bacteria

600 Million Years Ago

The appearance of *invertebrates* (*trilobites* were the most abundant) and of animals with shells.

1 Billion Years Ago

The ocean was full of life—*algae, worms, sponges, jellyfish.* They multiplied.

Jellyfish

Trilobite

480 Million Years Ago

The first *vertebrates* appeared—fish. The first fish, known as *Eusthenopteron*, had no jawbones. Its body was protected by a shell.

Eusthenopteron
(29.5 inches long)

Ichthyostega
(amphibian)

200 Million Years Ago

A period of extreme cold caused the disappearance of most large reptiles. Only the most resistant ones were able to adapt to the environment. Their blood became warmer. For about 130 million years, *dinosaurs* occupied the earth. After them, *birds* and *mammals* spread over the land.

Tyrannosaurus
(the largest carnivorous dinosaur)

Brontosaurus
(giant herbivorous dinosaur, 65 feet long and weighing up to 39 tons)

300 Million Years Ago

From sea to land. The first vertebrate ventured out of the water. It was an *amphibian*. The *ichthyostega* breathed with lungs and crawled on the ground. It had to return to the water to lay its eggs. Amphibians were succeeded by *reptiles*. *Dimetrodon* was a carnivore. *Pteranodon* was a flying reptile.

In 1974, the skeleton of an australopithecine was found in Africa. "Lucy" was about 1 meter (39 inches) tall and walked with her back hunched. Her brain was 1/3 the size of ours.

70 Million Years Ago

Dinosaurs disappeared. Mammals and birds multiplied. With the first *primates* the slow evolution toward human beings began.

Pteranodon
(18 to 26 feet)

Woolly Mammoth. It appeared about 300,000 years ago and was hunted by humans.

Dimetrodon
(6 to 9 feet)

Pantothere, ancestor of the marsupial and placental mammal. It was the size of a rodent.

Machairodus
(saber-toothed tiger, with awesome teeth)

Australopithecus

Homo sapiens (humans)

3 Million Years Ago

Australopithecus was the first primate that walked almost upright. He made and used a tool, the *chipped stone*, to kill animals and to defend himself against carnivorous mammals.

The evolution of *hominids* continued. Slowly, humans took on the appearance they have today.

An Overview of History

The Timeline
It shows the various periods in the history of humans.

It is divided into millennia (thousand-year periods) and into centuries (hundred-year periods).

In countries which have adopted Christianity, years are counted from the birth of Christ.

1,000,000 Years Ago

The first people lived in Asia, Africa, and Europe. They made tools from chipped stones and lived by hunting, fishing, and gathering.

800,000 Years Ago
They discovered fire and slowly learned to use it.

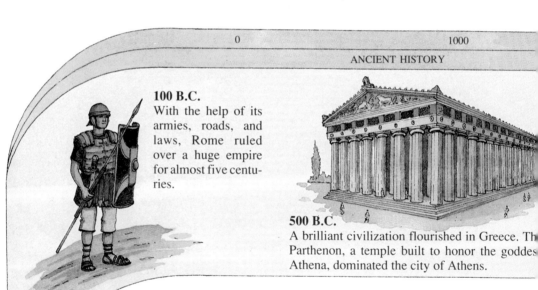

ANCIENT HISTORY

100 B.C.
With the help of its armies, roads, and laws, Rome ruled over a huge empire for almost five centuries.

500 B.C.
A brilliant civilization flourished in Greece. The Parthenon, a temple built to honor the goddess Athena, dominated the city of Athens.

THE MIDDLE AGES

1095
Religious faith caused the people of Europe to go to war to recover the Holy Land. These were the *Crusades*.

1450
The invention of the printing press made books less rare and less expensive.

7000

6000

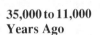

35,000 to 11,000 Years Ago
Tools were improved. People cut and shaped stone better and used the bones of animals they killed.

10,000 to 8,000 Years Ago
They became farmers and raised animals.

2000

3000

500 B.C.
The use of writing marked the beginning of recorded history.

4000 B.C.
(Before Christ)
The first organized societies appeared. Egyptian civilization began in the Nile Valley.

MODERN TIMES

1825
The invention of the steam engine in the late 1700s marked the beginning of great progress, especially in transportation. A steam railway began in 1825.

1969
The first human walked on the moon.

Cave Dwellers

Fireplace

Sculpture of a woman's head made from ivory of mammoth tusks

Horse engraved on a fragment of reindeer antler

Manufacturing of flint tools

Clothes were made of animal hides sewed together.

Wall painting. The artist used 16 different colors made from ground rocks. An oil lamp provided lighting.

The term "prehistory" refers to the long period of time between the appearance of humans on earth and the invention of writing. The Old Stone Age or Paleolithic Period goes back about one million years.

Life in the Caves

Paintings and sculptures, mostly representing animals, were found in many caves in France and Spain. The purpose of these beautiful, lifelike cave paintings is not known. However, it is generally thought that they had some religious significance and may have been part of rituals to bring success in hunting.

Caves were used for shelter only in winter. Their entrance was often marked by a small stone or by animal hides.

Already an Artist!

With the help of very simple tools, prehistoric men and women used ivory for sculptures and reindeer antlers for engravings. By stringing shells, small bones, and animal teeth, they made the first necklaces and bracelets.

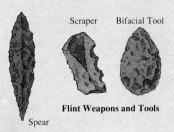

Scraper

Bifacial Tool

Flint Weapons and Tools

Spear

Harpoons

Human Beings Were Nomads

They moved from place to place and lived by hunting mammoths, bears, reindeer, horses), fishing, and gathering nuts, berries, and roots. They first carved their weapons and their tools from wood and flint, and then they became skilled enough to use the tusks and antlers of animals they killed to make spears, harpoons for fishing, and even needles for sewing animal hides.

At that time, people lived in groups of about ten persons.

Hunting the Woolly Mammoth.
With primitive weapons, hunters were not afraid to attack these powerful animals that provided them with most of the necessities of life. They hunted in groups.

During their trips, hunters camped underneath tents made of hides and supported by branches or mammoth tusks. A fireplace dug in the ground was kept burning at the campsite.

They Conquered Fire

Between 800,000 and 500,000 years ago, the life of early humans was transformed by the discovery of fire. They learned how to start and use it. In addition to protecting them against the cold, fire was also used for lighting, for cooking food, and for protection against wild animals.

Villages in Prehistoric Times

The New Stone Age or Neolithic Period: 10,000 Years Ago

A Real Revolution

During this period, human beings made great progress. Tools and weapons were more precisely shaped by polishing. They learned how to work the soil, to grow wheat, and to raise cattle and sheep.

Polished Stone Axes

Stones were polished by rubbing. The *polisher* was a hard rock, often a *sandstone*.

The First Villages

Humans were no longer nomads but *settled* permanent villages. In these early villages, various activities were distributed among people. Some farmed or raised livestock, wh others made tools. Still others wove baskets made sheep's wool into cloth. Some created first pottery for storing, heating, and transport food.

At the top of the hut, an opening was made for the escape of smoke produced by the central fireplace.

Sheep Raising

Beef cattle, pigs, and goats were also raised.

Agriculture
New tools were necessary (sickles, hoes).

The First Pottery

Fishing with Nets

Monuments

Dolmens and menhirs date from the age of polished stone. Dolmens were perhaps tombs and menhirs were certainly built for the worship of gods.

The word *dolmen* comes from two words in Breton: "table" and "stone." Dolmens weighed between 10 and 100 tons.

The Secret of the Menhirs

At Carnac in Brittany (France) stand 3,000 menhirs. The above picture shows how Neolithic people transported and built them.

A Dolmen

(23 to 33 feet high)

These monuments are usually called "megaliths." In France alone, there are 4,500 dolmens and 8,000 menhirs.

Metals

At the end of the Neolithic Age, metallurgy (the refining and use of metals) was begun. People made increasingly hard and efficient tools. They used copper, bronze, and then

Comparison of the duration of the various ages:

1. Age of Chipped Stone
2. Age of Polished Stone
3. Age of Metals

iron. For protection against the new metal weapons, they invented helmets and armor.

Weaving baskets for transportation of goods

In rivers, fish (carp, turbot, salmon, pike) were abundant.

Ancient Egypt

The Gift of the Nile

Egypt is divided by a very long river, the Nile. Every year, from June to October, the Nile overflows, producing a flood that waters the adjacent lands. The Egyptians have cultivated this area of fertile land for a very long time.

The Pharaoh—King and God

Egypt was ruled by a supreme master, the pharaoh. High priest and military chief, he was worshipped by his people as a god, equal to the Sun. Gifts were brought to him and he offered them to the gods. The people built a tomb for him, decorated by magnificent wall paintings and containing precious and familiar objects—everything that would make his afterlife pleasant.

During the course of Egyptian history, there were many pharaohs. Two of them have remained particularly famous:

Amenhotep IV, or Akhenaton, who introduced the worship of one god, the Sun.

Ramses II, the conqueror and builder of many monuments, ruled for 66 years!

The Gods

Egyptians spent their lives cultivating the land. They believed that everything was a gift from the gods whom one had to worship endlessly. These gods resembled both humans and animals. The most important were Amon-Re, the Sun god, Horus, protector of the pharaoh, and Osiris, king and judge of the dead.

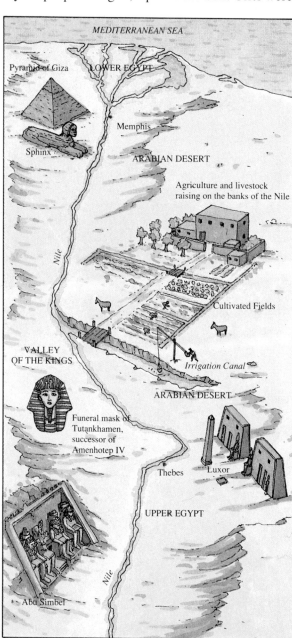

MEDITERRANEAN SEA

Pyramid of Giza

LOWER EGYPT

Memphis

Sphinx

ARABIAN DESERT

Agriculture and livestock raising on the banks of the Nile

Nile

Cultivated Fields

VALLEY OF THE KINGS

Irrigation Canal

ARABIAN DESERT

Funeral mask of Tutankhamen, successor of Amenhotep IV

Thebes

Luxor

UPPER EGYPT

Nile

Abu Simbel

Temple of the Pharaoh Khafre

Hieroglyphics Carved on an Obelisk (Solar Symbol)

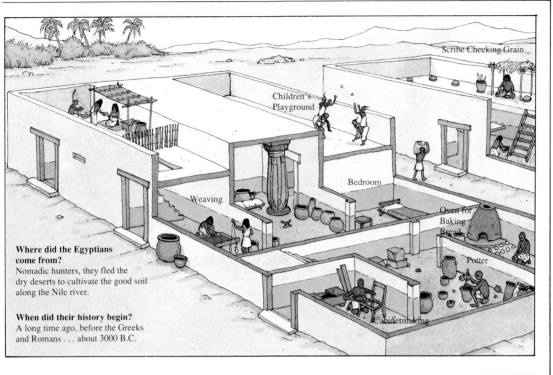

Scribe Checking Grain

Children's Playground

Bedroom

Weaving

Oven for Baking Bread

Potter

Where did the Egyptians come from?
Nomadic hunters, they fled the dry deserts to cultivate the good soil along the Nile river.

When did their history begin?
A long time ago, before the Greeks and Romans . . . about 3000 B.C.

Cabinetmaking

3,000 Years of History

The Old Kingdom, founded about 3200 B.C., had its capital in Memphis. During this age, great pharaohs such as Khufu (Cheops), Khafre (Khefren), and Menkure ruled.

The capital of the Middle Kingdom (2052-1770 B.C.) was in Thebes. The economy began to develop.

During the New Empire (1580-1085 B.C.), Egypt was more powerful than ever during the dynasties of the Ramses. The pharaohs conquered Syria and Palestine. However, gradually, the Empire fell first to the Assyrians, then to the Persians, the Greeks, and, finally, to the Romans during the 1st century B.C.

Hieroglyphics
Egyptians knew how to write. Therefore, we have been able to learn about their long history. They did not invent the alphabet. Instead, they drew sacred images called *hieroglyphics*. Scribes (writers) wrote on sheets of papyrus.

Pyramids, Tombs of Pharaohs
These huge monuments were each built for only one pharaoh who had a funeral chamber inside. In many temples, the statue of a god was worshipped.

Pyramid of Khafre

Transportation of a Huge Statue

The Oldest Civilizations

The Sumerians— Inventors of the Wheel

Sumerian civilization began between the Tigris and the Euphrates rivers, in Asia, about 3500 B.C.

Sumerians were the first to use writing. They knew how to cultivate the soil, how to spin and weave. They were experienced sculptors. They also knew how to melt and work metals. They founded cities. They divided the hour into 60 minutes and the minute into 60 seconds.

They invented the wheel.

The Cretans—Sailors

Cretan civilization started around 3000 B.C. on Crete, an island in the Mediterranean Sea. Its geographic location allowed contacts with other advanced civilizations (Egypt and the Near East).

Cretans excelled in architecture and decoration. Their art influenced the Greek world. They were outstanding sailors. They invented a system of writing about 2000 B.C.

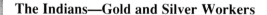

The Indians—Gold and Silver Workers

Indian civilization started in the Indus Valley about 2500 B.C.

Their writing appeared about 2300 B.C. as pictographs (sym-

bols). Indians farmed and raised livestock. They knew how to work metals (gold, silver) and were the first to use the potter's wheel.

The Chinese—Drew Ideographs

The Chinese civilization started in the lower valley of the Yellow River around 4000 B.C. They mastered the technique of

working bronze around 1600 B.C. By 1500 B.C., they used a type of writing consisting of ideographs (each symbol representing an idea or a thing). The first Chinese dynasty was founded by Yü the Great, well after the Egyptian empire, and a short time before the Sumerian empire.

What do we mean by the beginning of civilization?

The change from a primitive society to one in which human beings share work, raise livestock, and cultivate the land.

Where did the first civilizations begin?

In the Mediterranean region, in Mesopotamia, in India, and in China.

And the first nation states?

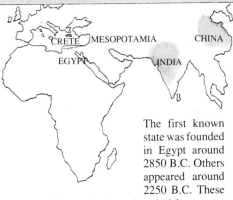

The first known state was founded in Egypt around 2850 B.C. Others appeared around 2250 B.C. These were the Chinese, the Sumerian, the Mycenaean, the Indian, and the Cretan states.

What did they have in common?

In all these civilizations, the people were forced to participate in the construction of great public works—palaces, dikes, the draining of swamps and the building of canals. Many remains of these great works have survived—the pyramids of Egypt, the palaces of Crete, the Great Wall of China.

Athens: The Greek Miracle

Athens

The city, surrounded by mountains, faces the Mediterranean Sea. It was founded during the 10th century B.C. At that time it was nothing more than a rock called the *Acropolis*, surrounded by twelve rival cities.

Athens was named for the goddess Athena, daughter of Zeus, and protector of the city. The Athenian citizen, born of an Athenian mother and father, was the only one able to participate in political life and to own land. The foreigners, or *metics*, were often merchants. Many slaves lived in the city.

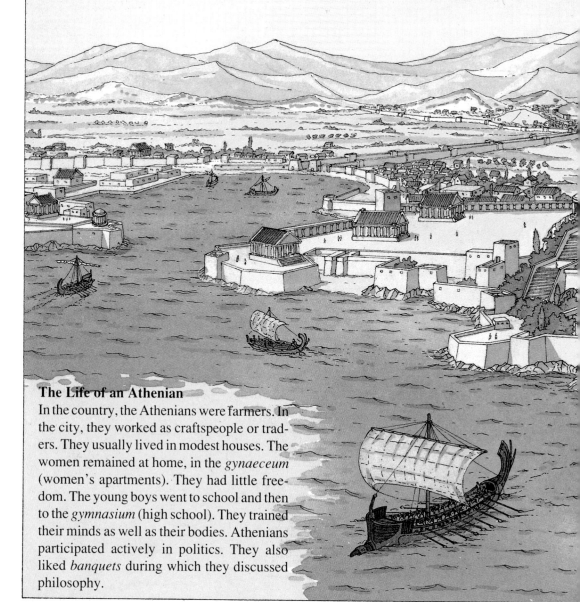

The Life of an Athenian

In the country, the Athenians were farmers. In the city, they worked as craftspeople or traders. They usually lived in modest houses. The women remained at home, in the *gynaeceum* (women's apartments). They had little freedom. The young boys went to school and then to the *gymnasium* (high school). They trained their minds as well as their bodies. Athenians participated actively in politics. They also liked *banquets* during which they discussed philosophy.

Athena

The Acropolis, Kingdom of the Gods
This hill, which dominates the city, was in the past only a fortress. In the 5th century B.C., it was transformed by Pericles into an immense sanctuary.

Magnificent temples such as the *Parthenon*, built in honor of Athena, or the *Erechtheum*, overlooked the city and made Athens the leading city of the Greek world.

Athens and Sparta—Enemy Cities

Sparta was the great rival of Athens. A strict government, an *oligarchy*, ruled the people. The education of young boys was especially strict because they were trained to become warriors.

Festivals
Gods such as Athena were honored during the Panathennea festivals, when a procession of maidens offered her a veil. The god Dionysius was honored during the great festivals held in open-air theaters.

Discus Thrower

Sports
Every four years each city participated in the Olympic Games held in honor of Zeus. Athletes competed in various events—chariot races, wrestling, discus throwing, javelin throwing.

Chariot Race

Athens, the artistic center of Greece, was the rival of this warlike society. In 404 B.C., the two cities fought the Peloponnesian War and Athens lost. It fell into the hands of the Spartan leader, Lysander.

Sea Trade
The Athenians sold the products of their land (oil, wine, figs) and from their workshops (vases, fabrics).

Rome—A Small Town Conquered the World

Legend and Truth

According to legend, Rome was founded in 753 B.C. by two  abandoned twins, *Romulus* and *Remus*, who were adopted and nursed by a she-wolf. This small town of Latium, after having fought its neighbors, in particular the Etruscans, finally conquered all of Italy.

Rome had three successive political systems in its history. These included:

- a royal kingdom in the beginning (until 509 B.C.)
- a republic during its period of conquest (until the 1st century B.C.)
- the Empire during its periods of triumph, followed by decline

Temple of Saturn
Temple of Jupiter
Court of Justice

Paved Square Closed to Chariots

Rome, the Capital of an Empire

After having conquered Italy, Rome gradually extended its rule over a vast empire.

The Roman Empire lasted almost *five centuries*!

The armed peace (called the *Pax Romana*), assured the prosperity of the Empire.

The Roman language, Latin, spread all over the Mediterranean.

Roman Empire

55,000 Miles of Highways

For the security of this huge Empire, the Romans organized a powerful army, the *legions*.

To ease their movements, they built a large *network of highways* (more than 55,000 miles). These highways improved trading between cities.

The Mediterranean Sea, center of the Empire, was an important communication link. Many Romans were sailors.

Tabularium (public archives)
Temple of Concord
Arch of Triumph of Septimius Severus
Via Sacra
m (Stage) for Public Speaking
Roman Forum (western section)

Power and Wealth

Like Athens before it, Rome was the center of important economic, artistic, and cultural development.

With its temples, theaters, public baths, circuses, schools, gymnasiums, gardens, libraries, marketplaces, and elegant villas, it became a rich city that neighboring towns tried to imitate.

The city of Rome was a very busy and exciting place to live. The streets were filled with people, chariots, and animals being brought to market. Outdoor markets were filled with food and goods for Romans to buy.

Ideas and learning were also important in Rome. Philosophers and poets gathered there to discuss the ideas of the earlier, great Greek philosophers.

Market in a Roman city. Merchants were sheltered by arcades. Raised stones allowed pedestrians to cross the street while the wheels of chariots ran between these stones.

Like the Athenians, the Romans were very religious. They adopted Greek gods, adding them to their own gods, but giving them different names. *Jupiter* (the equivalent of Zeus) was the supreme god.

Emperors ruled with absolute power. Upon their death, they were considered gods. Octavius, because of his skill and political insight, became master of the Roman world after defeating his rival Antony at Actium. Under the name of Augustus Caesar, this emperor brought the power of the "Roman Peace."

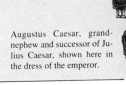

Augustus Caesar, grandnephew and successor of Julius Caesar, shown here in the dress of the emperor.

The Byzantine Empire

Rome Falls and the Eastern Empire Survives

Over the years, the Empire grew weak and it was divided into two parts—the Western Roman Empire and the Eastern Roman Empire. Invasions of the Roman Empire in the West caused it to fall in 476 A.D., and it was conquered by German tribes.

After the fall of the Western Roman Empire, the *Byzantine* or Eastern Roman Empire continued for 1,000 years. The Empire was located at the eastern tip of Europe, in Asia Minor, and in North Africa. The heart of the Empire was the city of Byzantium, or Constantinople, "Crossroads of the world."

Reasons for its long survival were its wealth, its location where Europe and Asia meet, and the strict rule of its emperors. This Empire preserved Roman law and kept alive classical civilization (Greek, Roman and Oriental). Its culture was Greek and Middle Eastern. It became the foundation of the later Russian and Balkan civilization.

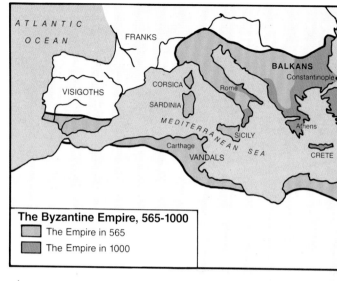

The Byzantine Empire, 565-1000

  The Empire in 565
  The Empire in 1000

A Rich Trading Empire

The Byzantine Empire grew rich through trade and industry. Skilled workers produced silk cloth, gold and silver jewelry, perfumes, tapestries, and fine glass. Merchants exported these luxuries to Italian cities and to Russia. They imported Far Eastern raw silk, spices, and precious stones.

The City of Constantinople

Constantinople was a magnificent city, with paved streets, beautiful homes, churches and palaces, fine parks, museums, libraries and schools. Artists adorned building interiors with brilliant *mosaics*—pictures or designs formed by fitting together small pieces of glass, stone or tile.

Decline of the Empire

For centuries, the Empire battled against various invaders: Lombards in Italy, Visigoths in Spain, Arabs in Africa and Asia Minor, and Turks in the Balkans. The Byzantine Empire ended when Constantinople fell to the Ottoman Turks in 1453.

Ancient India and China

Early Chinese Civilization

An important civilization developed in the Yellow River (Hwang Ho) Valley between 1000 and 200 B.C. Under the Chou *dynasty* (a line of kings from the same family), iron tools, written laws and metal coins were introduced (1000-256 B.C.). China was united for the first time under the Ch'in dynasty (256-206 B.C.). From *Ch'in* came the name *China*. The Great Wall was built to keep out northern invaders. It was 1,500 miles long.

The Rule of the Han

Under the Han rulers (206 B.C.-220 A.D.), literature, art, commerce and good government became highly developed. By 200 B.C., about 30 million people were living in China. They raised rice, tea and mulberry leaves (to feed silkworms). They made porcelain and silks, discovered how to make paper and gunpowder, studied eclipses, and created a modern solar calendar.

Statue of Buddha

Chinese Culture

The system of Chinese writing existed by 1500 B.C. In it, each of thousands of characters (originally pictures) represents a distinct idea or sound.

The Chinese lived mainly in large, close-knit families. The oldest person was the head of the family and he was always obeyed. Loyalty to the family was more important than loyalty to the nation.

For over 2,000 years, the Chinese people have followed the teachings of three wise men who lived in the 6th century B.C. *Confucius* and *Lao-Tse* were Chinese philosophers. *Buddha* was a native of India. Much of ancient Chinese philosophy consisted of written works by and about Confucius.

Confucius

Ancient Chinese art included decorated bronzes and ceramic vases, fine jewelry and figurines made of jade, and landscape paintings. A special Chinese structure was the pagoda—a many-storied, tapered temple with a series of upward-curving roofs.

The Great Wall of China

Ruins of an Early Fortified Indian City

A Carved Gateway to a Buddhist Shrine

Early Indian Civilization

The first Indian civilization developed in the Indus Valley. Between 2500 and 1500 B.C., the cities of Harappa and Mohenjo-Daro were the main centers of this civilization.

The Aryan Invasion

Between 2000 and 600 B.C., the Aryans crossed the northwest mountain passes from Persia, and invaded India. They conquered the people of the Indus Valley. During the Aryan period of rule the foundation of traditional Indian culture was developed. *Hinduism* and *Buddhism*, two of the world's important religions, also developed in this period. *Sanskrit* became the spoken and the literary language of India. The Aryans began a *caste* system of inferior and superior peoples.

Great Indian Empires

The Maurya dynasty, which ruled between 321 and 184 B.C., united much of present-day India for the first time. The emperor Asoka (273-232 B.C.) ruled over two-thirds of present India. As a ruler, he stressed truth, justice, charity, religious tolerance, and non-violence. Asoka became a Buddhist, and sent teachers to convert other people in Asia.

During the reign of the Guptas (320-535 A.D.), India reached its "golden age." There were great achievements in literature, science, art, and mathematics. Indian art included statues of humans and animals, cave-temple wall paintings, and ornate temple architecture. The stories of the "Arabian Nights" were written. Knowledge of chemistry was applied to dyeing cloth, tanning leather, making soap and glass, and refining iron ore. Math in India was advanced. It used the decimal system, the concept of zero, and the symbols for numbers we use today.

The God Shiva

Four Great Religions

2000 B.C.
Shiva, God of
Hinduism

1500 B.C.
The Seven-Branched
Menorah (Judaism)

1000 B.C.

500 B.C.
Buddha

Judaism

Moses descending from Mount Sinai where he received the Ten Commandments

The rabbi reads from the Torah in the synagogue.

This religion was born in *Palestine* 4,000 years ago and was revealed to the Jewish people by great prophets such as *Moses*. The Jews were the first people to worship only one God.

The teachings of Moses are found in the *Torah* (the first five books of the Bible), and contain the *Ten Commandments*.

Passover is a major Jewish holiday that celebrates the freedom of the ancient Israelites from slavery in the Egypt of the Pharaohs.

Religious services are conducted by a *rabbi* (teacher) in a *synagogue* (temple).

Some Jewish people await the arrival of the *Messiah* (a messenger of God), as promised by the prophets.

Christianity

The death of Jesus, crucified on Mount Golgotha

The priest celebrates Mass in the church.

At the beginning of the 1st century, *Jesus of Galilee* was recognized by some as the Messiah promised by the Hebrew prophets. He taught his doctrine to his disciples—love of God, love of one's fellow humans, and forgiveness.

He was crucified by the Romans.

After his death, he appeared to his disciples (Resurrection), who then began to preach the word of Christ throughout the world.

The *New Testament* (second part of the Bible) consists mainly of the *Gospel* which relates the acts and the words of Jesus.

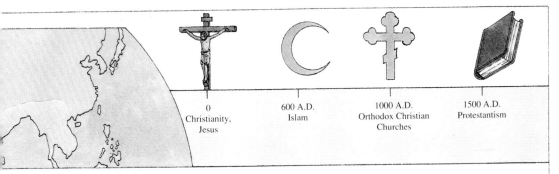

0 Christianity, Jesus	600 A.D. Islam	1000 A.D. Orthodox Christian Churches	1500 A.D. Protestantism

Islam

The angel Gabriel presents the Kaaba (sacred stone) to Abraham.

Praying Arabs turn toward Mecca.

Begun in Arabia in the 7th century, Islam follows a sacred book, the *Koran*, transmitted by *Mohammed*, who was born in *Mecca*.

Islam teaches that Mohammed is a prophet sent by God after Moses and Jesus. Its doctrine teaches the worship of a single God, *Allah*. It requires ritual prayer, fasting, charity, and a pilgrimage to Mecca. The services are conducted in *mosques*. Followers of Islam are called Moslems or Muslims.

Mohammed favored "*Holy Wars*." Those killed in such wars were promised the reward of heaven.

Buddhism

Prince Gautama (Buddha)

A Buddhist Temple

Practiced in many parts of Asia, Buddhism was founded in the 6th century B.C. in India by Gautama, the so-called *Buddha*, or the "Enlightened One."

After the "truth" was revealed to him, Buddha taught his disciples that people must overcome desire, the source of all pain, in order to attain *nirvana* (state of perfect peace).

Nirvana is the giving up of all desires—those who do not reach it are condemned to be reborn in another form, either human or animal. This is called *reincarnation*.

The way to achieve nirvana was to follow the *Middle Way*. This consisted of guidelines called the *Eightfold Path*.

Germanic Invasions

Because of its wealth and mild climate, Germanic peoples were attracted to the Roman Empire. They crossed the northern frontier of the Empire, and tried to settle. Starting in the 3rd century, the Roman legions could no longer defend the Empire's frontiers. The Roman Empire was about to go through a long period of invasions.

Germanic Invasions
(5th century)

Germanic People Invade the Roman Empire

Shortly before 400 A.D., the *Visigoths*, entered the Roman Empire and settled there. In the 400s, other Germanic peoples invaded the Empire: the *Franks*, the *Burgundians*, and the *Vandals*.

As the *Vandals* crossed Rome, they plundered it. The *Angles* and the *Saxons* invaded what is today Britain.

They were skilled craftspeople.
Germanic people knew how to make weapons and jewelry of high quality. Here is a masterpiece by a goldsmith. This jewelry box is made of gold, encrusted with precious stones, and decorated with enamel.

The Roman Empire came to an end in 476 A.D., and Germanic kingdoms were set up in Europe.

Invasion of the Huns (5th century), nomadic tribes which came from the steppes (plains) of Central Asia

The Huns Spread Terror

In 451 A.D., the *Huns*, led by *Attila*, invaded the Empire and terrorized its inhabitants. Roman armies and Germanic people joined to fight them. Finally beaten, the Huns retreated.

According to a Hunnic legend, a shepherd dug up a magnificent sword. He went to Attila's camp and presented it to him. The king of the Huns declared this mysterious weapon a sign from the sky entrusting him with the mission to conquer the world. This is the origin of his nickname, "Wrath of God"!

Arab Invasions (8th century)

The Muslim Empire extended from Arabia to Spain.

The Arabs Waged the Holy War

In the 8th century, the Arabs entered Europe. They tried to spread a new religion, *Islam*, preached by the prophet *Mohammed*. The Muslim invasion was halted by Charles Martel in 732 A.D.

The Vikings Raided and Terrorized Europe

During the 9th and 10th centuries, Vikings invaded Europe. They sailed up the major rivers with fast boats, called *drakkars*. They raided towns and villages throughout Europe and killed their inhabitants. To stop these massacres in France, the king gave them a territory in 911 A.D., which was called *Normandy*.

A few years later, in 1066, the Normans (the Vikings who settled in Normandy) began the conquest of England. The conquest was led by William the Conqueror. He and his Norman forces defeated the Saxons at the Battle of Hastings. William killed the English king, and was crowned King William I of England.

The drakkar was about 80 feet long and 16 feet wide. It held 35 rowers and as many passengers. It could reach a speed of 10 knots (about 11 miles per hour) and was able to navigate in high seas because it had a keel.

GREENLAND NORWAY

NORTH AMERICA ICELAND

Viking Invasions (9th century)

Clovis and Charlemagne

The Middle Ages

The period from the breakup of the Roman Empire to the rise of modern European nations is called the *Middle Ages* or the *Medieval Period*. The first half of the Middle Ages is often called the *Dark Ages* (500-1000 A.D.). Culture and learning almost disappeared in Europe as a result of the confusion and lack of organized government following the barbarian invasions. However, some highlights included the Medieval Church, the Byzantine Empire, and the age of Charlemagne.

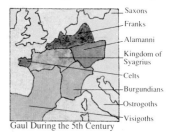

Gaul During the 5th Century

The Baptism of Clovis in 496

Clovis

The Franks were the first Germanic tribe to create a powerful and lasting kingdom during the Middle Ages. Clovis was only sixteen when he became king of the Franks (481-511). A capable military ruler, he conquered the other Germanic tribes in Gaul (France). When he converted the Franks to Catholicism, he gained the support of the Pope and of Gaul's large Christian population. His conversion was due to his wife's influence.

Charlemagne (Charles the Great)

Charlemagne (768-814) was the most important figure in the early Medieval Period. His grandfather, Charles Martel (the Hammer), led the Frankish army that stopped the Muslim invasion of Christian Europe. His father, Pepin, drove the Lombards out of Italy, and gave their lands to the Pope. That area, called the Papal States, was then ruled by the Church for 1,000 years. By conquest, Charlemagne expanded the Frankish kingdom, which had started as a small area around Belgium, into an empire that included most of western Europe.

A Great Empire

In the year 800, Charlemagne was the ruler of a vast territory. On Christmas day in Rome, the Pope crowned him emperor of the Holy Roman Empire. He divided his empire into provinces, each headed by a noble responsible to him. To keep control over them, he sent royal agents to report on the noble's loyalty and ability.

Charlemagne believed in education. The age of Charlemagne has been called "a light in the Dark Ages." Mon-

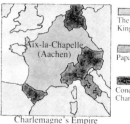

	The Frankish Kingdom in 768
	Papal States
	Conquests by Charlemagne

Charlemagne's Empire

Charlemagne, wearing the imperial crown (closed at the top) assisted at a workshop in which monks and laypeople participated.

astery schools were set up for the children of the nobility, and for children from less privileged families as well. He had scholars collect and copy Latin manuscripts to preserve ancient learning.

Charlemagne died in 814 at the age of 72, after ruling for 46 years. After his death, Charlemagne's empire was split into three parts. The western part was roughly similar in boundaries to modern France. The northeastern third included modern West Germany. The southeastern part included parts of modern Italy.

After Charlemagne's Holy Roman Empire came to an end, *feudalism* came into being. Feudalism was a system of local government, local protection and landholding in western Europe between 900 and 1400 A.D. It controlled much of everyday life for more than 500 years. During the feudal age, government in Europe was local. Powerful feudal lords ruled their own domains. Kings were usually figureheads.

The Feudal System

The Strong Protect the Weak

Under the feudal system, powerful lords provided protection to the less powerful nobles, their *vassals*. In exchange, each vassal pledged allegiance to his lord. He owed him obedience, and his main duty was to help in warfare.

The Lords Went to War

War was their main occupation. When they were not fighting, the knights organized violent games, called *tournaments*, or went hunting on their land.

The Rules of a Tournament

At a given signal, two knights on horseback rushed against each other, spear in hand. Each tried to unseat the other.

Many were wounded; some died. The winner received from the loser his armor and his horse.

A Fortified Castle

It provided good protection to the lord and inhabitants of the land. However, since it was poorly lit and badly heated, it was not a very comfortable place to live.

Peasants Did All the Work

They were the largest group of people. They farmed the lord's land and led a hard life.

Some of them, the *serfs*, did not have the right to leave the land of their master.

Serfs lived in poor huts and often fell victim to famine and disease.

The "Corvee" (a labor tax)
Peasants had the duty to work without pay for the lord at certain times. The life of peasants slowly improved because of technical progress in agriculture.

he Monks Prayed and Studied

fter the year 1000, numerous churches were
ilt in Europe. Religious faith was very im-
ortant.

Bishops lived as lords. The *priests* in the
llages taught the basic religious ideas to
e faithful. *Monks* lived in monasteries
d were the best educated people
that time. They divided their
me between prayer, studies,
d manual labor. Some monks
pied manuscripts.

Manuscript
is a book written by hand. At that time,
rchment made from tanned and rubbed
eep hides was used. These manuscripts are
hly decorated.

The Creation of National States

The Decline of Feudalism

There were many reasons for the decline of feudalism. Many nobles were killed in the frequent wars. The growth of towns and trade, starting in the year 1000, resulted in the rise of a middle class that sided with the kings against the nobles. Increased trade brought new products, methods and ideas to Europe.

Serfdom declined as many serfs fled from the manors to the towns.

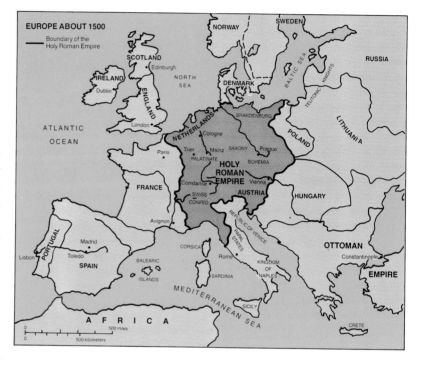

National States in the Middle Ages

As feudalism declined and the power of the nobles lessened, kings began to increase their power.

By the 1300s, after long struggles with the nobility, kings began to regain power, to establish strong central governments, and to win the allegiance of their people. They created *national states* out of feudal kingdoms. Loyalty was shifted from the nobles to the kings. As this happened, nation states were created in Europe.

England was one of the first countries to develop a national government. After the Norman conquest in 1066, *William the Conqueror* (1066-1087) ended Anglo-Saxon rule and forced the nobles to swear allegiance to him. He set up a strong central government. *King Henry II* (1154-1189) started a jury system and improved the courts.

In France, starting with *Hugh Capet* (987-996), capable French rulers took over the lands of the nobility, established royal courts, created a standing army, and centralized the government.

Most of central Europe was joined in a

A section of the Bayeux tapestry which shows the Norman invasion of England.

loose union, known as the Holy Roman Empire, that included the lands that later became Germany, Austria, and northern Italy. Prussia, one of the largest states, expanded its boundaries by conquest, purchase or inheritance, and tried to control this union of states.

Absolute Monarchs in Europe

During the 1500s and 1600s. European kings and queens gained great power. They developed strong armies that took the place of the private armies of the nobles. They took over more territory. Kings and queens created strong royal governments that began to have strict control over the lives of the people. They were known as *absolute monarchs*, that is, rulers who had complete authority over the government and the people.

In England, the popular and able Tudor monarchs built a world empire, and promoted trade and prosperity. *Henry VIII* (1507-1547), and his daughter *Elizabeth I* (1558-1603) also encouraged Renaissance learning.

France became an absolute monarchy under the Bourbon kings (1598-1792). Under *Louis XIV* (1643-1715), France became the leading power in Europe. The palace at Versailles became a cultural center for outstanding writers, artists, and scientists.

In Spain, the marriage of *Ferdinand of Aragon* to *Isabella of Castile* united that nation under their control. In the 1500s, Spain gained a vast empire in the New World from Mexico and the Caribbean islands to Argentina. Spain became rich and powerful.

In eastern Europe, Prussia and Austria became powerful national states. Rulers like *Peter the Great* of Russia (1682-1725), *Frederick the Great* of Prussia (1740-1786), and *Maria Theresa* of Austria (1740-1780) enlarged the size and power of their countries, and brought the nobles under royal control.

Louis XIV

Henry VIII

Elizabeth I

The Crusades

Reasons for the Crusades

The Crusades were a series of religious wars between 1095 and 1291. They were fought to free the Holy Land, Palestine, from the Muslim Turks. In the 11th century, the Seljuk Turks took Jerusalem, and prevented Christian pilgrims from visiting the tomb of Christ. When the Turks threatened to invade Constantinople, the Byzantine emperor appealed to the Pope (head of the Roman Catholic Church) for soldiers to defend his city and to take back the Holy Land.

Pope Urban II called on the nobles and all Christians to join together in a war to win back the Holy Land. Those who took part in the Crusades felt they were doing God's will. If killed, they were promised they would go to heaven. Some feudal nobles fought in the hope of conquest, wealth and adventure. Many serfs went along with their lords because they were promised freedom on their return.

The Major Crusades

The First Crusade, which lasted from 1096 to 1099, was the only successful one. It is known as the "Peasants' Crusade" because many peasants, or farmers, took part. Many of them joined this Crusade because they hoped to see something of the world and improve their harsh lives. Most of them were killed. French and Norman nobles led the army in the Crusade, which captured the city of Jerusalem.

The Second Crusade began in 1147 after the Muslims took back the city of Edessa, which was won in the First Crusade. The Second Crusade was led by King Louis VII of France and the Holy Roman Emperor Conrad III. It was a failure and the defeated armies returned to Europe.

Crusaders were rowed across the Mediterranean in ships called galleys.

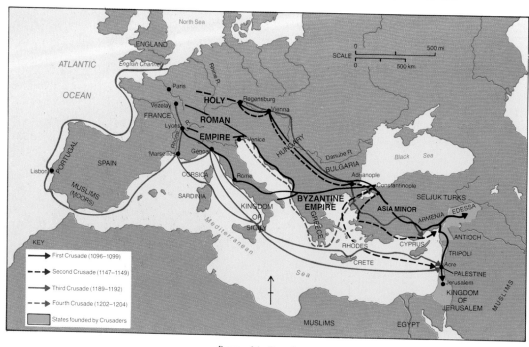

Routes of the Crusades

Crusaders kill the Muslim defenders of the city of Jerusalem.

The Third Crusade was fought from 1189 to 1192 to take back Jerusalem, which had been recaptured by the Muslims. It involved many famous rulers, including King Richard the Lion-Hearted of England, and Saladin, the able Muslim leader.

The Fourth Crusade (1202-1204) was organized by the merchants of Venice. They were not interested in defeating the Muslims, but wanted to destroy the competition for trade from Byzantine ships in the Mediterranean. This Crusade ended when the Crusaders invaded Constantinople in 1204 and set up their own kingdom. It took the Byzantines 50 years to win back Constantinople.

Results of the Crusades

The Crusades had important short-range results. Although the Christians took back the Holy Land for a short time, they failed to regain the Holy Land permanently. The Byzantine Empire was weakened by the attacks of the Crusaders, who looted Constantinople on their way to the Holy Land. Italian merchants and city-states such as Venice and Genoa grew rich by trading with the Crusaders and transporting them by ship to the Holy Land.

There were also important long-lasting results. Feudalism in Europe was weakened and never recovered. Kings increased their power. Many nobles were away from their land, and many lords died in the Crusades. Serfs left the lord's manor for the Crusades or to live in towns because "town air is free air." Cities and towns grew as trade and manufacturing increased.

Finally, Europeans came into contact with new ideas and products from the more advanced Muslim and Byzantine civilizations.

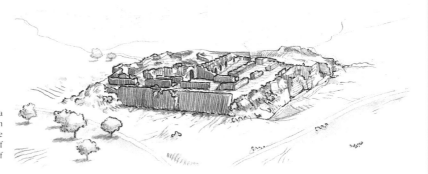

These are the ruins of a castle built by Crusaders in the Holy Land. The castle of Belvoir was on a cliff overlooking the Sea of Galilee.

Medieval Towns

Beginning in the 11th century, greater security on the roads allowed trade in Europe to start again, and towns began to develop.

Towns Were Free

After having been ruled by lords, the towns became free.

Master Potter and his Family   Cabinetmaker

Master Tailor

Each guild had apprentices (beginners), workers, and masters.

Towns were small and surrounded by walls. Merchants and craftspeople had their shops in narrow streets that were often dirty but very lively. Since most of the inhabitants could not read, shop signs had symbols that identified the various trades. Houses were built of wood and fires were common. The towns usually had a small population of no more than 10,000. Paris, at that time one of the largest cities in Europe, had only 100,000 inhabitants.

Burghers (inhabitants of towns) elected a *mayor* and a *council of municipal magistrates* to run the town.

Craftspeople and Merchants

All those who practiced the same trade belonged to organizations called *guilds*: blacksmiths, tailors, and so forth. Each guild had a set of regulations which defined working conditions and set prices and wages.

The Age of Cathedrals

During the 12th century, magnificent churches were built in the large cities of Europe. These were called *cathedrals*.

These churches were tall, bright, and delicately sculptured.

Their construction took a long time. It took 75 years (1160-1235) to construct Notre Dame in Paris.

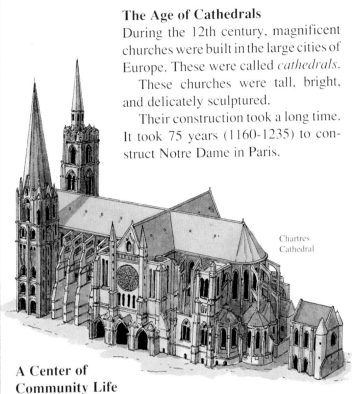

Chartres Cathedral

A Center of Community Life

At that time, a cathedral was not only a place of worship but also the site of meetings, a place to hide in case of danger, and even a shelter for merchants in case of rain. Plays were performed in the courtyard in front of the cathedral. These were called *mystery plays*. Jugglers and acrobats also performed there.

The Age of Great Discoveries

Beginning in the 15th century, great inventions (printing and paper manufacturing, to name two) and discoveries (the route to India, the discovery of America) changed people's lives.

From Manuscript to Printed Book

Two hundred sheep for a manuscript! That was the price paid by the Countess of Anjou. It is said that King Charles V of France tied his books to his desk with a chain for fear of thieves!

Until the 15th century, books were rare and very expensive because months and sometimes years were needed to copy a manuscript.

Printing Shop at the Time of Gutenberg

Gradually, Everything Changed

Then a remarkable new invention, printing, which was started in China, was introduced. At first, books were printed from carved wooden blocks that were inked and pressed on paper. By the 1440s, movable type was invented in Germany. Movable type consisted of small pieces of metal engraved with a letter that could be combined to form words and sentences. They could be used again and again. In 1450 Johann Gutenberg of Germany invented a printing press that used movable type. He was the first to print a book in Europe. Printing spread rapidly.

Invention of paper

The Chinese invented paper in the 2nd century A.D. At first, writing was done on papyrus, a plant whose stem was crushed.

Later it was done on parchments (animal skins). After the 10th century, rags were used to manufacture paper. Today, wood pulp is used.

Cannon Powder and Firearms

The invention of gunpowder (probably in China) led to the use of the first cannons and the manufacture of the first individual firearms.

Adventurers and Caravels

By using the *compass*, borrowed from the Chinese and the Arabs, navigators sailed the oceans in powerful ships, called *caravels*. They searched for new routes to reach the lands that were rich in spices and gold.

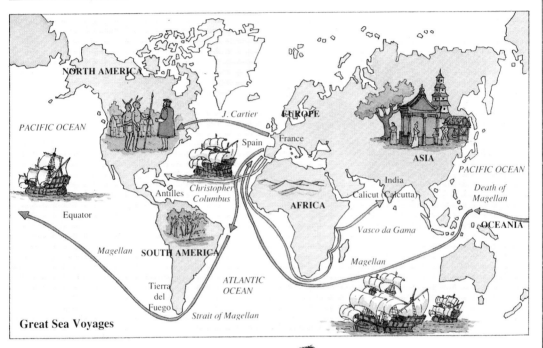

Great Sea Voyages

1492

Christopher Columbus, searching for the western route to India,

1498

The Portuguese *Vasco da Gama* discovered the most direct route to India. He sailed around the southern tip of Africa.

1519-1522

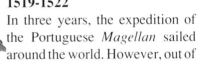

In three years, the expedition of the Portuguese *Magellan* sailed around the world. However, out of the five sailing ships and 234 sailors that left Spain, only one ship and 18 survivors returned. Magellan himself died along the way. This expedition proved that the earth is round.

1534

The Frenchman, *Jacques Cartier*, discovered Canada.

America or India?

Christopher Columbus was convinced he had reached India when he landed on the American continent on October 12, 1492, after 70 days at sea. Therefore, he gave the name "Indians" to the first Native Americans he met.

The Renaissance

The Renaissance Starts in Italy

The word *Renaissance* is French for rebirth. The period from the 14th to the 16th centuries was a time of the cultural rebirth of Europe, and the beginnings of modern times.

The Renaissance began in Italy as Italian writers and artists began to show a new curiosity about human beings and the world in which they lived. Why did it begin here? Starting with the Crusades, trade and commerce grew in the area around the Mediterranean Sea. The large Italian cities such as Rome, Florence, Venice and Genoa grew very rich. Wealthy merchants became the patrons, or supporters, of painters, architects, sculptors and writers. These artists and writers studied the works of ancient Greece and Rome and drew upon them for inspiration. Their creative genius caused the rebirth of a brilliant civilization. Later, the Renaissance spread to northern and western Europe.

Great Artists

Artists such as Raphael, Michelangelo, and Leonardo da Vinci were the creative geniuses of the Italian Renaissance.

The greatest artist of northern Europe was *Rembrandt van Rijn*, a Dutch Master.

Leonardo da Vinci (1452-1519) excelled in many fields, as a painter, musician, sculptor, poet and scientist. As an inventor, he drew up plans for airplanes, submarines, and military weapons.

Michelangelo (1475-1564) was another many-talented Renaissance genius. He worked in Florence and Rome, and was a fine painter, sculptor, poet and architect. He painted scenes from the Bible on the ceiling of the Sistine Chapel in the Vatican. He sculpted the *Pietà* showing Mary with Jesus, and carved huge, lifelike statues of Moses and David. Michelangelo designed the vast dome of St. Peter's Cathedral in Rome.

Renaissance Literature

During the Renaissance, writers began to use their own spoken languages instead of writing in Latin.

Dante Alighieri wrote *The Divine Comedy* in Italian verse.

Miguel Cervantes wrote his novel, *Don*

Quixote, in Spanish.

François Rabelais wrote his satires in French.

Desiderius Erasmus criticized the Church in Dutch.

William Shakespeare wrote all his world-famous plays in English.

The Scientific Renaissance

A *scientific revolution* came along with the Renaissance. The way in which people viewed themselves and the world changed a great deal.

Renaissance scientists emphasized direct observation of nature, and experimentation.

Copernicus, a Polish astronomer, came to believe that the sun, rather than the earth, is the center of the solar system.

The Flemish *Vesalius* advanced knowledge of human anatomy.

William Harvey, in England, discovered the circulation of the blood.

Isaac Newton, also English, showed the law of gravity as a mathematical formula.

These findings were important discoveries in the scientific revolution.

Changes Brought by the Renaissance

An emphasis on reason, a questioning attitude, and scientific experimentation began to replace the medieval concern with faith, authority and tradition.

A spirit of freedom, inquiry, and interest in the pleasures of *this* world replaced the earlier emphasis on preparing oneself for salvation and the *next* world.

By the end of the 1500s, countries on the Atlantic Ocean became cultural centers of the Renaissance. England, France and Spain also spread their literature and learning to their empires overseas.

The Renaissance signaled an end of the medieval world in Europe, and the beginning of the modern era.

America Is Colonized

Why England Established Colonies

- English merchants wished to make profits from trading with colonies in the New World. They imported raw materials—cotton, tobacco and lumber—and sold manufactured goods.
- Overseas colonies were an outlet for the growing English population, and a place to settle dissatisfied religious groups.
- The English rulers wanted to increase England's power and prestige.

The English Colonies in America

By the 18th century, England had established 13 colonies along the Atlantic seaboard of North America. Several more were established in the West Indies (Bahamas, Barbados, Jamaica). By 1763, there were two mil-

The Pilgrims gather for church services.

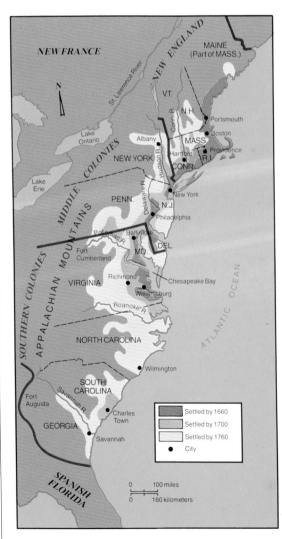

lion people living in the English colonies in America. More than one-third of the population was non-English, including Scotch-Irish, German, French, Swiss, Dutch, and African slaves.

Jamestown, 1607

The first permanent English colony in the Americas was settled at Jamestown, Virginia, in 1607. By 1619, after a shaky beginning, Virginia was a successful colony with a thriving tobacco trade. It had also established the first representative assembly, or law-making group (the Virginia House of Burgesses). In 1619, the first group of English women arrived, as did the first group of Africans. The Africans were later made slaves.

Plymouth, 1620

The Pilgrims landed at Cape Cod, Massachusetts, and stepped onto Plymouth Rock. They left England because they wanted religious freedom. They wished to separate completely from the Church of England (Anglican Church) and have their own church. Before landing, the leaders of the 41 families aboard signed the *Mayflower Compact*. This was an agreement to make "just and equal laws" that they all promised to obey. This compact is the first example of self-government in the New World.

The Puritans, 1630

The Massachusetts Bay Colony was founded in and near Boston in 1630. The *Puritans* who settled this colony wanted religious freedom. They did not wish to separate from the Anglican Church. Instead, they wished to purify it, and so were called Puritans. Their colony grew quickly and was a great success.

The Colony of Jamestown

Other English Colonies

In 1623, the colonies of New Hampshire and Maine were begun. Massachusetts took over Maine and the southern towns of New Hampshire.

William Penn

In 1624, the Dutch founded the colony of New Amsterdam, which included New York and New Jersey. England took over both colonies in 1664. New Jersey became a separate colony in 1738.

Maryland began in 1634 as a colony where Catholics were free to practice their religion. In 1636, Roger Williams left Massachusetts to start Rhode Island. This was the first colony to grant religious freedom to all religions and even to non-believers. Connecticut was founded that same year.

In 1638, the Swedes settled in Delaware. That colony, was conquered by England in 1664.

Individual English proprietors, or owners, who were granted land by the English king, founded the other four colonies:

1665—North and South Carolina. They became separate colonies in 1711.

1683—Pennsylvania. William Penn began a Quaker settlement at Philadelphia.

1733—Georgia. This became a buffer between Spanish Florida and the Carolinas.

William Penn signs a treaty with the Indians.

A Colonial Plantation in South Carolina

The American and French Revolutions

American Colonists Demand Independence

Britain's American colonies along the Atlantic seaboard were separated from the mother country by 3,000 miles of ocean, which proved to be a barrier to understanding and compromise. After the British drove the French out of the Ohio Valley in the *French and Indian War* (1754-1763), the British government wanted the colonists to help pay the cost of that war and they began to tax the colo-

The Boston Tea Party

nists. They also began to control the colonies more strictly. In time, Britain's new policy toward the colonies and new taxes caused the colonists to revolt. The result was an independent United States of America.

Causes of the American Revolution

- Colonial manufacturers and merchants rejected the idea that the colonies existed to make the parent country rich.
- The colonists felt the taxes voted by the British Parliament (law-making body) were unfair. They claimed that since they did not send representatives to Parliament, it was "taxation without representation."
- After living in the New World, many colonists considered themselves Americans, not British subjects. Non-English colonists (Dutch, French, Irish) came from nations hostile to Britain.

The ideas of philosophers like *John Locke* of England, and later *Jean-Jacques Rousseau* of France, influenced colonial leaders. These philosophers wrote that the purpose of government was to protect the rights of the people to life, liberty, and property. They said that when the government failed to live up to its purpose, the people had the right to change or end that government, even by force.

After several years of conflict between Britain and the colonies, compromise proved impossible.

In 1776, the Second Continental Congress, representing the various colonies, adopted the Declaration of Independence. The colonies had to fight the British to win their independence. The American Revolution came to an end in 1781 with an American victory. A new nation, the United States of America, was created.

Democratic Effects of the American Revolution

- The Constitution of the United States (1789) created the basis for a democratic government that has lasted over 200 years.
- The American Revolution inspired the colonies of Spain and Portugal in Central and South America to revolt in the early 1800s, and win their independence. In Europe, it inspired Greece and Belgium to gain their independence by 1830.
- It led to a change in British policy toward its colonies. England granted self-govern-

George Washington

On July 14, 1789, a Paris mob stormed and captured the Bastille, the hated royal prison. In France, every July 14 is celebrated as Bastille Day, or the beginning of French independence It is a national holiday, simliar to Independence Day (July 4) in the United States.

ment to Canada in 1867, and later to most of its other possessions.

In France, the American example encouraged the French people to replace their absolute monarchy in the French Revolution of 1789.

Causes of the French Revolution

The French Revolution was an attack upon the *unlimited power* of the king and nobles in the 1700s. Like most other European kings of that time, *King Louis XVI* ruled as an absolute monarch. The nobility had all the privileges and received the high government positions, but they paid few taxes. The middle class merchants, the poor workers, and the peasants (small farmers) made up over 90% of the population. They did all the hard work and paid most of the taxes, but had no voice in the government.

When the French treasury became bankrupt in 1789, representatives of *all* classes in France formed a National Assembly, which made far-reaching reforms:

- All remaining feudal privileges (of the nobles and Church leaders) were ended.
- The new Constitution of 1791 (France's first) limited the powers of the king.
- The power to make and enforce laws was put into the hands of a Legislative Assembly. Its members were to be elected.

The "Reign of Terror"

In 1791, the French Revolution turned violent and the so-called "Reign of Terror" began. Radical, or extreme, leaders who did not want a king came to power. The king and queen and many nobles were put to death. Order was restored when *Napoleon Bonaparte* gained control of the French government. His wars made him the master of Europe for a time and he carried the reforms of the French Revolution to other parts of Europe.

Washington and the American army retreat.

The United States Constitution

Washington presides over the Constitutional Convention.

The Constitutional Convention

The Constitution was written in Philadelphia in the spring and summer of 1787. The fifty-five delegates at the Constitutional Convention came from every state except Rhode Island. They included some of the nation's most able leaders, such as *George Washington* and *Benjamin Franklin*, the oldest delegate. The Founders made compromises on important points in order to form a government that all could agree to. The Constitution they wrote has been our nation's plan of government for over 200 years.

Important Ideas in the United States Constitution

- The central, or national, government was given certain powers (to coin money, to make war), while the state governments kept other powers (to regulate marriage and education). This division of powers between the national government and the state governments is called a *federal system.*
- The three branches of the national government are *separated,* so that none of them can gain too much power:

the *legislature*, Congress, makes the laws for the whole country;

the *executive branch*, president and advisers, enforces or executes the laws;

the *judicial branch*, Supreme Court and other federal courts, sees that the laws are carried out. The courts interpret, or say, what the laws mean.

- Each branch has certain checks on the actions of the other two branches in order to prevent any abuse of power and to prevent any one branch from becoming too powerful. For example, the Supreme Court can declare a law passed by Congress or an executive act to be *unconstitutional.* That stops it.
- A major compromise at the Constitutional Convention was to form a Congress made up of two houses. In the *Senate*, each state is equally represented and has two senators. In the *House of Representatives*, the number of each state's representatives is determined by that state's population. All laws must be passed by both houses of Congress and approved by the president.
- The *Bill of Rights* is included in the first ten amendments (or additions) to the

George Washington is inaugurated as the nation's first president.

The Declaration of Independence was written by Thomas Jefferson. It has become one of the important documents in history. Its ideas of human rights have inspired people all over the world for more than 200 years.

Constitution. The Bill of Rights was added to clearly spell out the rights of citizens. It prevents the government from interfering with such basic American liberties as freedom of religion, freedom of the press, freedom from unlawful imprisonment, and trial by jury.

Ben Franklin, over 80, was the oldest delegate. Weak and in pain, he often had to be carried to meetings.

Thomas Jefferson could not attend the Convention because he was in France but many of his ideas may be found in the document.

Important American Leaders

Thomas Jefferson, author of the Declaration of Independence in 1776, was not present at the Constitutional Convention. At the time he was serving as the American minister to France. He approved the Constitution, but only *with* a Bill of Rights included.

James Madison is considered the "Father of the Constitution." He kept a careful record of the secret discussions at the Constitutional Convention. He also helped to write the *Federalist Papers*, a series of essays, to answer the objections people had to the new Constitution.

George Washington, military hero of the American Revolution, was the chairman of the Convention, and was elected the first president of the United States. He was "first in war, first in peace, and first in the hearts of his countrymen."

The Industrial Revolution

Numerous inventions revolutionized human life during the 18th and 19th centuries. These changes, which began in Great Britain, marked the beginning of the modern world in the United States and Europe. They were so important that they are called the *Industrial Revolution*.

A New Force—Steam

The *leading principle* is that water in a boiler produces steam. The controlled escape of steam provides a usable force. In the 18th century steam engines were invented. They were perfected and their use became widespread. At the end of the 19th century, their number reached *more than 73,000*.

From Stagecoach to Railroad

The British and Americans constructed the first steam locomotives capable of pulling carriages on rails.

The *railroad* was certainly the most popular invention of the century. By 1850, traveling was faster (almost 32 miles an hour) and more comfortable. Large amounts of goods were also transported. Starting in 1842, railroads were built to connect major cities.

Ships Without Sails and Oars

Starting in 1819, steamships began to cross the Atlantic. They brought the continents closer together and encouraged trade. The crossing lasted about 15 days, whereas a sailing ship took between 30 and 40 days.

The First Factories

Agriculture also used the power of engines, which made farming easier. However, technical progress took place mostly in industry. In countries rich in coal necessary to run the engines, the first *factories* were built and attracted many workers.

Hundreds of poor farmers left their villages for the cities to become *workers*, but living conditions were miserable. They worked 12 to 14 hours a day for low salaries. Even seven-year-old children were em-

The First Factories
They replaced small workshops and represented industrial development. Their number increased rapidly.

Steam Thresher
Steam moved the engine of threshers. Work became easier and faster.

Airplanes
At the end of the 19th century, humans went up in the sky in strange machines.

Ships
The pressure of steam-propelled huge paddle wheels moved ships.

Steamboat, around 1850

The Rocket, 1830

Cars
Their performance became incredible. In 1894, they could travel at a speed of 13 miles an hour. In 1903, they reached speeds of 65 miles an hour.

ployed. Living conditions improved only at the end of the 19th century.

The First Cars

Just before 1900, the first gasoline-powered cars appeared. Coughing and backfiring, they frightened people and their horses. However, motor cars were soon perfected and became a way of life for everyone. The auto industry kept developing better cars.

A Mysterious Force—Electricity

Electrical energy was first used in the middle of the 19th century and progress in developing electricity was rapid. By the end of the century, many machines were powered by electricity. The lighting of cities by gas was gradually replaced by electricity.

Other Discoveries of the 19th Century

1807   *Fulton* built the first successful *steamboat.*

1825   *Niepce* invented *photography.*
        Stephenson built the first successful *steam locomotive.*

1834   *McCormick* patented the *reaper* for farming.

1837   *Morse* invented the *telegraph.*

1846   *Howe* made the first successful *sewing machine.*

1855   *Bessemer* manufactured *steel* from cast-iron.

1859   *Drake* drilled the first successful *oil well.*

1865   *Lister* used *antiseptic* methods in surgery.

1869   *Gramme* invented a machine to produce *electricity.*

1869   *Berguès* produced electrical current by means of a waterfall (*hydroelectric power*).

1876   *Bell* invented the *telephone.*

1879   *Edison* made the first *electric light bulb.*

1880   *Edison* invented the *phonograph.*

1885   *Daimler* and *Benz* produced the first *automobile.*

1888   *Pasteur* produced a vaccine against *rabies.*

1896   *Marconi* invented *wireless telegraphy.*

1890s   *Roentgen* discovered *X-rays.*

1896   *Henry Ford* produced his first successful *car.*

1897   *Ader* constructed an engine-driven flying machine: the *airplane.*

America Develops in the 1800s

Westward Expansion

Americans began to move west from the time of the first settlements. Most were attracted by cheap, fertile land and the chance to improve their lives. After the Revolution, some pioneers settled in the western areas of New England, New York, and Pennsylvania. Others pushed across the mountains and down the Ohio Valley into Ohio, southern Indiana, and Illinois. Western settlement soon brought statehood to Vermont, Kentucky, Tennessee, Ohio, and Louisiana.

Between 1812 and 1861, eastern settlers and European immigrants settled the areas

In New York, the *Erie Canal* (1825) joined the Hudson River at Albany to Lake Erie at Buffalo. This opened eastern markets to farm products from the Midwest and helped immigrants to settle there.

Railroads built in the Northeast between 1830 and 1860 linked the cities along the Atlantic Coast with the cities of the upper Midwest.

Frontier Life

Life on the frontier was primitive, hard and lonely. Most pioneers were poor farmers who struggled to support their families. They lived

Settlers traveling west stop at an inn along the National Road.

east of the Mississippi River. They also crossed into Iowa, Minnesota, the Dakotas, the Oregon Territory, and California. During those years, 17 new states entered the Union.

Internal Improvements

In the early 1800s, poor roads made transportation difficult. This need for improved transportation led the government and private companies to build roads and canals. The *National* or *Cumberland Road* went from Cumberland, Maryland, across the Appalachians to Wheeling (now West Virginia) by 1818. It was later extended to Vandalia, Illinois. Further south, the *Wilderness Road* ran westward into Tennessee and Kentucky.

in crude log cabins (or sod houses in the Dakotas), made their own clothing, furniture and utensils, and had few neighbors, schools or churches.

The Sections

In the 1800s, the three sections, the Northeast, South, and West, developed in different ways. By the 1840s the *Northeast*, the nation's chief manufacturing region, produced textiles, leather goods, iron implements, utensils and machinery. The South and West were a growing market for its factory goods.

The *South* had many small-scale farmers, but was dominated by a small number of

A Slave Auction

wealthy and influential plantation owners. On their land, black slaves raised cash crops—cotton, tobacco, sugar cane and rice—for the market.

After *Eli Whitney's* invention in 1793 of the cotton gin, which separated the cotton fiber from seeds, cotton became king. American cotton production grew from two million pounds a year in the 1790s to 330 million pounds by 1826.

The *West* consisted of small, family-sized farms in the North Central states. Farmers sold their surpluses of wheat, rye, corn and meat to cities in the North.

By the mid-1820s, the three sections held differing viewpoints on various (economic) issues. Because

Abraham Lincoln

of their differences, sectional loyalty began to replace loyalty to the nation.

The Civil War

The biggest conflict between the sections developed over the issue of the *extension of slavery* into new territories and states. The Southern planters insisted upon it. Northern workers and farmers opposed it. After the *Mexican War* (1846-1848), the United States gained a vast amount of new territory. This opened new areas to the possibility of slavery and caused conflict between the North and South. Great bitterness developed. Many Northerners were opposed to slavery on moral grounds. In 1854 the Republican Party was formed, pledged to prevent the further expansion of slavery.

The election of a Republican, *Abraham Lincoln*, as president in 1860, caused seven Southern states to *secede*, or leave, the Union (the United States). They formed the *Confederate States of America*. They claimed the North wanted to destroy both slavery and the Southern way of life. The North and South fought each other in the *Civil War*. The immediate cause of the Civil War was a Confederate attack upon a Union fort—Fort Sumter in the harbor of Charleston, South Carolina. This war was the most destructive in American history, and ended both slavery and the previous Southern way of life.

The Battle of Antietam (1862)

Colonialism

The Race for Colonies

Colonization is the takeover and control of other lands by a given country. It started in the 16th century and increased so much during the 19th century that some countries established vast empires.

Europeans took possession of a large portion of the world in the late 1800s, especially in Africa and Asia.

By 1914, Great Britain ruled an empire containing one-fourth the world's population. France then governed an area 28 times its own size.

The map below indicates the extent of British and French colonialism in 1914, just before World War I.

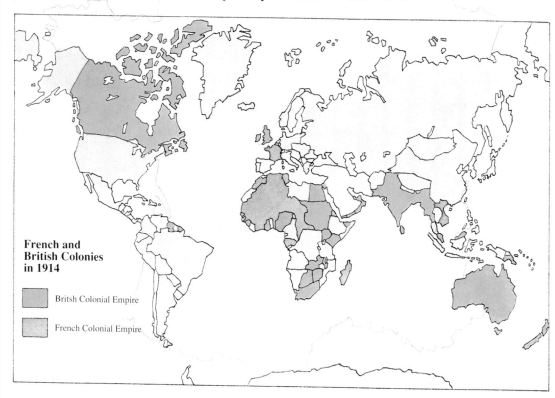

French and
British Colonies
in 1914

British Colonial Empire

French Colonial Empire

Why the Need for Colonies

To assert authority, to exploit the riches of the conquered lands (many types of raw materials), to find outlets for industry and trade, and to "civilize" other people by spreading one's language, beliefs, and techniques.

In 1914, Europe and the United States were the center of the world. Europeans settled many colonies in Africa and in Asia. The United States had colonies in the Pacific.

Gathering of Rubber

Ruins of Angkor Wat in Cambodia

A Missionary in an African Village

of them led to *genocides* (extermination of native populations).

The Partition of Africa

During the 19th century, the African continent was the site of European colonial expansion. Each country tried to carve out its own empire. In 1914, *seven European countries* had African colonies. The largest areas belonged to France and Britain.

Missionaries and Explorers

They often started the conquests. They explored the poorly known parts of the world and tried to convince the native people to put themselves under the protection of their countries.

These conquests were sometimes *peaceful*, but more often they were *violent* (Algeria, Indochina). Some

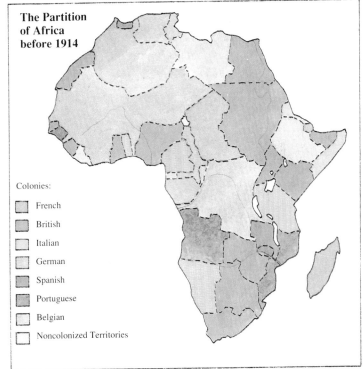

The Partition of Africa before 1914

Colonies:

- French
- British
- Italian
- German
- Spanish
- Portuguese
- Belgian
- Noncolonized Territories

Rafting Logs in Equatorial Africa

India and Canada

France and Britain were rivals for colonies in the 18th century. By 1763 Britain gained control and drove the French out of India, Canada, and the Ohio Valley.

India was the "jewel" of the British Empire. Queen Victoria of Great Britain was proclaimed Empress of India. In 1867, Canada became the first self-governing territory, or *dominion*, in the British Empire.

American Colonization

In the late 1800s, the United States acquired the Midway Islands in the Pacific (1867) and annexed Hawaii (1898). After the American victory in the Spanish-American War of 1898, Spain turned over to the United States its colonies of Puerto Rico, Guam, and the Philippines. The United States then had a colonial empire, and had become an important world power.

1914-1918: World War I

A Shooting Starts the War

The event that led to World War I took place in Austria-Hungary, located in south-eastern Europe. A group of people called *Serbs* lived here but did not like Austrian rule. They wanted to become part of the nation of Serbia. On June 28, 1914, in the city of Sarajevo, a Serb shot and killed *Archduke Franz Ferdinand*, who was to become the next emperor of Austria-Hungary. Four weeks later, on July 28, 1914, Austria-Hungary declared war against Serbia. One by one, most of the nations of Europe entered the war.

The Assassination of Archduke Franz Ferdinand

Why the War?

Two alliances of powerful European nations opposed each other and quarreled for economic and political reasons. On one side was France, Russia, and Britain; on the other side, Germany, Austria-Hungary, and Italy. When Germany declared war on Russia, all their allies entered the war.

August 1914

Germany declared war on France and invaded. Shortly afterward, Great Britain came into the war. British and French troops stopped the advancing German army at the Marne River, near Paris, France.

The Underground Armies

From 1914 to 1917, soldiers lived in mud, cold, and terror, at the bottom of *trenches* which they left only for attacks. The opposing armies' trenches were separated by an area called "No Man's Land," where the fighting took place.

Losses in human lives were enormous.

Soldiers are shown here leaving a trench and crossing barbed wire under enemy fire—shells, grenades, and machine-gun bullets.

700,000 dead in 5 months!
This was the death toll of one of the worst battles in history between French and German soldiers at *Verdun* in 1916.

With neither side able to win a decisive battle, German troops and French and British troops remained in their facing line of trenches.

American Reinforcements
The *United States* joined the war in 1917. They joined allied troops under the French general *Foch* and managed to stop the Germans.

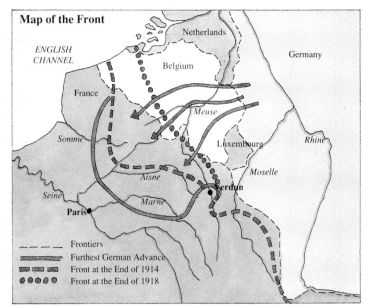

Map of the Front

ENGLISH CHANNEL
Netherlands
Germany
Belgium
France
Meuse
Somme
Rhine
Luxembourg
Aisne
Moselle
Seine
Marne
Verdun
Paris

- – – – Frontiers
━━━ Furthest German Advance
▬ ▬ ▬ Front at the End of 1914
◉◉◉◉◉ Front at the End of 1918

Signing the Armistice on November 11, 1918
Allied leaders (seated at the table) met the German officers who came to surrender in a railroad coach at Rethondes in France.

November 11, 1918
This was the end of the war. Germany signed the *armistice*. The following year, at the *Treaty of Versailles*, Germany had to give up territory and colonies, and agreed to pay war damages.

The Price of War
In four years, at least 10 million soldiers died in the war and 1 million were wounded. Millions of people on the home front also were killed and there was tremendous property damage.

Why did Russia leave the war in 1917?

While there was a stalemate in the trench warfare on the western front, the Germans invaded Russia on the eastern front. Suffering from problems caused by their government, which was an absolute monarchy, poverty, and military defeat, the Russians overthrew their king (the Czar) in 1917, and made a separate peace with Germany.

The World Facing Nazism

Adolf Hitler (1889-1945), called the "Fuhrer" (leader), became ruler of Germany in 1933. He was eager for revenge and conquest.

high prices enabled Hitler to play on the hopes, fears and hatreds of the German people, who felt unjustly blamed and punished for causing World War I. He seized power in 1933 during a world-wide depression.

Dictatorships in Europe

After World War I, dictatorships were established in Russia, Italy and Germany. In Russia, the Communists seized power in 1917. In Italy, *Benito Mussolini* set up a *Fascist* government in 1922. In Germany, *Adolf Hitler* founded the "National Socialist" or *Nazi* party. Too few jobs and sky-

Nazi Aggression

Hitler rebuilt the German army, and announced his intention to take over the countries bordering Germany and, in 1938, Hitler joined Austria to Germany. In 1939, he took over Czechoslovakia.

Blitzkrieg

In 1939, Hitler invaded Poland. Great Britain and France declared war on Germany.

Suddenly, in April 1940, Germany struck and defeated Norway and Denmark. Then, on May 10, 1940, the Germans invaded France,

Europe before November 11, 1942

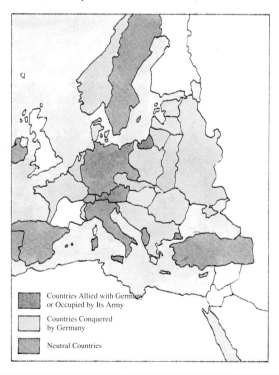

Countries Allied with Germany or Occupied by Its Army

Countries Conquered by Germany

Neutral Countries

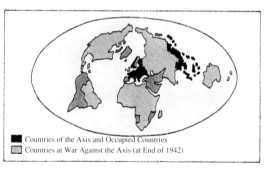

Countries of the Axis and Occupied Countries
Countries at War Against the Axis (at End of 1942)

Belgium, the Netherlands, and Luxembourg. The invasion could not be stopped. In less than 40 days, France was defeated. Only Great Britain remained to oppose Germany.

In the spring of 1941, Hitler invaded the Soviet Union. Germany was now fighting Great Britain and the Soviet Union.

The Japanese attack Pearl Harbor.

The United States Enters the War

On December 7, 1941, Japan, an ally of Germany, attacked the United States. It bombed the American naval base at Pearl Harbor, Hawaii. This "sneak attack" completely stunned the nation and caused tremendous casualties in lives, property, and airplanes. The next day, the United States declared war on Japan. Germany and Italy then declared war on the United States, which had been providing the British with supplies to help in their fight against Hitler.

Concentration Camps

Hitler's police, the *Gestapo* and the *S.S.*, arrested, tortured, and imprisoned in concentration camps millions of men, women, and children, especially Jews, whom the Nazis wanted to kill for racial reasons.

Ten million people died, among them *six million* Jews. As a result of this horrible massacre of innocent people, known as "The Holocaust," the major Nazi leaders were sentenced to death as "war criminals" after the war.

Germany Defeated

In 1941, the war spread throughout the world. The United States and the Soviet Union fought against Germany and its allies, Italy and Japan. On *June 6, 1944*, "D-Day," the British and Americans landed on the coast of Normandy to fight the Germans. It was the beginning of the liberation of occupied Europe.

Hitler committed suicide on April 30, 1945 and Germany surrendered on May 7.

The war ended three months later when the United States dropped the *atomic bomb* on Hiroshima and Nagasaki, in Japan.

World War II had caused almost *50 million* deaths and tremendous suffering and destruction.

June 6, 1944 (D-Day)

With the support of air cover, landing craft brought American, British, and French troops to the beaches.

East-West: The Two Blocs

Occupied Germany

In February, 1945, a conference was held at *Yalta* in the Soviet Union, among the Brit-

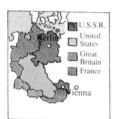

Churchill, Roosevelt, Stalin

ish, the Americans, and the Soviets, to decide upon the occupation of Germany. The German territory was divided into two parts:

in the East, a zone to be occupied by the Soviet army
in the West, a zone to be occupied by American, British, and French armies.

The Western and Eastern Blocs

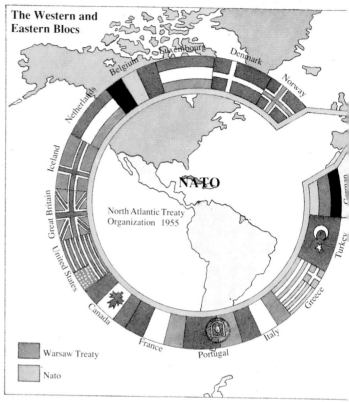

NATO

North Atlantic Treaty Organization 1955

Warsaw Treaty

Nato

The Victors Divide

The four occupied zones in Germany and Austria after surrender

The Soviet Union, the center of communism, extended its influence over a large part of eastern Europe. The dividing line was called the "Iron Curtain."

The United States, to prevent further communist expansion, gave financial help to the countries of western Europe to help them recover from the war.

From then on, two blocs, the Soviet and the Western bloc, opposed each other, and the danger of a new world war threatened the world.

The United Nations

The United Nations (U.N.) was founded on July 26, 1945 to avoid new wars and to encourage international cooperation. Its headquarters are in New York City. Today, 158 countries are members of the U.N. It can send troops, supplied by member nations, to troubled areas to restore order.

A U.N. health agency, WHO, has helped wipe out smallpox. UNICEF, the U.N. Children's Fund, has helped millions of underprivileged children.

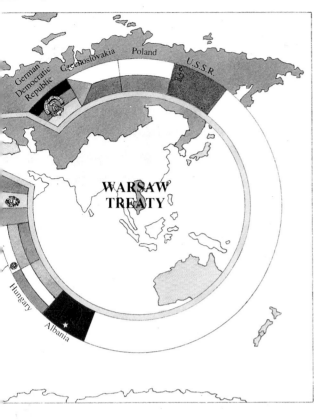

WARSAW TREATY

military defense treaty. Others joined later.

Similarly, in 1955, seven eastern European countries, including Poland, Hungary, East Germany, Rumania, and Bulgaria, signed a treaty of military alliance with the Soviet Union.

The blocs have never fought directly. However, they have supported opposing sides in wars in the Third World of developing nations.

A Wall 27 Miles Long

Constructed in 1961 by the authorities of East Germany, this wall divides Berlin in two, preventing the people of

What Is the "Cold War"?

It is a political and economic rivalry that began after World War II between the two superpowers, the Soviet Union and the United States. Today, the two nations have begun to work together and have signed a treaty to limit some weapons. However, tension and distrust still remain.

In 1949, 12 countries of the Western bloc signed a

East Berlin from going to the West. This wall is the symbol of the opposition between the two blocs.

Tchernenko Brezhnev Nixon Boumedienne Kadhafi Reagan Mitterrand Gorbachev

Tse-tung De Gaulle Hussein Pompidou Golda Meir Arafat Thatcher Pope John-Paul II

Major Changes in the Post-War World

The End of Western Colonialism
After World War II, the colonial peoples of Asia and Africa demanded and obtained freedom from European rule. From 1950 to 1970, more than 35 newly independent nations emerged in Africa. Today, white control exists only at the southern tip of Africa in the Republic of South Africa.

The Vietnam War
In Vietnam, which is located in southeast Asia, first France (1946-1954), then the United States (1954-1973) opposed a communist-led independence movement. The result was a long and costly war which the United States was not able to win. In the *Vietnam War* 46,000 Americans were killed and 300,000 wounded. About $140 billion was spent on this war, which severely divided the American people. It caused terrible hardship and thousands of deaths in Vietnam, Laos and Cambodia (formerly French Indochina).

The Marshall Plan (1948-1952)
Undamaged by World War II, the United States developed a generous program of economic aid to help the European nations (including its former enemies, Germany and Italy) recover from wartime destruction. This program, the *Marshall Plan*, sought to improve living standards, reestablish European trade with America, and lessen the danger of the spread of communism in western Europe. It also encouraged cooperation among the European nations, and helped build the trust needed to form the European Economic Community (Common Market).

Abuse of the Environment
The *greenhouse effect* is a general warming of temperatures on earth, along with drier conditions. It is the result of the loss in the

Europe lay in ruins after the war.

An Atomic Explosion

ozone layer over the earth. This thinning of ozone is caused by burning fossil fuels like coal and gasoline products, fluorocarbons used in spray cans and air conditioners, and by rapid cutting down of forests. If allowed to continue it may cut down the world's food supply and lead to floods along our low-lying coastlines.

Rain forests such as those in Brazil and southeast Asia, contain two-thirds of the known species of plants and animals on earth. In 1988, an area of the Amazon rain forest equal to the size of Nebraska was purposely burned. This rapid loss of the rain forests is a serious problem. Cutting down the trees means less oxygen in the environment. Also, some of the plants there may be the key to our future survival.

The first person walks on the moon.

Refugees

Wars and natural disasters have made millions of persons *refugees*—individuals who have lost their homes and who need help to rebuild their shattered lives. Recent wars in Afghanistan, southeast Asia, and the Middle East have created countless refugees. In Indochina, since 1975, more than one million Vietnamese, Cambodians, and ethnic Chinese have had to flee for their lives.

Hô-Chi Minh

Spread of Nuclear Weapons

In the 1950's, only the United States and the Soviet Union had atomic bombs. In 1968 those two nations agreed on a treaty limiting the spread of nuclear weapons.

Unfortunately, the arms race between America and the Soviet Union has continued. Moreover, other nations have obtained nuclear weapons and Third World nations have paid industrial powers to provide them with nuclear plants, fuel and technology. Some are also trying to build nuclear bombs.

Terrorism

Extremist groups have used modern technology as well as crude weapons in terrorist attacks—deliberate violence against innocent civilians—to further their political goals. This has included hijacking and blowing up airplanes, and murdering diplomats, Olympic athletes and school children. The governments of Libya, Syria and Iran have been accused of aiding terrorist groups.

Emerging World Powers

After 1945, there began great economic growth everywhere in the world. New partners appeared ready to join the three economic and commercial powers—the United States, the Soviet Union, and Europe.

The Japanese Miracle

Defeated and ruined in 1945, Japan began an extraordinary industrial growth and twenty years later, it became the third economic power in the world!

Because of its population—about 120 million inhabitants—Japan has a vast market and a large pool of skilled workers. Its production in machinery, optics, and electronics is exported in great quantity.

Hitachi, Toyota, Mitsubishi, Honda—these brand names have become familiar to the Western world since the Japanese started to produce television sets, videotape recorders, stereo equipment, motorcycles and automobiles.

However, Japan is confined to a very small living space of 145,856 sq. mi. and must fight continuously against pollution caused by its vast industries. Korea, Japan's neighbor, is becoming another industrial power in Asia.

A Robot in Action
One of the marvels of Japanese electronics. A camera reads the screen and transmits orders to mechanical hands which press the keys of the keyboard.

NORTH AMERICA

SOUTH AMERICA

Brazil: Its Power and Its Weakness

Once a Portuguese colony, this country, *almost as large* in area as the United States, is populated by *125 million inhabitants*. It witnessed fast changes after 1965. Cities developed following the American model and large industries were created.

Agriculture and cattle raising occupy immense newly-cleared lands.

However, profits of this extraordinary economic growth are poorly distributed and *4 out of 10 Brazilians go hungry!*

Ever since 1980, Brazil has known a severe crisis. Today it is one of the countries with the highest foreign debt in the world. Its economy is in urgent need of reorganization: 50% of all lands which could be used for agriculture are still unused; they represent the greatest reserve in the world. However, burning areas of the Amazon jungle to clear the land has destroyed plant species, animal habitat, and the ozone in the atmosphere.

Land of Contrast
These hovels (called *favelas*) are adjacent to modern buildings in the rich section of the city.

The Birth of a Giant: China

China, with *one billion inhabitants* in a huge nation, gradually became modernized. Until 1949, constant warfare held back its development and caused it to fall behind other industrial countries. After 1949, China, led by Mao Tse-tung, became a communist nation. In 1958, it broke off relations with the Soviet Union and followed its own ideas. However, progress did not come overnight because, besides some modern industrial techniques, China still kept many traditional ones. Furthermore, China counted only upon its own power to exploit its important natural riches.

More than a billion persons marching toward progress!

After the death of Mao, China adopted a more open policy toward the world and increased its commercial ties. Since 1979, diplomatic and trade ties between the United States and China have been restored.

ASIA

OPE

AFRICA

India: The Will to Succeed

This very heavily populated land of *775 million inhabitants*—one billion is forecast for the year 2000—changed very slowly.

Although agricultural methods have become increasingly modern, India is still part of the Third World and suffers great hunger and poverty. Overpopulation and the export of most of its farm products are the principal causes of these problems. Efforts are being made to overcome these difficulties. Being careful to keep its neutrality, India has nevertheless accepted help from the great industrial powers.

Hindi is the official language. English and sixteen regional languages are recognized by the Indian Constitution. Some 4,000 languages and unofficial dialects also are spoken in India.

A Very Slow Industrialization
Only the military sector enjoys important technical advances.

Who was Gandhi?

Called the "Mahatma," "the Great Soul," he led the fight against the British for independence and preached "non-violence." He was murdered in 1948. He inspired the non-violent U.S. civil rights movement in the 1960s.

Technological Revolution

Since 1945, many discoveries and important technological advances have revolutionized human life.

Life Span Has Been Lengthened

Medicine has made great breakthroughs. *Vaccines* have been discovered to eliminate and prevent dangerous diseases, such as tuberculosis, tetanus, and polio. New medications, such as *antibiotics*, bring relief to many sick people. The first *organ transplants* (heart, kidneys) were tried and succeeded.

A CAT Scan
This is a device for examining a body, an organ, or a tissue for exact information about their functioning.

Machines Replace Humans

Thanks to *automation*, work has become easier. Agriculture and industry have been modernized. The first "*robots*" have appeared.

Computers, capable of solving very complicated problems in a few seconds, represent a new stage in this development.

Automated Assembly Line
This robot alone solders pieces together.

Peaceful Atoms

Atomic power is not only used for destruction. Today, great *nuclear plants* use atomic energy to produce electricity.

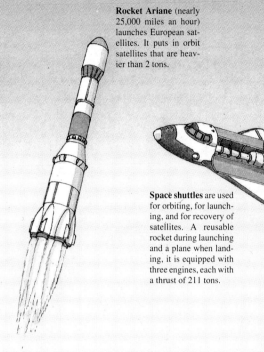

Rocket Ariane (nearly 25,000 miles an hour) launches European satellites. It puts in orbit satellites that are heavier than 2 tons.

Space shuttles are used for orbiting, for launching, and for recovery of satellites. A reusable rocket during launching and a plane when landing, it is equipped with three engines, each with a thrust of 211 tons.

Nuclear Plant
Atomic energy plants have helped replace the burning of fossil fuels (coal and oil), which pollute the atmosphere.

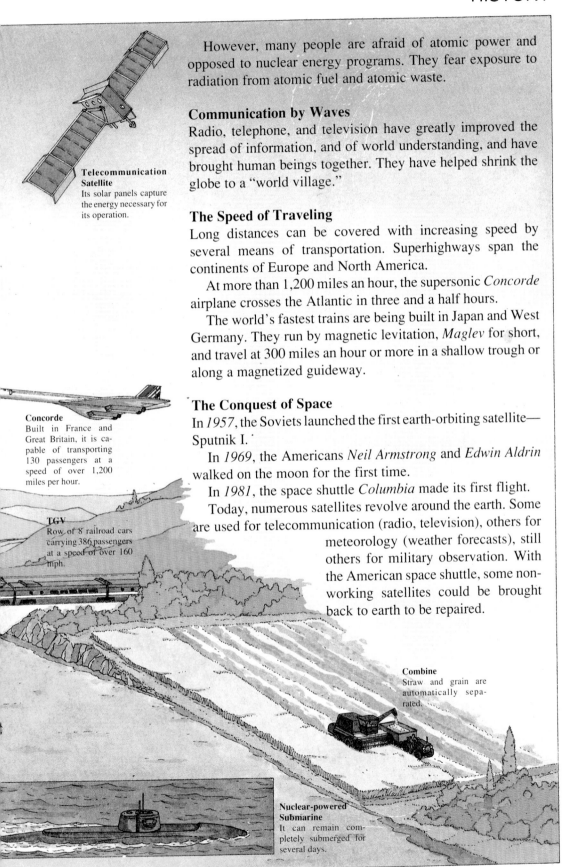

However, many people are afraid of atomic power and opposed to nuclear energy programs. They fear exposure to radiation from atomic fuel and atomic waste.

Communication by Waves

Radio, telephone, and television have greatly improved the spread of information, and of world understanding, and have brought human beings together. They have helped shrink the globe to a "world village."

The Speed of Traveling

Long distances can be covered with increasing speed by several means of transportation. Superhighways span the continents of Europe and North America.

At more than 1,200 miles an hour, the supersonic *Concorde* airplane crosses the Atlantic in three and a half hours.

The world's fastest trains are being built in Japan and West Germany. They run by magnetic levitation, *Maglev* for short, and travel at 300 miles an hour or more in a shallow trough or along a magnetized guideway.

The Conquest of Space

In *1957*, the Soviets launched the first earth-orbiting satellite— Sputnik I.

In *1969*, the Americans *Neil Armstrong* and *Edwin Aldrin* walked on the moon for the first time.

In *1981*, the space shuttle *Columbia* made its first flight.

Today, numerous satellites revolve around the earth. Some are used for telecommunication (radio, television), others for meteorology (weather forecasts), still others for military observation. With the American space shuttle, some non-working satellites could be brought back to earth to be repaired.

Telecommunication Satellite
Its solar panels capture the energy necessary for its operation.

Concorde
Built in France and Great Britain, it is capable of transporting 130 passengers at a speed of over 1,200 miles per hour.

TGV
Row of 8 railroad cars carrying 386 passengers at a speed of over 160 mph.

Combine
Straw and grain are automatically separated.

Nuclear-powered Submarine
It can remain completely submerged for several days.

Human Rights Today

In 1948, the General Assembly of the United Nations adopted the *Universal Declaration of Human Rights*. It was inspired by the American *Bill of Rights* and the French *Declaration of the Rights of Man*.

Although the ideals expressed will not soon be realized throughout the world, they provide a "standard of achievement for all peoples and all nations," including the 158 member nations of the U.N.

The flag of the U.N. symbolizes peace in the world.

The Declaration states that all human beings are born free and equal, and are entitled to:
- *civil rights*: life, liberty, freedom of religion, speech and assembly; and a voice in their government
- *legal rights*: freedom from arrest without cause, and the right to a fair trial
- *economic rights*: a job, enough to live on, private property, and leisure time
- *social rights*: an education, and a cultural life.

Distinction Between Races

The idea of a superior race is a violation of article 2 of the Declaration. *Racism* is an attitude of hostility or persecution toward individuals of different races. In the name of that difference, Nazis killed *millions of human beings* during World War II.

Today, in the Republic of South Africa, a white government rules over the black majority of the country with a policy of *apartheid*, that is of "separate development." Black and white Africans have different rights and blacks are treated as "second class citizens."

Imprisoned Because of Their Opinions

The Declaration of Human Rights says in article 2 that freedom of political opinion and religion must be respected.

However, in some countries, especially those ruled by dictators, these freedoms are not recognized. Those opposed to the government are hunted down and imprisoned. Sometimes they are killed.

Many people are forced to flee their own country for political and economic reasons.

Amnesty International

Founded in 1961 by an English lawyer, *Peter Benenson*, this independent organization works closely with governments and tries to arouse international opinion in its fight against the death penalty and all forms of torture. It brings help and assistance to victims imprisoned because of their ideas, their beliefs, or their origin.

Since its founding, more than *7,000 prisoners* were set free because of the intervention of Amnesty International. Every year, it publishes a report denouncing governments that do not respect human rights.

The Red Cross

This humanitarian organization was founded in 1863 by the Swiss *Henri Dunant* to help war casualties regardless of nationality. The Red Cross intervenes today in many fields—catastrophies, helping the elderly, the handicapped, and the refugees (International Committee of the Red Cross).

Torture

Even today, bodily violence is used against certain prisoners to punish them or to pressure them to admit to, denounce, or give up their ideas.

These barbaric practices are condemned by most large states.

This poster symbolizes hope for freedom.

UNESCO

(United Nations Educational, Scientific, and Cultural Organization).

This is one of the many agencies of the U.N. It works to maintain peace by encouraging cooperation among nations in education, science, and culture. To carry out that purpose, it developed a worldwide program to *teach reading and writing*, thus responding to article 26 of the Universal Declaration of Human Rights: "Everyone has the right to an education."

The permanent headquarters of UNESCO are in Paris.

Children learn reading and writing in an African village.

Even in Democratic Nations

Every democracy must be careful to see that racism does not develop among its own population. Humanitarian movements, such as the National Conference of Christians and Jews, are in charge of this task. Human rights are very fragile and always in danger of being jeopardized.

Planet Earth

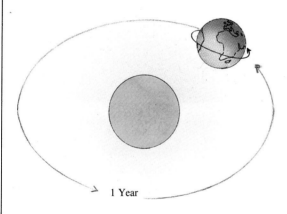

1 Year

Important Facts

Only a small blue dot in the universe, the earth was born about 4.6 billion years ago.

Shaped like a ball that is slightly flattened at the poles, its circumference (width around) at the Equator is about 25,000,000 miles.

It weighs 6.6 trillion tons. Its surface is 196,950,000 square miles and its volume is 260,000,000,000 (billion) cubic miles.

The earth turns on its axis from west to east in 23 hours, 56 minutes, and 4 seconds.

At the same time, it orbits (circles) the sun in 365 days and 6 hours, thus traveling 581.25 million miles at a speed of almost 67,000 miles per hour (over 18.6 miles per second!).

Distinctive Feature: life exists on earth. Our planet contains 5 billion inhabitants (world census of July 8, 1986).

The Lines of the Earth

Imaginary lines help to locate where we are on earth.

The *Equator* divides our globe into two hemispheres— the Northern Hemisphere and the Southern Hemisphere.

Lines running parallel to the Equator are called *parallels of latitude*.

Lines joining the *North* and *South Poles* are called *meridians of longitude*.

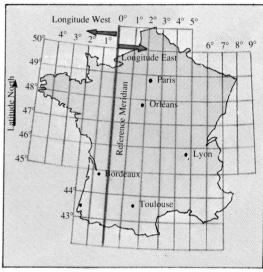

The grid formed by the intersection of parallels and meridians provides the precise location of a particular place.

The *latitude* of a place is the distance between the parallel on which its particular measurement is taken and the Equator.

The *longitude* of a place is the distance between the meridian on which its particular measurement is taken and some reference meridian such as that of Greenwich, or meridian 0°.

Latitude and longitude are measured in degrees.

Any place on earth can be located exactly by its latitude and longitude. These are the *geographical coordinates*.

Geographical coordinates of Paris:
48° 50 latitude north.
2° 20 longitude east.

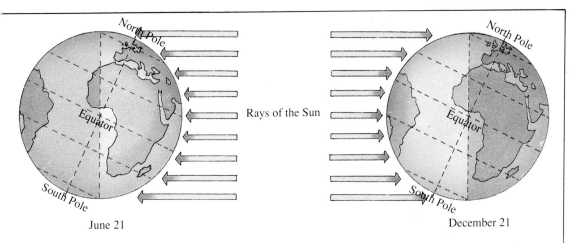

June 21   Rays of the Sun   December 21

Day and Night

The rotation of the earth on its axis (once every 24 hours) and its revolution around the sun gives us day and night.

All through the year, their length varies. In the Northern Hemisphere, the longest day is on June 21 and the shortest day is on December 21. In the Southern Hemisphere, it is the other way around.

The Seasons

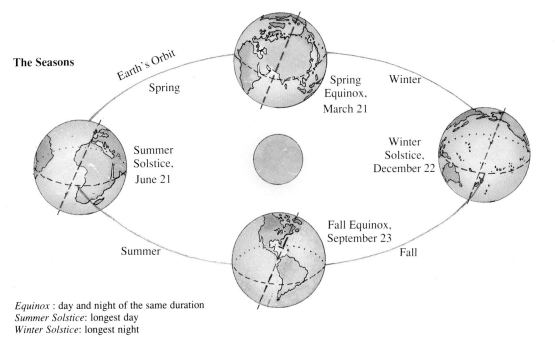

Equinox : day and night of the same duration
Summer Solstice: longest day
Winter Solstice: longest night

From One Season to the Other

Because of its revolution around the sun, the amount of the sun's rays that the earth receives changes according to its position. This explains the change in seasons. The shorter the distance crossed by the sun's rays in the atmosphere, the warmer the climate and vice versa.

Since the earth turns on a tilted axis, it is alternatively the Northern and then the Southern Hemisphere which is tilted toward the sun and receives most of the heat.

Time Around The World

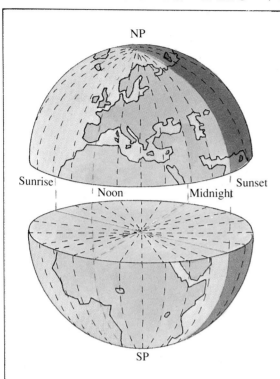

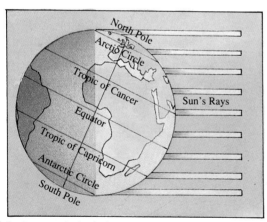

Sun's rays at the beginning of summer (June 21)

What Is Solar Time?

Each position of the sun in the sky corresponds to a precise time— solar time —which is the same for all places located on the same half-circle passing by the poles, the *meridian*.

Same Time All Over the Earth?

Impossible! Because of the rotation of the earth, the sun does not rise at the same time at all points on the globe.

Time Zones

The world is divided into 24 basic *time zones*. The illustration shows these time zones. Each zone is one hour earlier or one hour later than the one next to it.

Meridians of Longitude

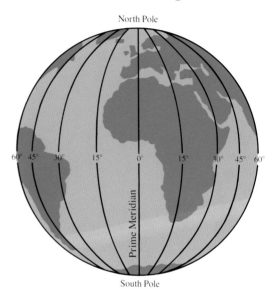

Since the day contains 24 hours, the earth's sphere of 360° is divided into 24 parts. The rotation of the earth pushes it through 15° of longitude each hour. The Prime Meridian (0°) was chosen to be the starting position in the 24-hour day. Thus, when it is noon at 0° longitude, it is 1 PM at 15° East, 2 PM at 30° East, and so forth. It is one hour earlier at 15° West and so on. When it is 4 AM in Los Angeles, it is 5 PM in Bombay, India.

Time in different parts of the world is measured from the Prime Meridian or the Greenwich Meridian, located near London. The time there is called G.M.T. (Greenwich Mean Time).

Each time zone is bounded by two meridians. The territories belonging to the same time zone have the same time— *standard time*. Time Zones generally follow national boundaries.

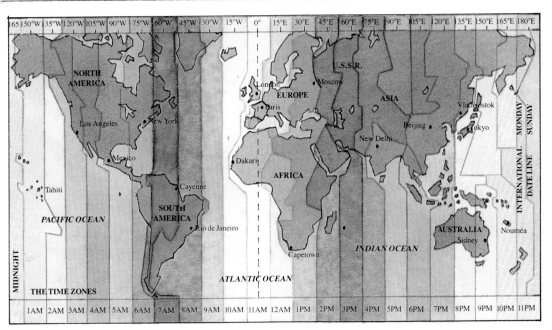

165°150°W 135°W 120°W 105°W 90°W 75°W 60°W 45°W 30°W 15°W 0° 15°E 30°E 45°E 60°E 75°E 90°E 105°E 120°E 135°E 150°E 165°E 180°E

NORTH AMERICA

Los Angeles

New York

Mexico

Tahiti

PACIFIC OCEAN

SOUTH AMERICA

Cayenne

Rio de Janeiro

London
EUROPE
Paris

Moscow

U.S.S.R.

ASIA

Vladivostok

Beijing

Tokyo

New Delhi

Dakar

AFRICA

Capetown

ATLANTIC OCEAN

INDIAN OCEAN

AUSTRALIA
Sidney

Nouméa

INTERNATIONAL DATE LINE

MONDAY

SUNDAY

MIDNIGHT

THE TIME ZONES

1AM 2AM 3AM 4AM 5AM 6AM 7AM 8AM 9AM 10AM 11AM 12AM 1PM 2PM 3PM 4PM 5PM 6PM 7PM 8PM 9PM 10PM 11PM

Clock and sundial on the front of an old house. The sundial indicates solar time

Always Be On Time!

When changing from one time zone to another, the time on one's watch has to be changed as follows:

- It is set *back* by one hour when moving west (against the rotation of the earth).
- It is *set ahead* by one hour when moving east (with the rotation of the earth).

Planes and Time Changes

Examples of flights of the *Concorde*:
1. Paris–New York (the plane flies westward)
   Departure from Paris: 11:00 A.M. Arrival New York: 8:45 A.M.
2. New York–Paris (the plane flies eastward)
   Departure from New York: 1:00 P.M. Arrival Paris: 10:45 P.M.

What Is A Sundial?
Invented by an ancient Greek scholar around the 6th century B.C., the sundial consists of a fixed rod and a flat surface that is divided into 24 parts. Each part corresponds to an hour and there are 15° triangles, each one representing the 24th portion of the circumference (360°). The shadow cast by the sun indicates time.

Is it true that certain countries have several time zones?
Yes, it is true for large countries. The United States has 7 time zones, and the U.S.S.R. has 11 time zones.

Further complications!
For economic reasons (in particular to save electricity) certain countries do not use the actual time of their time zone. The United States, for instance, sets its standard time ahead by one hour from May to October and observes "daylight savings time."
    Sundials indicate solar time, that is true local time.
    Watches indicate standard time.

The World We Live In

Waters of the World

More that two-thirds of the earth's surface is covered by water.

This huge amount of water consists of four great oceans that are interconnected:

- the Atlantic Ocean
- the Pacific Ocean
- the Indian Ocean
- the Arctic Ocean

and numerous other seas which are smaller and shallower, and flow into the oceans such as:

- the Caribbean Sea
- the Mediterranean Sea
- the North Sea
- the Red Sea

or totally enclosed:

- the Caspian Sea
- the Aral Sea

The Earth's Land Surface

About one fourth of the earth's surface is land. The land is in large areas called *continents*. They are:

ARCTIC OCEAN

ASIA

AMERICA

PACIFIC

OCEAN

PACIFIC ISLANDS

AUSTRALIA

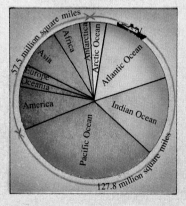

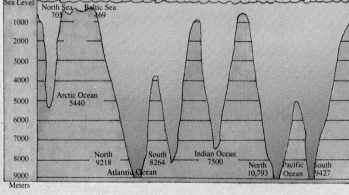

- *Europe* and *Asia* which make up *Eurasia*
- *Africa*
- *North America* and *South America* which make up the *American* continent
- *Antarctica*
- *Oceania* which includes Australia and the islands of the Pacific

1/10th of all the earth's land above water is covered by ice.

High Mountains and Great Depths

The surface of the earth above and below the water displays many similarities— deep valleys, mountain chains, plains, and plateaus.

Islands are emerged summits of gigantic underwater mountains.

The greatest difference of relief occurs in the ocean depth (Marianna Trench: 36,000 feet below sea level) and surpasses the record of the "top of the world" (Mount Everest: 29,028 feet, or 5.5 miles above sea level, in the Himalayas.

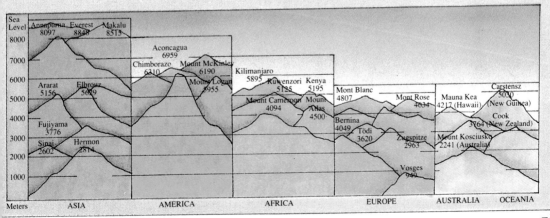

The Climates of the Earth

Variable Heat of the Sun

The movements of the earth, its spherical shape, and the tilt of its axis, all cause uneven distribution of heat by the sun's rays.

Heat is greater where the sun's rays strike the surface vertically, and less where they are slanted:

Hence, three major climate zones exist:
- the tropical zone, the hottest
- the polar zone, the coldest
- the temperate zone, intermediate

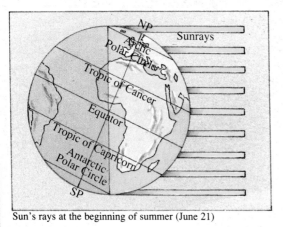

Sun's rays at the beginning of summer (June 21)

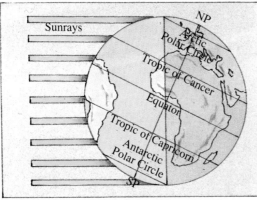

Sun's rays at the beginning of winter (December 21)

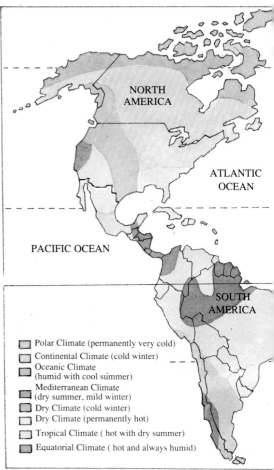

Polar Climate (permanently very cold)
Continental Climate (cold winter)
Oceanic Climate (humid with cool summer)
Mediterranean Climate (dry summer, mild winter)
Dry Climate (cold winter)
Dry Climate (permanently hot)
Tropical Climate (hot with dry summer)
Equatorial Climate (hot and always humid)

Varied Climates

Inside the same climate zone, temperatures and the distribution of rain and wind are sometimes uneven,

Thus, the tropical zone consists of:
- an equatorial climate, hot and humid all year round
- a tropical climate which has only one dry season

Similarly, the temperate zone has:
- an oceanic climate, mild and humid
- a Mediterranean climate, warm and dry in summer, mild and humid in winter.
- a continental climate, very warm in summer, very cold in winter

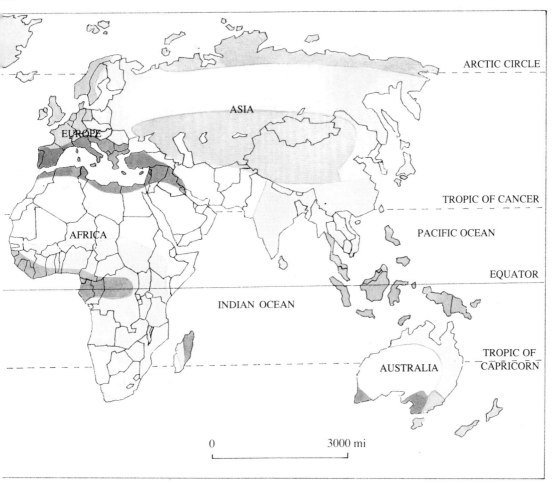

ARCTIC CIRCLE

ASIA

EUROPE

TROPIC OF CANCER

PACIFIC OCEAN

AFRICA

EQUATOR

INDIAN OCEAN

TROPIC OF
CAPRICORN

AUSTRALIA

0   3000 mi

Adapting to the Environment

In order to survive, human beings have to adapt to a great variety of geographical environments, some quite unfriendly. Differences in the economy, habitat, food, and clothing characterize the many different life styles in the world. However, as a result of technological progress and improved communication, certain limitations of the natural environment have been gradually lessened (opening of permanent bases at the poles, digging of wells in desert areas, irrigation). But difficulties still remain and adaptation is not always possible. For instance, today, African populations flee the advancing desert. This is the drama of the Sahel (area south of the Sahara).

Temperature Regions in the United States

No Summer, Long Winter

Short, Not Hot Summer, Cold Winter

Hot Summer, Cold Winter

Hot Summer, Mild Winter

Long Hot Summer, No Winter

Temperate

This map shows important variations in temperature in the 48 "mainland" states of the United States.

The Earth Is Moving

The effects of an earthquake in a village: the ground opens, causing houses to collapse since they no longer rest on stable foundations.

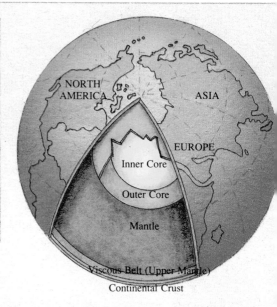

The Face of the Earth Changes

Volcanic eruptions and earthquakes regularly modify the surface of the earth (faults, fractures), sometimes causing great catastrophes. These movements are difficult to forecast and can be explained by the composition of the interior of our planet.

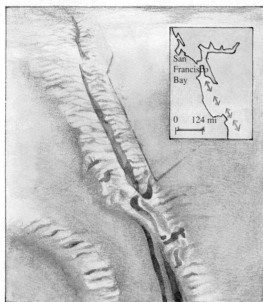

The San Andreas Fault in California (airview). 595 miles long, it runs from north of San Francisco to Southern California! (inset:) San Francisco Bay

What Is Inside the Earth?

A succession of superimposed layers (placed one above another):

- the earth's crust (continental and oceanic plates)
- the mantle
- the core (inner and outer)

The earth's crust consists of rigid crystal rocks (granite), and its thickness varies from 3 to 56 miles. The ocean crust (basalt) is much thinner.

- The mantle is about 1,800 miles thick.
- The core, a huge mass in fusion at a temperature of 10,000°F forms the center of the earth.

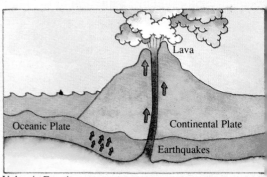

Volcanic Eruption

Like Drifting Rafts

The earth's crust consists of moving plates on which the continents stand and which glide continuously over the mantle. This slight

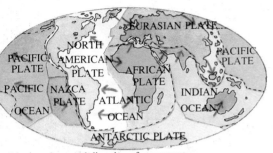

Moving plates and direction of movement

broke apart like the pieces of gigantic puzzle. A new set of individual continents appeared.

movement of the continents is called "continental drift." When the plates collide, they cause earthquakes and volcanic eruptions.

Proof – the Fitting Together of Africa and America

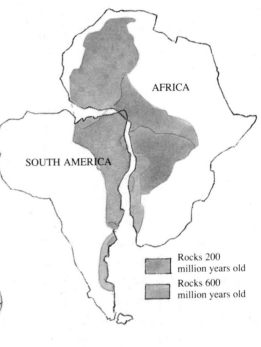

AFRICA

SOUTH AMERICA

Rocks 200 million years old

Rocks 600 million years old

180 Millions Years Ago...

The surface of our planet was completely different.

The supercontinent breaks up and separates into individual continents.

Each continent drifts in its own direction.

Present-day shape and position of continents. Plates continue to move.

It is possible to measure the intensity of earthquakes by using instruments called *seismographs.* Scales consisting of different degrees indicate the intensity of the tremors (shaking). The *Richter scale* consists of 9 degrees. Above degree 6, buildings can collapse.

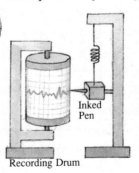

Inked Pen

Recording Drum

In 1906, the San Francisco earthquake caused 2,000 deaths, injured 15,000, and destroyed the fifth largest city in the United States.

At that time, the continental mass, which had earlier formed a single supercontinent,

Coming Soon – 6 Billion People

More and More Inhabitants

The population of the earth is continuously growing.

- 2,000 years ago— 250 million inhabitants
- In the year 1000— 450 million inhabitants
- In 1800— one billion inhabitants
- In 1900— one billion 650 million inhabitants

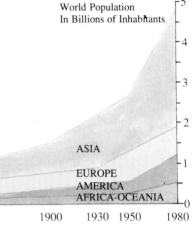

World Population In Billions of Inhabitants

ASIA
EUROPE
AMERICA
AFRICA-OCEANIA

1650   1700   1750   1800   1850   1900   1930   1950   1980

Today, we have reached a population of 5 billion.

At the end of the century, there will be about *6 billion, 500 million* inhabitants on earth

In one century, a demographic explosion has taken place, caused in part by a longer life expectancy. Each day, *200,000 more people* have to be fed. Today, 90 percent of all the earth's inhabitants live on only 20 percent of its land. One inhabitant out of 10 lives in the Southern Hemisphere.

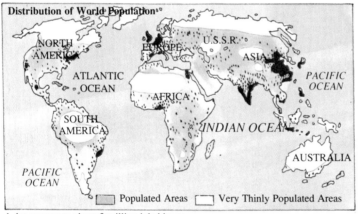

Distribution of World Population

NORTH AMERICA — EUROPE — U.S.S.R. — ASIA — ATLANTIC OCEAN — AFRICA — PACIFIC OCEAN — SOUTH AMERICA — INDIAN OCEAN — AUSTRALIA — PACIFIC OCEAN

☐ Populated Areas   ☐ Very Thinly Populated Areas

1 dot represents about 2 million inhabitants

Unequal Resources, Unequal Development

The various countries which share our planet do not have the same opportunities for development. These depend mainly on relatively favorable climate conditions, soil fertility,

An Unevenly Distributed Population

Mainly because of climate, extensive regions of the world are underpopulated:

- cold regions (Siberia, Canadian Northern Territories)
- arid regions (Sahara, Sahel, steppes)

On the other hand, there are areas of heavy population:

- East Asia, India, Europe, Indonesia

The Ten Most Populated Countries in the World

(in millions of inhabitants, 1984 census)

1.	China	1,023
2.	India	730
3.	U.S.S.R.	272
4.	United States	234
5.	Indonesia	156
6.	Brazil	131
7.	Japan	119
8.	Bangladesh	96.5
9.	Pakistan	95.7
10.	Nigeria	84.2

Most of the farmers of the Third World use primitive tools and methods to cultivate the soil.

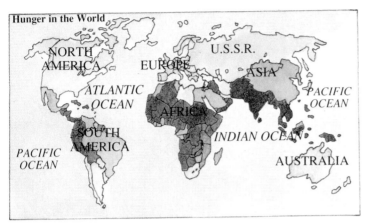

Hunger in the World

- ■ Insufficient daily food supply
- ▨ Barely sufficient daily food supply
- □ Normal or plentiful daily food supply

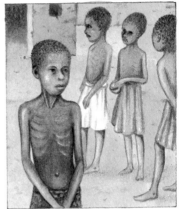

Because of undernourishment, many children are weak and have low resistance to diseases. The number who die before one year of age is twenty times higher in the Third World.

richness of mineral resources, and surface features like rivers and harbors. Many countries are dependent on others.

A Serious Problem – Hunger

This unequal development often has dramatic consequences.

More than two thirds of the human beings in the *Third World* (underdeveloped countries) suffer from lack of food. This situation is made worse by the high birth rate in these poor countries. More than 100 million babies are born each year compared to 30 million deaths!

Through international organizations such as UNICEF and UNESCO, these countries receive help from the richest ones. However, it is believed that only a policy of self-development by these countries will enable them to solve their difficulties. Birth control is also considered.

Working Children!

Hunger and poor living conditions force many young children to work for miserably low pay. Today, more than 50 million children work all over the world. Most of them do not attend school.

Children are often employed in hard labor that is not related to their physical abilities. Such conditions are worsened by insufficient food.

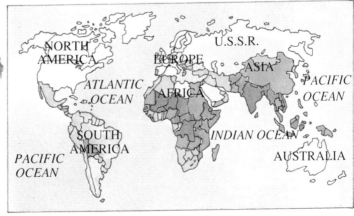

- □ All children go to school
- ▨ 9 out of 10 children go to school
- ▨ 2 out of 3 children go to school
- ▨ 1 out of 2 children goes to school

The African Continent

Location in the World

Important Facts

Area: 11.8 million square miles
Population: 600 million inhabitants (1987)
Density of population: 40 inhabitants per square mile
It is the hottest continent in the world.

Africa has:

the largest desert in the world—the *Sahara*, and the longest river in the world— the *Nile* (4,160 miles in length).

The highest African mountain, *Kilimanjaro* is 19,320 feet high.

The continent is rich in natural resources but is still largely underdeveloped.

Africa has many human problems— food shortage, epidemics, racial discrimination (in the Republic of South Africa).

In an attempt to solve these problems, African countries have formed an organization, the O.A.U. (Organization of African Unity), with headquarters in Addis Ababa (Ethiopia).

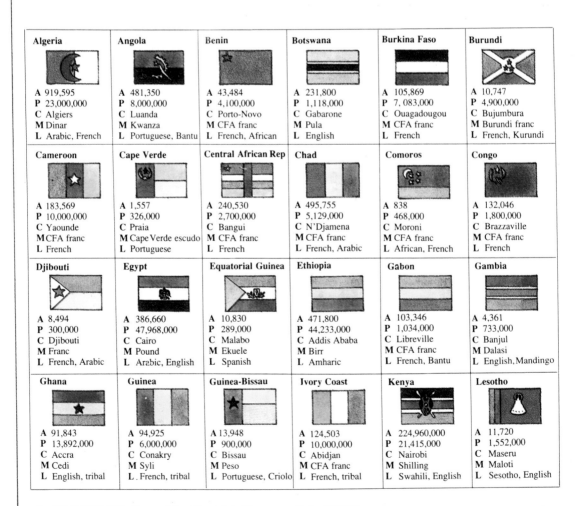

Algeria	Angola	Benin	Botswana	Burkina Faso	Burundi
A 919,595	A 481,350	A 43,484	A 231,800	A 105,869	A 10,747
P 23,000,000	P 8,000,000	P 4,100,000	P 1,118,000	P 7,083,000	P 4,900,000
C Algiers	C Luanda	C Porto-Novo	C Gabarone	C Ouagadougou	C Bujumbura
M Dinar	M Kwanza	M CFA franc	M Pula	M CFA franc	M Burundi franc
L Arabic, French	L Portuguese, Bantu	L French, African	L English	L French	L French, Kurundi

Cameroon	Cape Verde	Central African Rep	Chad	Comoros	Congo
A 183,569	A 1,557	A 240,530	A 495,755	A 838	A 132,046
P 10,000,000	P 326,000	P 2,700,000	P 5,129,000	P 468,000	P 1,800,000
C Yaounde	C Praia	C Bangui	C N'Djamena	C Moroni	C Brazzaville
M CFA franc	M Cape Verde escudo	M CFA franc	M CFA franc	M CFA franc	M CFA franc
L French	L Portuguese	L French	L French, Arabic	L African, French	L French

Djibouti	Egypt	Equatorial Guinea	Ethiopia	Gabon	Gambia
A 8,494	A 386,660	A 10,830	A 471,800	A 103,346	A 4,361
P 300,000	P 47,968,000	P 289,000	P 44,233,000	P 1,034,000	P 733,000
C Djibouti	C Cairo	C Malabo	C Addis Ababa	C Libreville	C Banjul
M Franc	M Pound	M Ekuele	M Birr	M CFA franc	M Dalasi
L French, Arabic	L Arabic, English	L Spanish	L Amharic	L French, Bantu	L English, Mandingo

Ghana	Guinea	Guinea-Bissau	Ivory Coast	Kenya	Lesotho
A 91,843	A 94,925	A 13,948	A 124,503	A 224,960,000	A 11,720
P 13,892,000	P 6,000,000	P 900,000	P 10,000,000	P 21,415,000	P 1,552,000
C Accra	C Conakry	C Bissau	C Abidjan	C Nairobi	C Maseru
M Cedi	M Syli	M Peso	M CFA franc	M Shilling	M Maloti
L English, tribal	L French, tribal	L Portuguese, Criolo	L French, tribal	L Swahili, English	L Sesotho, English

A = area in square miles, P = population, C = capital, M = money unit, L = language

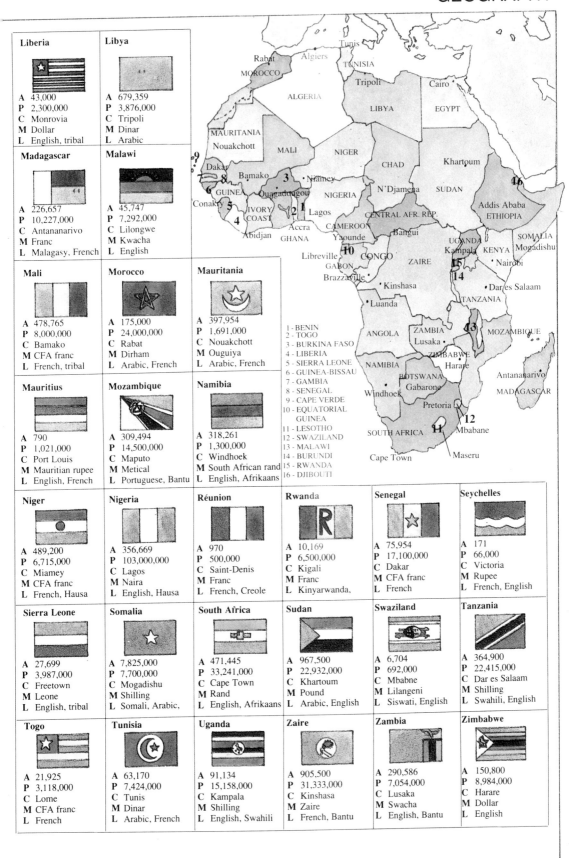

Liberia

A 43,000
P 2,300,000
C Monrovia
M Dollar
L English, tribal

Libya

A 679,359
P 3,876,000
C Tripoli
M Dinar
L Arabic

Madagascar

A 226,657
P 10,227,000
C Antananarivo
M Franc
L Malagasy, French

Malawi

A 45,747
P 7,292,000
C Lilongwe
M Kwacha
L English

Mali

A 478,765
P 8,000,000
C Bamako
M CFA franc
L French, tribal

Morocco

A 175,000
P 24,000,000
C Rabat
M Dirham
L Arabic, French

Mauritania

A 397,954
P 1,691,000
C Nouakchott
M Ouguiya
L Arabic, French

Mauritius

A 790
P 1,021,000
C Port Louis
M Mauritian rupee
L English, French

Mozambique

A 309,494
P 14,500,000
C Maputo
M Metical
L Portuguese, Bantu

Namibia

A 318,261
P 1,300,000
C Windhoek
M South African rand
L English, Afrikaans

1 - BENIN
2 - TOGO
3 - BURKINA FASO
4 - LIBERIA
5 - SIERRA LEONE
6 - GUINEA-BISSAU
7 - GAMBIA
8 - SENEGAL
9 - CAPE VERDE
10 - EQUATORIAL GUINEA
11 - LESOTHO
12 - SWAZILAND
13 - MALAWI
14 - BURUNDI
15 - RWANDA
16 - DJIBOUTI

Niger

A 489,200
P 6,715,000
C Miamey
M CFA franc
L French, Hausa

Nigeria

A 356,669
P 103,000,000
C Lagos
M Naira
L English, Hausa

Réunion

A 970
P 500,000
C Saint-Denis
M Franc
L French, Creole

Rwanda

A 10,169
P 6,500,000
C Kigali
M Franc
L Kinyarwanda,

Senegal

A 75,954
P 17,100,000
C Dakar
M CFA franc
L French

Seychelles

A 171
P 66,000
C Victoria
M Rupee
L French, English

Sierra Leone

A 27,699
P 3,987,000
C Freetown
M Leone
L English, tribal

Somalia

A 7,825,000
P 7,700,000
C Mogadishu
M Shilling
L Somali, Arabic,

South Africa

A 471,445
P 33,241,000
C Cape Town
M Rand
L English, Afrikaans

Sudan

A 967,500
P 22,932,000
C Khartoum
M Pound
L Arabic, English

Swaziland

A 6,704
P 692,000
C Mbabne
M Lilangeni
L Siswati, English

Tanzania

A 364,900
P 22,415,000
C Dar es Salaam
M Shilling
L Swahili, English

Togo

A 21,925
P 3,118,000
C Lome
M CFA franc
L French

Tunisia

A 63,170
P 7,424,000
C Tunis
M Dinar
L Arabic, French

Uganda

A 91,134
P 15,158,000
C Kampala
M Shilling
L English, Swahili

Zaire

A 905,500
P 31,333,000
C Kinshasa
M Zaire
L French, Bantu

Zambia

A 290,586
P 7,054,000
C Lusaka
M Swacha
L English, Bantu

Zimbabwe

A 150,800
P 8,984,000
C Harare
M Dollar
L English

The American Continent

Location in the World

The American continent spreads over many latitudes and extends 9,400 miles from north to south. Hence, the variety of land forms.

America contains the most important river as measured by its rate of flow— the *Amazon* (in Brazil).

The highest American mountain, *Mt. Aconcagua* (at the border of Argentina and Chile), reaches 23,080 feet above sea level.

The Americas are characterized by a great variety of population and by great social inequalities. Racial groups include whites, blacks, Native Americans, and many people of mixed background including Mestizos and Amerindians.

The continent is greatly influenced by the *United States*, the leading agricultural and industrial power of the world.

The *United States* is a federation of 50 states.

Canada, the world's second largest country, is made up of ten provinces and two territories. Many countries of Central and South America suffer from social tensions and civil wars.

Important Facts

Area	in millions of square miles
North America	8.50
Central America	1.05
South America	6.81
Total	16.36

Population	in millions of inhabitants
North America	300
Central America	90
South America	260
Total	650

Density of population: 31 inhabitants per square mile.

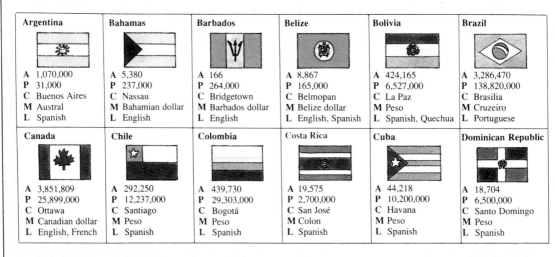

Argentina	Bahamas	Barbados	Belize	Bolivia	Brazil
A 1,070,000	A 5,380	A 166	A 8,867	A 424,165	A 3,286,470
P 31,000	P 237,000	P 264,000	P 165,000	P 6,527,000	P 138,820,000
C Buenos Aires	C Nassau	C Bridgetown	C Belmopan	C La Paz	C Brasilia
M Austral	M Bahamian dollar	M Barbados dollar	M Belize dollar	M Peso	M Cruzeiro
L Spanish	L English	L English	L English, Spanish	L Spanish, Quechua	L Portuguese
Canada	Chile	Colombia	Costa Rica	Cuba	Dominican Republic
A 3,851,809	A 292,250	A 439,730	A 19,575	A 44,218	A 18,704
P 25,899,000	P 12,237,000	P 29,303,000	P 2,700,000	P 10,200,000	P 6,500,000
C Ottawa	C Santiago	C Bogotá	C San José	C Havana	C Santo Domingo
M Canadian dollar	M Peso	M Peso	M Colon	M Peso	M Peso
L English, French	L Spanish	L Spanish	L Spanish	L Spanish	L Spanish

A = area in square miles, P = population, C = capital,   M = money unit, L = language

Ecuador
A 104,510
P 10,000,000
C Quito
M Sucre
L Spanish

El Salvador
A 8,260
P 5,286,000
C San Salvador
M Colon
L Spanish

French Guiana
A 35,126
P 78,336
C Cayenne
M Franc
L Creole

Grenada
A 133
P 116,000
C St. George's
M Caribbean dollar
L English

Guadeloupe
A 687
P 300,000
C Basse-Terre
M Franc
L French, Creole

Guatemala
A 42,042
P 6,939,000
C Guatemala City
M Quetzal
L Spanish

Guyana
A 83,000
P 844,000
C Georgetown
M Dollar
L English

Haiti
A 10,714
P 6,033,000
C Port-au-Prince
M Gourde
L French, Creole

Honduras
A 42,277
P 4,525,000
C Tegucigalpa
M Lempira
L Spanish

Jamaica
A 4,250
P 2,437,000
C Kingston
M Dollar
L English, Creole

Martinique
A 431
P 300,000
C Fort-de-France
M Franc
L French, Creole

Mexico
A 761,600
P 80,709,000
C Mexico City
M Peso
L Spanish

Nicaragua
A 50,193
P 3,342,000
C Managua
M Cordoba
L Spanish, English

Panama
A 29,760
P 2,227,000
C Panama City
M Balboa
L Spanish, English

Paraguay
A 157,047
P 4,119,000
C Asunción
M Guarani
L Spanish, Guarani

Peru
A 496,222
P 20,207,000
C Lima
M Sol
L Spanish, Quechua

St. Pierre/Miquelon
A 93
P 6,041
C St. Pierre
M Franc
L French

Surinam
A 63,037
P 381,000
C Paramaribo
M Guilder
L Dutch, Creole

Trinidad/Tobago
A 1,980
P 1,204,000
C Port-of-Spain
M Dollar
L English

United States
A 3,615,123
P 246,000,000
C Washington, D.C.
M Dollar
L English

Uruguay
A 68,037
P 3,000,000
C Montevideo
M New Peso
L Spanish

Venezuela
A 352,143
P 18,000,000
C Caracas
M Bolivar
L Spanish, Indian

Map labels:
Alaska, North America, CANADA, Ottawa, UNITED STATES, Washington D.C., MEXICO, Mexico City, Central America, CARIBBEAN SEA, Caracas, VENEZUELA, COLOMBIA, Bogota, Quito, ECUADOR, Lima, PERU, BRAZIL, Brasilia, La Paz, BOLIVIA, PARAGUAY, Asuncion, PACIFIC OCEAN, CHILE, ARGENTINA, URUGUAY, Montevideo, Santiago, Buenos Aires, South America, ATLANTIC OCEAN, Cape Horn

1 - BELIZE
2 - GUATEMALA
3 - EL SALVADOR
4 - HONDURAS
5 - NICARAGUA
6 - COSTA RICA
7 - PANAMA
8 - GUYANA
9 - SURINAM
10 - FRENCH GUIANA
11 - HAITI
12 - DOMINICAN REPUBLIC
13 - CUBA
14 - JAMAICA
15 - ANTIGUA

89

The Asian Continent

Location in the World

extending over one third of the earth's land surface.

It is also the most populated (containing more than half the world's population) and has the greatest population growth.

Its extent in latitude (5,625 miles) from north to south, divides the continent into three climatic zones:

- Cold Asia in the north
- Arid Asia in the center and in the west
- Monsoon Asia in the south

Asia has the highest mountain in the world—*Mount Everest,* (29,028 feet) in the Himalayas.

A great variety of ethnic groups, with white, yellow, brown and black skin, live in Asia.

In Asia, over *100 languages and different dialects* are spoken.

All the great religions began there; Islam, Hinduism, Buddhism, Judaism, and Christianity.

Many countries in this vast continent are faced with overpopulation, malnutrition, and underdevelopment.

Important Facts

Area:
17.2 million square miles (not including the western part of U.S.S.R)
Population:
2 billion 370 million inhabitants not including U.S.S.R.
Density of population:
130 inhabitants per square mile.
It is the largest continent of the world,

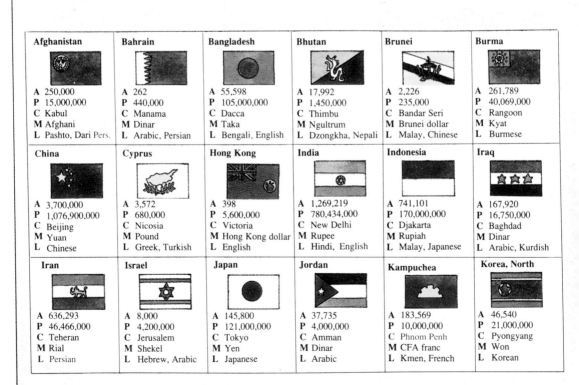

Afghanistan	Bahrain	Bangladesh	Bhutan	Brunei	Burma
A 250,000	A 262	A 55,598	A 17,992	A 2,226	A 261,789
P 15,000,000	P 440,000	P 105,000,000	P 1,450,000	P 235,000	P 40,069,000
C Kabul	C Manama	C Dacca	C Thimbu	C Bandar Seri	C Rangoon
M Afghani	M Dinar	M Taka	M Ngultrum	M Brunei dollar	M Kyat
L Pashto, Dari Pers.	L Arabic, Persian	L Bengali, English	L Dzongkha, Nepali	L Malay, Chinese	L Burmese

China	Cyprus	Hong Kong	India	Indonesia	Iraq
A 3,700,000	A 3,572	A 398	A 1,269,219	A 741,101	A 167,920
P 1,076,900,000	P 680,000	P 5,600,000	P 780,434,000	P 170,000,000	P 16,750,000
C Beijing	C Nicosia	C Victoria	C New Delhi	C Djakarta	C Baghdad
M Yuan	M Pound	M Hong Kong dollar	M Rupee	M Rupiah	M Dinar
L Chinese	L Greek, Turkish	L English	L Hindi, English	L Malay, Japanese	L Arabic, Kurdish

Iran	Israel	Japan	Jordan	Kampuchea	Korea, North
A 636,293	A 8,000	A 145,800	A 37,735	A 183,569	A 46,540
P 46,466,000	P 4,200,000	P 121,000,000	P 4,000,000	P 10,000,000	P 21,000,000
C Teheran	C Jerusalem	C Tokyo	C Amman	C Phnom Penh	C Pyongyang
M Rial	M Shekel	M Yen	M Dinar	M CFA franc	M Won
L Persian	L Hebrew, Arabic	L Japanese	L Arabic	L Kmen, French	L Korean

A = area in square miles. P = population. C = capital. M = money unit. L = language

ATLANTIC OCEAN
ARCTIC OCEAN

EUROPE

U.S.S.R

Ankara
TURKEY
Baghdad
IRAQ
Teheran
IRAN
Kabul
AFGHANISTAN
Islamabad
SAUDI ARABIA
Riyadh
U.A.E
Muscat
NORTH YEMEN
Sana
SOUTH YEMEN
Aden
OMAN
AFRICA

Ulan Bator
MONGOLIA

NORTH KOREA
Pyongyang
Seoul
SOUTH KOREA
Peking
CHINA

Tokyo
JAPAN

PACIFIC OCEAN

PAKISTAN
New Delhi
INDIA
INDIAN OCEAN

BURMA
Rangoon
THAILAND
Bangkok

Hanoi
VIETNAM

Manila
PHILIPPINES

14
15

SRI LANKA
Colombo

MALAYSIA
Kuala Lumpur
16
INDONESIA
Djakarta

17

1 - LEBANON
2 - SYRIA
3 - ISRAEL
4 - JORDAN
5 - BHUTAN
6 - BANGLADESH
7 - NEPAL
8 - LAOS
9 - KAMPUCHEA
10 - CYPRUS
11 - KUWAIT
12 - BAHRAIN
13 - QATAR
14 - TAIWAN
15 - HONG KONG
16 - SINGAPORE
17 - BRUNEI

Korea, South
A 38,025
P 43,000,000
C Seoul
M Won
L Korean

Kuwait
A 6,880
P 1,800,000
C Kuwait
M Dinar
L Arabic, English

Laos
A 91,429
P 3,679,000
C Vientiane
M Kip
L Lao, French

Lebanon
A 4,015
P 2,674,000
C Beiruit
M Pound
L Arabic, French

Malaysia	Mongolia	Nepal	Oman	Pakistan	Philippines
A 127,320	A 604,250	A 54,362	A 82,030	A 310,403	A 115,830
P 15,820,00	P 1,942,000	P 17,422,000	P 1,300,000	P 103,000,000	P 58,091,00
C Kuala Lumpur	C Ulan Bator	C Katmandu	C Muscat	C Islamabad	C Manila
M Ringgit	M Tugrik	M Rupee	M Omani Rule	M Rupee	M Peso
L Malay, English	L Mongolian	L Nepali	L Arabic, Urdu	L Urdu, English	L Filipino, English

Qatar	Saudi Arabia	Singapore	Sri Lanka	Syria	Taiwan
A 4,400	A 840,000	A 224	A 25,332	A 71,498	A 13,900
P 305,000	P 11,519,000	P 2,600,000	P 16,638,000	P 10,931,000	P 19,601,000
C Doha	C Riyadh	C Singapore	C Colombo	C Damascus	C Taipei
M Riyal	M Riyal	M Dollar	M Rupee	M Pound	M Dollar
L Arabic, English	L Arabic	L Chinese, English	L Sinhala, Tamil	L Arabic, Kurdish	L Chinese

Thailand	Turkey	U. Arab Emirates	Vietnam	Yemen (North)	Yemen (South)
A 198,456	A 301,381	A 32,000	A 128,000	A 75,290	A 128,559
P 52,438,000	P 51,819,000	P 1,400,000	P 62,000,000	P 6,339,000	P 2,275,000
C Bangkok	C Ankara	C Abu Dhabi	C Hanoi	C Sana	C Aden
M Baht	M Lira	M Dirham	M Dong	M Rial	M Dinar
L Thai	L Turkish, Kurdish	L Arabic	L Vietnamese	L Arabic	L Arabic

The European Countries

Location In the World

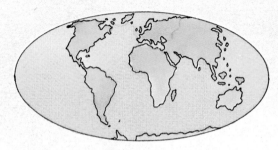

Europe has a great variety of topography— old mountains, great plains, and high mountain chains. The highest peak is *Mont Blanc* (15,623 feet), in France.

Located almost entirely in the temperate zone, with the exception of northern Scandinavian, Europe has three climate zones— oceanic, Mediterranean, and continental.

Densely populated, its population nevertheless is not growing as fast as that of the rest of the world.

Its population is a mix of people, cultures, religions, and languages.

Attempts at unification began on January 1, 1958 when the European Economic Community (E.E.C.) was founded.

Important Facts

Europe is not a separate continent, but the western part of the vast Eurasian continent. It extends from the Atlantic Ocean to the Ural mountains.

Area:
4 million square miles
Population:
761 million inhabitants
Density of population:
160 inhabitants per square mile

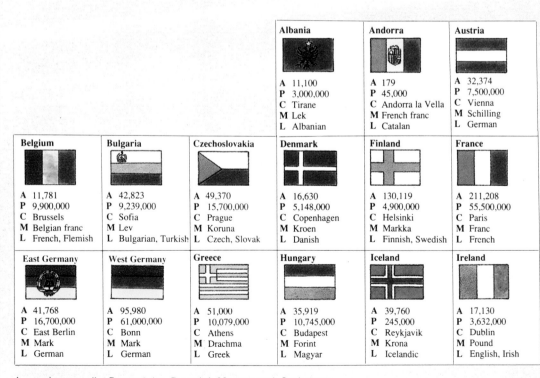

Albania	Andorra	Austria
A 11,100	A 179	A 32,374
P 3,000,000	P 45,000	P 7,500,000
C Tirane	C Andorra la Vella	C Vienna
M Lek	M French franc	M Schilling
L Albanian	L Catalan	L German

Belgium	Bulgaria	Czechoslovakia	Denmark	Finland	France
A 11,781	A 42,823	A 49,370	A 16,630	A 130,119	A 211,208
P 9,900,000	P 9,239,000	P 15,700,000	P 5,148,000	P 4,900,000	P 55,500,000
C Brussels	C Sofia	C Prague	C Copenhagen	C Helsinki	C Paris
M Belgian franc	M Lev	M Koruna	M Kroen	M Markka	M Franc
L French, Flemish	L Bulgarian, Turkish	L Czech, Slovak	L Danish	L Finnish, Swedish	L French

East Germany	West Germany	Greece	Hungary	Iceland	Ireland
A 41,768	A 95,980	A 51,000	A 35,919	A 39,760	A 17,130
P 16,700,000	P 61,000,000	P 10,079,000	P 10,745,000	P 245,000	P 3,632,000
C East Berlin	C Bonn	C Athens	C Budapest	C Reykjavik	C Dublin
M Mark	M Mark	M Drachma	M Forint	M Krona	M Pound
L German	L German	L Greek	L Magyar	L Icelandic	L English, Irish

A = area in square miles, P = population, C = capital, M = money unit, L = language

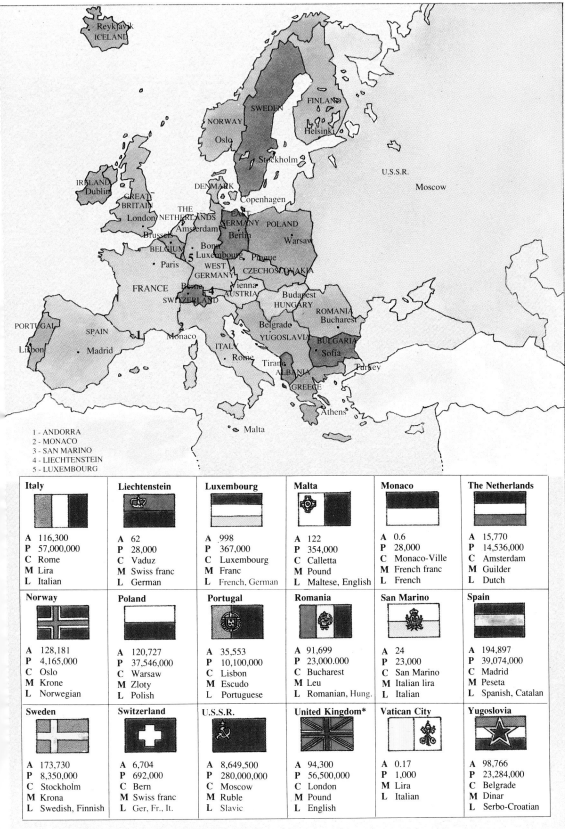

1 - ANDORRA
2 - MONACO
3 - SAN MARINO
4 - LIECHTENSTEIN
5 - LUXEMBOURG

Italy	Liechtenstein	Luxembourg	Malta	Monaco	The Netherlands
A 116,300	**A** 62	**A** 998	**A** 122	**A** 0.6	**A** 15,770
P 57,000,000	**P** 28,000	**P** 367,000	**P** 354,000	**P** 28,000	**P** 14,536,000
C Rome	**C** Vaduz	**C** Luxembourg	**C** Calletta	**C** Monaco-Ville	**C** Amsterdam
M Lira	**M** Swiss franc	**M** Franc	**M** Pound	**M** French franc	**M** Guilder
L Italian	**L** German	**L** French, German	**L** Maltese, English	**L** French	**L** Dutch
Norway	**Poland**	**Portugal**	**Romania**	**San Marino**	**Spain**
A 128,181	**A** 120,727	**A** 35,553	**A** 91,699	**A** 24	**A** 194,897
P 4,165,000	**P** 37,546,000	**P** 10,100,000	**P** 23,000.000	**P** 23,000	**P** 39,074,000
C Oslo	**C** Warsaw	**C** Lisbon	**C** Bucharest	**C** San Marino	**C** Madrid
M Krone	**M** Zloty	**M** Escudo	**M** Leu	**M** Italian lira	**M** Peseta
L Norwegian	**L** Polish	**L** Portuguese	**L** Romanian, Hung.	**L** Italian	**L** Spanish, Catalan
Sweden	**Switzerland**	**U.S.S.R.**	**United Kingdom***	**Vatican City**	**Yugoslovia**
A 173,730	**A** 6,704	**A** 8,649,500	**A** 94,300	**A** 0.17	**A** 98,766
P 8,350,000	**P** 692,000	**P** 280,000,000	**P** 56,500,000	**P** 1,000	**P** 23,284,000
C Stockholm	**C** Bern	**C** Moscow	**C** London	**M** Lira	**C** Belgrade
M Krona	**M** Swiss franc	**M** Ruble	**M** Pound	**L** Italian	**M** Dinar
L Swedish, Finnish	**L** Ger., Fr., It.	**L** Slavic	**L** English		**L** Serbo-Croatian

*The United Kingdom of Great Britain consists of England, Wales, Scotland, and Northern Ireland.

Oceania And The Polar Lands

Oceania – Location In the World

Scarcely populated, Oceania consists of numerous islands of very different size spread over the Pacific Ocean. *There are between 20,000 and 30,000 of them!*

Australia makes up *85%* of all the land and contains *50%* of the population of Oceania.

Besides the continent of Australia, there are three main island groups in Oceania. They are:

- Melanesia, "land of the black islands," and New Zealand
- Micronesia, "land of small islands"
- Polynesia, "land of many islands"

Area:
3,492,000 square miles
Population:
24 million inhabitants
Density of population:
6.9 inhabitants per square mile

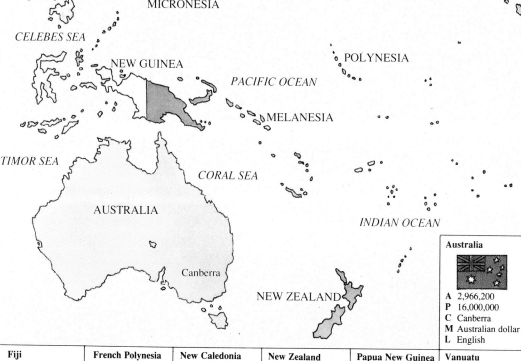

Australia	
A	2,966,200
P	16,000,000
C	Canberra
M	Australian dollar
L	English

Fiji		French Polynesia		New Caledonia		New Zealand		Papua New Guinea		Vanuatu	
A	7,056	A	1,544	A	7,374	A	103,736	A	178,260	A	5,700
P	700,000	P	200,000	P	200,000	P	3,305,000	P	3,395,000	P	136,000
C	Suva	C	Papeete	C	Nouméa	C	Wellington	C	Port Moresby	C	Vila
M	Dollar	M	CFA franc	M	CFA franc	M	Dollar	M	Kina	M	Vanuatu franc
L	English, Fijian	L	French	L	Melanesian	L	English, Maori	L	English	L	Bislama, Fr., Eng.

A = area in square miles, P = population, C = capital,
M = money unit, L = language

Polar Lands –
Location In the World

Arctic Lands

Antarctic Lands

The climate of the polar lands is extremely harsh. In summer, the average temperature does not rise above 10° (50°F) because of the high degree of slanting of the rays of the sun.

A Difference

The North Pole is a dot in the middle of the Arctic Ocean. It is surrounded by islands and lands.

The South Pole is a dot located on the continent of Antarctica.

Arctic Area

This vast region includes the largest island in the world – *Greenland*, a Danish territory with an area of 854,000 square miles and a population of 53,000 inhabitants, mostly Eskimos. Of its surface, 9/10th is covered by a sheet of ice averaging 5,000 feet thick. The Arctic area also includes Spitzbergen (Norway), Lapland (the northern part of Scandinavia, Finland, and northwestern U.S.S.R.), Alaska, and the northern part of Canada.

Antarctica

It is the largest ice desert in the world – more than five million square miles. The environment is very harsh. The coldest temperature on record was reached there – *minus* 88.3°C (-191°F) in 1960.

The sheet of ice has a thickness of about 13,000 feet. There are very strong winds (record speed: 204 mph).

Human beings live only in a few recently opened scientific stations.

ARCTIC LANDS

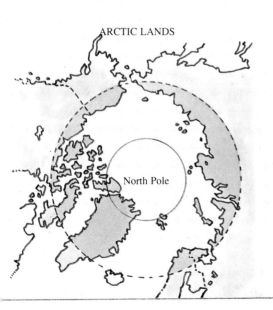

North Pole

ANTARCTIC LANDS

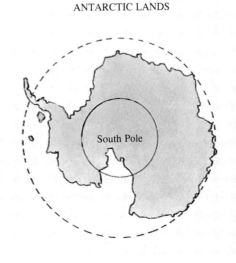

South Pole

The United States

Important Facts

Location:

The United States occupies the central one-third of the North American continent. Alaska is at the extreme northwest of the continent, and Hawaii lies in the Pacific.

Area:

3,628,150 square miles

Population:

246,000,000 persons (1988, est.)

United States (Political)

Government:

A *federal republic*, with an elected president, an elected two-house Congress and an appointed Supreme Court. The powers of government are divided between the 50 state governments and the nation's federal, or central, government which is located in Washington, D.C.

Borders:

North—Canada
South—Mexico, Gulf of Mexico
East—Atlantic Ocean
West—Pacific Ocean

The United States is divided into eight physical regions. They can also be grouped as Eastern, Interior, and Western regions.

United States (Physical)

Eastern Regions

Eastern Coastal Lowlands

The Atlantic Coastal Plain curves along the east coast of the United States from Long Island and New Jersey in the northeast to Texas on the Gulf of Mexico in the southwest. Along the Gulf of Mexico, from Florida to Texas, this lowland plain is called the *Gulf Coastal Plain*. It also stretches inland along the Mississippi River Valley from Louisiana to the southern tip of Illinois, and to the western edge of Kentucky.

The land is generally low and flat, with a few areas of rolling hills. It is crossed by many slow-moving rivers and is heavily wooded, with large areas of swampland along the coast. The climate is rainy, with long, hot summers, and short, mild winters. Tourism, manufacturing and agriculture are important. Major cities are Houston, Dallas, New Orleans and Miami.

Piedmont

The *Piedmont* (pĕd´mont) is an area of rolling hills that lies between the coastal plain and the mountains. It extends from southern New York south to Alabama. The climate is like that of the nearby coastal plain. The region's eastern edge, where fast-flowing rivers from the Appalachians fall sharply onto the coastal plain, is known as the "fall line." Here are found such large cities as Philadelphia, Washington, Richmond and Atlanta. Both agriculture and manufacturing are important.

Appalachian Mountains

The *Appalachian* (ap´e lā chē n) *Highlands* lie west of the Piedmont and extend from Ala-

bama to Maine, and on to Newfoundland in eastern Canada. They are made up of low, rounded mountain ranges and plateaus such as the Blue Ridge and Great Smokies in the south, and the Alleghenies, Catskills and White Mountains in the north. This region includes most of New England (Maine, Vermont, New Hampshire, Massachusetts, Connecticut and Rhode Island), as well as large parts of the Middle Atlantic states of New York, Pennsylvania and Maryland.

In the north, summers are shorter and winters longer and colder. There are heavily-wooded mountains, and well-populated river valleys and lowlands. Manufacturing and coal mining are important. Major cities include Pittsburgh, Pennsylvania and Atlanta, Georgia. The point at which the Appalachians, the Piedmont and the Atlantic coastal plain all meet is New York City.

The United States

St. Louis, Missouri

Steamboat on the Mississippi River

Interior Regions

Central Plains

The *Central Plains* cover a very large area from the Arctic coastal plain in Alaska and northwest Canada to the Appalachians. They include much of the Mississippi River basin, and the St. Lawrence valley in northwest New York. The land is fairly flat and partly forested. Tall grasses once covered the entire region. Agriculture is very important. The region is highly industrialized and heavily populated. It includes many large cities, such as Minneapolis, Kansas City, St. Louis, Milwaukee, Chicago, Detroit, Cleveland, and Buffalo.

High Plains

The *High Plains*, which are also called the *Great Plains*, lie between the Central Plains and the Rocky Mountains. They extend from the Dakotas and Montana in the north all the way south to Texas. The region is higher and drier than the Central Plains, but is important for agriculture despite an undependable water supply. There is scattered industry. The region is moderately populated, with Denver and San Antonio the largest cities.

Western Regions

Rocky Mountains

The *Rocky Mountains* extend in a long belt from Alaska to New Mexico. They contain many high mountain ranges that are a major barrier to transportation. The Rockies often reach higher than 14,000 feet above sea level, and contain some of the most beautiful forests

The Great Plains

The Badlands

The Grand Canyon

A Western City

The Western Desert

California Seacoast

and lakes in the United States. While the winter climate is harsh, the region is important for tourism, ranching and mining. Its largest population centers, Denver and Salt Lake City, actually lie *outside* the region.

Intermountain Region

To the west of the Rocky Mountains is a lower, flatter area called the *Intermountain Region*. It lies between the Rockies and the two mountain ranges near the west coast, the Cascade Range and the Sierra Nevada. This long, broad area extends from Alaska to Mexico. The region has isolated mountain ridges, high plateaus, and desert basins. It includes the Colorado River and deep gorges such as the Grand Canyon. The region is rich in minerals and water power, and has some irrigated agriculture. Its largest cities are Spokane, Phoenix, and Salt Lake City.

Pacific Mountains and Valleys

The *Pacific Mountains and Valleys* lie along the Pacific Coast from northern Washington to southern California. The region includes both high and low mountain ranges, coastal lowlands, and interior valleys. With a mild climate and rich soils, the region has some very fine agricultural land. Fishing and forestry are important in the north. The coastal lowlands, especially in California, are heavily populated and industrialized. The region's largest cities are Seattle, Portland, San Francisco, Los Angeles, and San Diego.

The United States

A Nation of Immigrants

President John F. Kennedy called the United States a nation of immigrants. All Americans have either personally come here from another country or are descendents of immigrants. They came to make a better life—to find land to farm, religious freedom, and jobs to support their families.

The first immigrants were the ancestors of the American Indians. Starting about 100,000 years ago, they crossed a land bridge from Asia (now covered by the Bering Sea) into Alaska, and spread down into what are now Canada and the United States. Thousands of years after the American Indians settled here, the first immigrants from Europe arrived.

In the last few hundred years since the first American colony was settled at Jamestown in 1607, millions of immigrants have come from all parts of the world. The American population in 1790 was four million; by 1990 it is expected to reach over 246 million.

Between 1790 and 1860, most immigrants came from northern and western Europe. Many came from England, Scotland and Wales. Others arrived from Ireland, France, the Netherlands (Holland and Belgium), Germany and Sweden. However, between the 1880s and 1940, most immigrants came from southern and eastern Europe—Italy, Austria-Hungary, Poland, Russia, and Greece.

Before the slave trade was outlawed in 1808, some three million black Africans were brought to this country as slaves. They were owned by other people, and forced to work for their owners without payment or hope of freedom.

Many immigrants have also come from Asia. In the late 1800s, many people (mostly men) from China and Japan came to the United States in search of jobs. Today, the United States has immigrants from all parts of Asia. Thousands have come from Korea, the Philippines, India, Vietnam, Hong Kong, and

Most Americans live in cities.

Most American suburbs are growing rapidly.

Immigrants arrive in America in the early 1900s.

many areas of the Middle East.

In recent years, more immigrants have come to the United States from other parts of the Americas than from anywhere else. They come from Mexico, from Central and South America, from islands in the Caribbean Sea, and from Canada.

Where Americans Live

From 1790 on, during the early years of the United States, most Americans made their living by farming. The country's few cities were small. About 90% of Americans lived on farms or in small towns in rural areas.

By the middle of the 1800s, this pattern of settlement changed greatly. There were many cities, and they grew rapidly. By 1920, more than half of all Americans were living in urban (city) areas. Now, *more than two-thirds* of all Americans live in urban areas. An urban area includes a city and its *suburbs*, or smaller communities built around the city.

The United States has become a nation of cities. The reason for this is that fewer and fewer farmers are needed to grow the nation's food. Using machinery and scientific farming methods, it now takes less than 10% of the population to feed the rest of the nation.

Americans come from all over the world.

The United States

New England States

The *New England states* of Maine, New Hampshire, Vermont, Massachusetts, Rhode Island and Connecticut are located largely in the Appalachian highlands. The farms are small because the land is hilly and the soil is rocky. Farms near large cities raise fruits and vegetables. Dairy farms, poultry farms and fruit orchards dot the landscape. Fishing is an important industry.

Manufacturing is a major activity of its cities. Boston is the largest industrial center and busiest port in New England.

Once known as the textile and leather center of the United States, New England now produces electronic equipment and complex machines.

Middle Atlantic States

New York, New Jersey, Pennsylvania and Delaware make up the *Middle Atlantic states*. These are leading industrial states because the region has many natural resources, a good location, and a large number of workers. About one-third of the population here works in manufacturing. This group of states manufactures chemicals, electrical equipment and paper products.

New York City is one of the five largest cities in the world, and the home of the United Nations. Many corporations and banks have their headquarters in this world financial center. New York is an important fashion and cultural center. Publishing is another important industry. The Port of New York is one of

Chief Industrial Regions of the New England States and the Middle Atlantic States

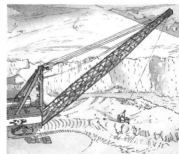

the world's largest and busiest harbors.

Pittsburgh, Pennsylvania, which is near coal mines and iron ore deposits, is one of the world's greatest steelmaking centers. It also produces large amounts of aluminum, machinery, plate glass and safety equipment.

As in New England, dairy farming, poultry farming and fruit orchards help supply city people with the fresh food they need. Both deep-sea and inshore fishing are carried on all along the coast. In the shallow, quiet waters off Long Island and Delaware, oysters, scallops, and other shellfish are harvested.

Southeastern States

The *Southeastern states* are Virginia, West Virginia, Maryland, North Carolina, South Carolina, Georgia, Kentucky, Tennessee, Alabama, Mississippi, and Florida. This area was once called the "land of cotton." Today, cotton and tobacco fields share the land with fruit orchards (Georgia peaches), and fields of soybeans, peanuts, corn, and sweet potatoes.

Forests grow fast in the warm climate of the Southeast, and one-fourth of America's lumber comes from this region. The largest coal field in the world is also in this region, under the Appalachian Highland. Kentucky and West Virginia mine the largest amounts of bituminous (soft) coal.

Many northern factories moved to the Southeast during the 1900s to take advantage of the area's rich raw materials, good climate and transportation, and large numbers of workers and markets. After iron and coal were found near Birmingham, Alabama, it became a steel manufacturing center.

Beginning in the 1930s, the *Tennessee Valley Administration* built a series of dams here to control floods, to generate cheap electric power in five states, and to make the rivers navigable year-round. In 1985, a waterway was completed in Mississippi and Alabama to connect the Tennessee and Tombigbee Rivers. This Tenn-Tom Waterway connects 16,000 miles of navigable waters. Goods can be shipped from the industrial cities of the North Central states to seaports on the Gulf of Mexico.

Other leading industries in the region are food processing (Florida citrus juices), chemicals (phosphate fertilizers), and textiles (linens and cotton clothing).

The nation's capital, Washington, in the District of Columbia, is in this region. Atlanta, Georgia, a center of trade and transportation, has one of the nation's busiest airports.

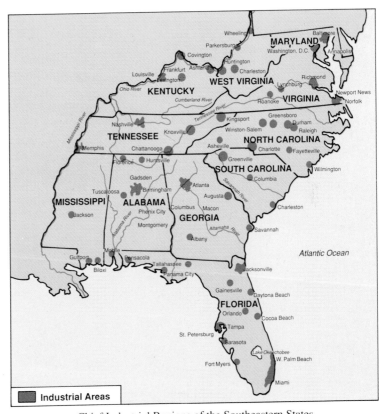

Chief Industrial Regions of the Southeastern States

The United States

North Central States

"Middle America" is made up of Ohio, Indiana, Illinois, Michigan, Wisconsin, Minnesota, Iowa, Missouri, North Dakota, South Dakota, Nebraska, and Kansas. This region has some of the world's best corn and wheat lands. The *corn belt* stretches from Ohio to central Nebraska. Most of the corn is fed to animals (beef cattle, hogs and poultry) because meat brings a higher price than grain.

With less rain, the Dakotas, Nebraska and Kansas grow a great deal of wheat. Modern harvesters *reap* and *thresh* the grain. Winter wheat is sown in autumn and harvested in summer. Centered in Kansas, the winter wheat region extends into Nebraska, Colorado, Oklahoma and Texas.

The heart of the spring wheat region is in North Dakota. This region extends into Minnesota, South Dakota, Montana and Canada.

Because of the cold winters the wheat is sown in the spring and harvested in late summer.

Our nation's greatest iron-mining region is near the western end of Lake Superior and important soft coal fields are found in Indiana, Illinois, and eastern Ohio. Because of these resources and good transportation, the *North Central states* have become a great industrial region. Indianapolis, capital of Indiana, uses iron and steel for automobile parts, trucks, airplane motors and heavy machinery. Automobiles and auto parts are manufactured in the Michigan cities of Detroit, Flint, Pontiac and Lansing.

Chicago is the most important marketing center for the rich farming region around it. It is also the greatest railroad center and air center in the United States. Located on Lake Michigan, it is easily reached by lake freighters, river barges, and trucks. Chicago leads in

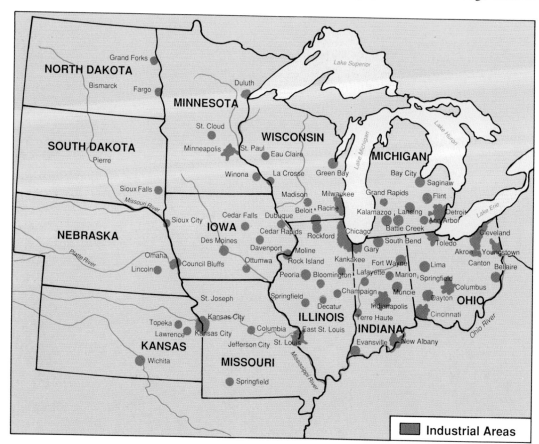

Chief Industrial Regions of the North Central States

the manufacture of farm machinery and other iron and steel products.

The Mississippi provides a waterway to the sea. Barges can move bulk products south from this region to New Orleans and the Gulf of Mexico. St. Louis, Missouri, is the Mississippi's most important inland port. The St. Lawrence Seaway permits ocean-going ships to move between the Great Lakes and the Atlantic Ocean.

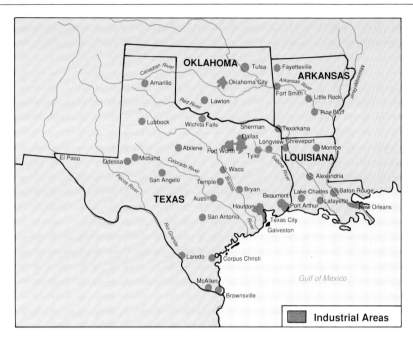

Chief Industrial Regions of the South Central States

South Central States

The four states in this region are Arkansas, Louisiana, Oklahoma and Texas. The eastern part of this region is like the Southeast. It has the same climate and crops. Cotton, rice and sugar cane are important crops. Texas has more cattle, sheep and goats than any other state.

Forests cover about half of Louisiana and Arkansas. Their tall, straight cypress trees make fine lumber. Eastern Texas and eastern Oklahoma also produce much lumber.

Texas, Louisiana and Oklahoma are among the leading oil-producing states. Some oil fields are deep underground on land. Others are offshore in the Gulf of Mexico. From petroleum we get gasoline,

kerosene, fuel oils, and lubricants, or smoothing oils. Natural gas is often found with petroleum. Texas and Louisiana are leading producers of natural gas.

Much of the world's supply of *sulfur* comes from the Louisiana and Texas Gulf Coast. This yellow mineral is important in making many products from steel and newsprint to rayon. Arkansas has some of the largest deposits of *bauxite* in North America. This is the ore from which aluminum is made. It is used for airplanes and kitchen utensils.

The cities of this region are chiefly trade and transportation centers. New Orleans is the trade and shipping center for the lower Mississippi Valley. Houston is a center for the United States space program.

The United States

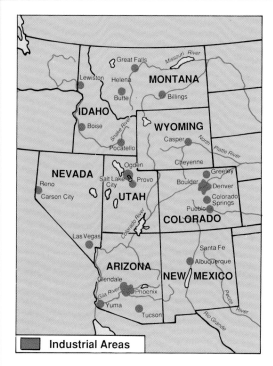

Chief Industrial Regions of the Rocky Mountain States

Rocky Mountain States

The *Rocky Mountain states* are Colorado, Montana, Wyoming, Idaho, Nevada, Utah, Arizona, and New Mexico. Many people here earn their living by farming and by raising livestock. The leading crops are wheat and cotton. Since rainfall is uncertain, farms are often irrigated with water from dammed-up rivers. These dams also control flooding, and provide hydroelectricity for power for industry. *Dry farming* is used where there is little rain and no supply of water for irrigation. Crops are planted on a plot of land only every other year, so the land at rest conserves its moisture.

Cattle and sheep feed on the tough grass that covers much of the land especially in Montana and Wyoming.

The Rocky Mountains are rich in minerals. Gold and silver are mined in every state in the region. Uranium from Colorado is used in nuclear energy plants. Arizona is the largest producer of copper. Coal, lead, zinc, petroleum and natural gas are also found here.

Many tourists visit the national parks in the Rockies to enjoy their beautiful scenery. The oldest and best-known is Yellowstone, which is located mostly in northwestern Wyoming. Huge natural fires took place there in 1988. South of Yellowstone is Grand Teton National Park. To the south, Utah has five national parks, including Bryce Canyon and Zion. The Grand Canyon in Arizona was carved out by the waters of the Colorado River. It is one of the world's greatest wonders.

Denver, Colorado is the state capital and a major transportation and trade center for the Rocky Mountain region.

Pacific States

The five *Pacific states* are California, Oregon, Washington, Alaska and Hawaii. The Imperial Valley of Southern California and the Central Valley to the north have rich farmland that needs irrigation to produce fine crops of fruit, vegetables and cotton. More than half the world's supply of raisins (sun-dried grapes), and 75% of the wine used in the United States come from the Central Valley. Washington is the chief apple-growing state in the nation. The Willamette Valley is one of

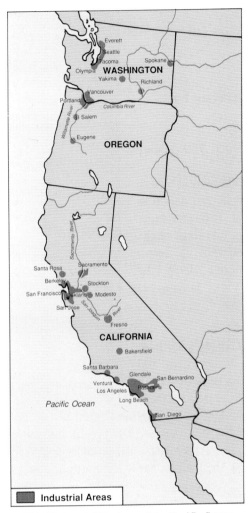
Chief Industrial Regions of the Pacific States

the leading fruit and vegetable canning centers in our country.

Oregon is the leading lumber state in the country. Many West Coast workers earn a living in farming, timber products, mining and fishing.

Southern California has large aircraft and defense factories. Other California factories process foods (canning tuna, freezing fruits and vegetables), and make machinery, cars and computers. Shipbuilding and tourism are also important.

Los Angeles is the largest city in population in the United States. It is the industrial center of southern California. Hollywood, a section in Los Angeles, is the nation's capital for filmmaking and television production.

ALASKA and HAWAII

Alaska is the largest state in area, but one of the smallest in population. In 1977, an 800-mile pipeline was built across Alaska to transport oil to port cities.

Alaska and **Hawaii** became states in 1959. Tourism is the main industry in Hawaii, which is located in the central Pacific Ocean. Beautiful scenery and warm weather make Hawaii a tropical paradise.

Canada

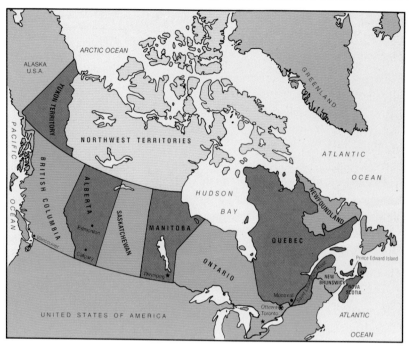

Canada's Provinces and Territories

Important Facts

Area:

    3,851,790 square miles

    The world's second largest nation in area. It covers more than one-third of the continent of North America. Only the Soviet Union is larger.

Borders:

    Canada's northern tip is less than 500 miles from the North Pole, and its southern boundary borders on the United States. This boundary is the world's longest unguarded border. To the east is the Atlantic and to the west, the Pacific. Far to the north lies the icy Arctic Ocean.

Population:

    26,000,000

    About 90% of its people live within 200 miles of the United States border. Most Canadians speak English and many have the same customs as the people of the United States.

Regions::

    Canada can be divided into four main regions: Eastern, Central, Northern, and Western regions.

Fishing Village in Canada's Eastern Region

Toronto

Eastern Regions

Maritime Region

This part of eastern Canada is almost completely surrounded by water. It includes New Brunswick, Nova Scotia, and Prince Edward and Newfoundland Islands. Like neighboring New England in the United States, it is part of the Appalachian Region. It too has old, worn-down mountains, and thin, rocky soils, some fertile valleys, and rocky coasts. There are many farms and fishing villages.

Great Lakes-St. Lawrence Lowlands

The *Great Lakes-St. Lawrence lowland* region is the most densely populated part of Canada. More than half of the Canadian people live here and Canada's two largest cities, Montreal and Toronto, are located here. Quebec, home to many French-speaking Canadians, is also here.

The western half of this lowland region is almost surrounded by three of the Great Lakes: Lake Huron, Lake Erie, and Lake Ontario. Much of the countryside is rich farming and grazing land. The eastern half of this region lies along the St. Lawrence River, where the land is flat and fertile.

The Great Lakes and the St. Lawrence River have been linked together by canals and locks to form the Great Lakes-St. Lawrence Waterway.

Central Region

Canadian Shield

The *Canadian Shield* of eastern and central Canada covers almost half the country. It extends from the Great Lakes and the Gulf of St. Lawrence north to the Arctic Ocean. The region is a heavily forested area of rocky plateaus, lakes, swamps, and hills. It is rich in minerals (iron ore, cobalt, copper, nickel, platinum, etc.) and water power. The population is small, and concentrated in the extreme south. There are no large cities.

The government of Canada

Canada is a federation, or union, of ten *provinces* and two *territories*. This federal form of government is similar to that of the United States. Canada has a national, or central, government in Ottawa and each province has its own government. Unlike the United States, Canada does not have three separate branches of government: legislative, executive and judicial. Instead, it has a *cabinet* system in which the legislative and judicial branches are united. The *Prime Minister* and members of the Cabinet are usually members of the *House of Commons*, the Canadian legislature.

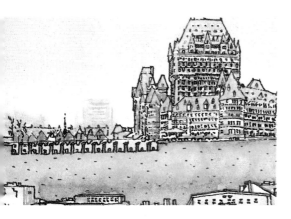

Quebec

Farm in Great Lakes—St. Lawrence Lowlands

Canada

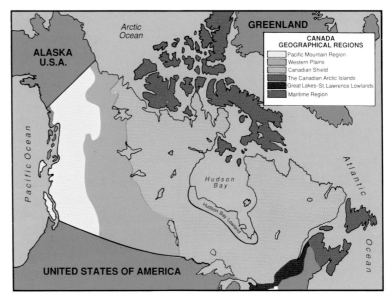

CANADA
GEOGRAPHICAL REGIONS
Pacific Mountain Region
Western Plains
Canadian Shield
The Canadian Arctic Islands
Great Lakes-St.Lawrence Lowlands
Maritime Region

Northern Regions

Canada's huge and valuable northland stretches west from Baffin Island and Hudson Bay to Alaska. It covers almost one-third of the country. It is divided into two territories, the Yukon and Northwest Territories.

Arctic Coastal Plain

The Hudson Bay lowland, which cuts into the Canadian Shield, is one section of Canada's *Arctic Coastal Plain*. The other section is the Arctic coast of the Northwest Territories and the Yukon Territory. The region is very cold and is largely a treeless plain known as *tundra*. (This Arctic Coastal Plain includes the northeast coast of Alaska, whose petroleum is an important natural resource of the United States.)

Canadian Arctic Islands

The *Canadian Arctic Islands* lie almost entirely within the Arctic Circle. The largest is Baffin Island. The northernmost is Ellesmere Island. Here mountain peaks rise 10,000 feet above sea level. They are covered with snow and ice for most of the year.

For two months during the winter, the sun does not rise above the Arctic horizon. Yet, in summer, lands north of the Arctic Circle receive twenty or more hours of sunlight daily. Then a bright blanket of poppies, buttercups and other colorful flowers covers the ground in many places.

Eskimos, or Inuit, are among the few people who live on the Arctic Islands.

Western Regions

Western Plains

Canada's *Western Plains* are part of a huge region of plains that extends across the conti-

Rocky Mountains

The Arctic Coastal Plain

110

nent of North America from the Arctic Ocean to the Gulf of Mexico. The southern part of Canada's Western Plains is very important for agriculture. The broad, flat plains are ideal for wheat because of the fertile soils, the warm summer growing season, and light rainfall.

Winds from the Arctic bring cold winters to all of Canada east of the Rockies. At times, a warm, dry wind called the "chinook" blows down the eastern slopes of the Rockies. The chinook can raise the temperature on the plains as much as forty degrees in a few hours. Then the heavy snows melt quickly, and the grainfields are exposed. In summer, the Western Plains are warm and usually dry.

The largest city in area is Winnipeg, in Manitoba province. Most *prairie* wheat comes eastward by train to Winnipeg, then goes by rail to Lake Superior, and by freighter to Montreal. There it is made into flour, or shipped to other countries.

Pacific Mountain Region

Like the mountainous western part of the United States to the south, Canada's *Pacific Mountain Region* also has several parts. In the east are the Rocky Mountains, with jag-ged, snow-capped peaks rising more than 11,000 feet above sea level. West of the Rockies lie rugged uplands with deep river valleys like that of the Fraser River, which flows from north to south toward Vancouver. Further west are the Coast Mountains, the Pacific shoreline, and many islands. The largest island is Vancouver Island, which lies between the United States and Canada. The Pacific Mountain Region covers most of the province of British Columbia, as well as of the Yukon Territory to the north.

Canada's west coast has the mildest winter temperatures of the whole country. The high mountains shelter this coast from the icy arctic winds. Also, a warm ocean current called the *North Pacific Drift* flows along the western coast of Canada. Westerly winds from the Pacific Ocean bring over 60 inches of rainfall each year to much of the Pacific coast of Canada. Dense forests of tall ever-green trees grow on the rainy slopes of the Coast Mountains. This mild, rainy coastal climate is also found along the southwest coast of Alaska, and in the northwest states of Washington and Oregon. All these Pacific coast areas enjoy cool, clear summers because of the westerly winds.

Wheat Farming

The City of Vancouver

Canada

The People of Canada

Although Canada is the second largest country in the world, it has about one-tenth as many people as has the United States:

Canada 26 million people (1988)
U.S.   246 million people (1988)

Ninety percent of all Canadians live within 200 miles of the United States border, because the climate in southern Canada is milder, and the land is more fertile.

Canada is the home of many different people. Canadian Indians and Eskimos (Inuit) have lived in North America for thousands of years. Others have come to Canada from many lands during the last 400 years. More than two-fifths of Canadians are descendants of people from England, Ireland, Scotland and Wales (the British Isles). Nearly one-third of Canada's people are of French descent. They live mainly in the province of Quebec, but are also found in New Brunswick, Ontario and Manitoba. Thousands have come from the United States, and from the European nations of Germany, the Netherlands, Norway, Sweden, Poland, Italy, Greece, and Portugal. Other Canadians have ancestors who came from the Asian countries of China, Japan, India and Tibet. Black people of African descent also live in Canada. Many of these came to Canada from the island of Jamaica in the West Indies.

Earning a Living

Farming

Canada is one of the world's great food-producing countries, but only a small part of this vast nation is used to raise crops and livestock. Most farms and ranches are in southern Canada, where there are enough warm days for many kinds of crops to grow, and where the most fertile soil is found.

In the Fraser River Valley in the Pacific Mountain Region, dairy farms and vegetable gardens help feed the people of Vancouver. On other hillside slopes, apple, peach and pear orchards are found.

Canada's richest farmland, and one of the best wheat-growing areas in the world, is the southern part of the flat, wide Western Plains. Farmers in this area also grow oats, barley, sugar beets and potatoes. Many beef and dairy cattle are raised in this region.

The southern part of the province of Ontario is another rich farming area. It is almost surrounded by three of the Great Lakes. Dairy herds and vegetable farms feed the people in the cities nearby. In Quebec province, nine-

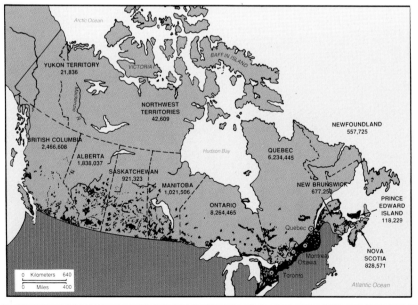

Canada's Population
Dots show concentrations.

Lumbering is an important industry in Canada.

tenths of Canada's maple syrup and maple sugar are produced. The Maritime Region yields fish from the Grand Banks, potatoes, oats, hay, and large, sweet apples.

Forest Products

Canada's vast forests may be divided into three regions:

1. The western forest region lies in the southern half of the Pacific Mountain region. Sixty to 100 inches of rain a year help to grow tall Douglas fir, spruce, hemlock, and cedar trees for lumber that is used in building.

2. The northern forest region is the largest of the three. It stretches from Alaska east to the Atlantic. The trees of this great forest are spruce, balsam fir and jack pine. Much of this popular wood is made into paper and cardboard.

3. The eastern forest spreads from the Great Lakes eastward along the St. Lawrence Valley to the Atlantic. Here, there are evergreen trees such as pine and spruce as well as maple, birch and aspen. The trees of this region are used to make woodpulp for paper and lumber for building.

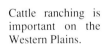

Cattle ranching is important on the Western Plains.

Canada

Earning a Living

Fishing and Furs

Canada is one of the world's leaders in fishing. Fish are caught off Canada's Atlantic and Pacific coasts, and in inland lakes and rivers. Many Canadians earn their living by fishing or by working in plants that process fish by freezing, salting, drying, or canning. The most important Atlantic fishing grounds are the Grand Banks, where cod, haddock, hake, halibut, pollack, herring, mackerel and shellfish are caught. Salmon fishing is important on the Pacific coast.

Fur trappers and fur farms bring skins to market. Canada's forests produce mink, muskrat, fox, beaver, otter and ermine.

Waterpower and Minerals

Waterpower is one of Canada's most important natural resources. Hydroelectric power plants use the force of rushing water to produce electric power. They produce about three-fourths of Canada's electricity. Vast deposits of petroleum and natural gas lie under the Western Plains in and near Alberta. Giant pipelines carry the oil and natural gas to many parts of Canada and the United States. The coal mined in Alberta and British Columbia is another important Canadian energy fuel.

Many important metal ores are mined in Canada. Rich deposits of iron ore are found near Labrador City. Copper and nickel are mined near Sudbury, Ontario. Canada is the world's leading producer of zinc and mines large amounts of gold, silver, and platinum.

Industry

Canada has large iron and steel mills at the Great Lakes ports of Sault Ste. Marie and Hamilton, Ontario. It manufactures aluminum using ore brought by ship from South

Steel Mills

Dams are used for hydroelectric power.

America and Jamaica. Windsor, Ontario, is called the "Detroit of Canada" because so many automobile factories are located there. Airplanes, ships and trucks are also made in Canada, as are machines and equipment used in farming, mining, paper manufacturing and food processing.

Near Canada's western oil wells are factories that make medicines, paints and plastics from petroleum. Here also are refineries that make gasoline and fuel oil from petroleum. Canada's pulp and paper mills produce more newsprint than any other country. Other

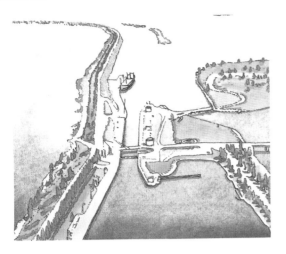

St. Lawrence Seaway

Fish Processing Plant

wood products include alcohol, fertilizer, plywood and rayon. Many textile and clothing factories are found in southern Quebec and Ontario.

Transportation and Communication

The Great Lakes-St. Lawrence Waterway permits ocean-going ships to travel from the Atlantic Ocean along the St. Lawrence River, and through the Great Lakes to the western shores of Lake Superior. The Trans-Canada Highway, which is about 5,000 miles long, extends across the entire country from the eastern coast of Newfoundland to the west coast of Canada.

About 30% of Canada's freight moves by rail. The two transcontinental railways are the Canadian National (CN), which is government-owned, and the privately owned Canadian Pacific (CP). Two major airlines serve Canada.

Newspapers, magazines, radio and television bring news and entertainment to the 26 million Canadians. Canada uses modern space communications, including satellite transmission of television programs.

Canada and the United States

Trade

About three-fourths of Canada's exports are sold to the United States. These products include oil and natural gas, iron ore, fish, wood pulp, and many manufactured goods. In return, Canada imports a great deal from the United States, including machinery, chemicals, and food products. A free trade agreement signed in 1988 will make more goods available to people in both countries.

Acid Rain

A growing problem between the United States and Canada is that of "acid rain." Large factories and power plants near their common border, but mostly in the United States, burn coal which gives off harmful chemicals of sulfur and nitrogen. When these chemicals combine with falling rain they produce a weak acid that pollutes lakes and streams. It kills fish, plants, and even many trees.

Canada wants the United States to require factories to install equipment to prevent harmful chemicals from escaping into the air. However, this would cost a great deal of money.

Expressing Oneself—Communicating

Spoken

Speech or Language?

The collection of sounds, organized into words or sentences, represents speech, which allows human beings to express themselves and to communicate. Human speech varies according to countries and people. Each variety of speech is called a *language*. There are close to *4,000 spoken languages* in the world.

Major Languages

The table below shows the most common languages in the world (nearly 5 billion human beings).

A Common Language

For better communication between people, a common language was needed. Ever since the 1700s, hundreds of languages have been developed to enable people all over the world to communicate, but none has had great success.

The most famous of these is *esperanto* which is used presently by 3 million people in 100 countries. Today, English is the language most often used for international communication.

Written

In the 1700s, a famous writer claimed that, "Writing is the painting of the voice." For over 5,000 years, humans have used signs or symbols to express themselves and to communicate.

3000 B.C. The Sumerians carved pictographs on clay tablets.

Original	Modified	Babylonian	Assyrian
Bird			
Fish			
Sun/Day			
Seed			
Orchard			

Evolution of pictographs in the Near East. They became more and more abstract.

Original	4th to 3rd Century B.C.	Modern
Man		
Hill		
Tree		
Dog		
Moon		

Evolution of Chinese pictographs. A pictograph became an ideograph or a symbol. Chinese writing has more than 3,000 ideographs!

One Symbol, One Idea

The Egyptian pictograph ⊏⊐ (sky) which indicates both clouds and paradise is an *ideograph*.

One Symbol, One Sound

In later Egyptian writing, each symbol also had a phonetic value and represented one, two, or three sounds. There were no vowels, only consonants. For instance: ⊂⊃ (mouth) means "r," ⌂ (loaf of bread) means "t," ⌡ (throne) means "s + t" and is pronounced "set."

Today, in order to indicate how a word sounds, we use phonetic symbols that are grouped together in an alphabet, called the International Phonetic Alphabet (I.P.A.).

EXAMPLE

[əp] = up   [läk] = lock   [dā] = day
[ēzē] = easy

The Alphabet

The introduction of the alphabet simplified writing considerably. The Phoenicians were the first to use it about 1000 B.C.

Finally, the invention of the printing press by Johann Gutenberg in the 1400s increased the number of books and made them more widespread and available.

North-Semitic	Early Phoenician	ⱅ 𝟫 𝟣 ◁Ⅎ⅂ Ɏ	I⊟⊕⅄	↓⌇Ɛϟ ⅀ⱦ⊘⅂	⅄ W+						
	Phoenician	ⱅ 𝟫 𝟣 ◁Ⅎ⅄	I⌿⊗Z	Ɏⱡ⋔ᵞ O⋔ ꟼ⅄ w t x							
Greek	Early	◁ 𝟪 𝟣 ◁Ⅎ⅂	I⌐⊗⅃	⅄↑⋔ᵞ O⋔MꟼⱯ ⅄X							
	Classical	A Β Γ Δ E	Z H θ I	K Λ M N Ξ O ⊓ P Σ T Y							
Etruscan	Classic	A ⅃ ⅂⅂	⅄⊞⊙I	⅄↓⋔ᵞ⋈ ⅂M Q ⅄ ⅄↑∨							
Latin	Early	A ▽⅂⅂	⊟ I	↓ ⋔⅄ O Γ ϟ ∨							
	Classical	A B C D E F G H I	K L M N O P Q R S T V								
Modern Capitals	Roman	A B C D E F G H I J K L M N O P Q R S T U V W									

Signs and Symbols

The spoken and written word are not the only ways to communicate. Visual symbols can also be used.

Sign Language

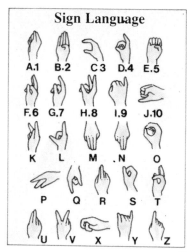

A.1 B.2 C.3 D.4 E.5
F.6 G.7 H.8 I.9 J.10
K L M .N O
P Q R S T
U V X Y Z

Morse Code

A · —	M — —	Z — — · ·
B — · · ·	N — ·	
C — · — ·	O — — —	
Ch — — — —	P · — — ·	1 · — — — —
D — · ·	Q — — · —	2 · · — — —
E ·	R · — ·	3 · · · — —
F · · — ·	S · · ·	4 · · · · —
G — — ·	T —	5 · · · · ·
H · · · ·	U · · —	6 — · · · ·
I · ·	V · · · —	7 — — · · ·
J · — — —	W · — —	8 — — — · ·
K — · —	X — · · —	9 — — — — ·
L · — · ·	Y — · — —	0 — — — — —

? · · — — · ·
! — · — · — —
() — · — — · —

Road Signs

 Parking

 No Right Turn

 No Trucks

 No Turn on Red

 Speed Limit 55

Winding Road

 Narrow Bridge

Stop

 No Left Turn

Yield

 No U-Turn

 Railroad Crossing

Keep Right of Divider

 Do Not Enter

Right Lane Ends Merge Left

Divided Highway Ends

 Traffic Signal Ahead

Two-Way Traffic

Merging Traffic Entering from Right

Hill Ahead

Slippery When Wet

Men at Work

Flagman Ahead

 Gas

 Detour

One-Way

Dangerous Intersection Ahead

 Road Work 1000 Ft

 Hospital

Navy Flag Signals

Arm signals are usually given with two small flags, one in each hand.

A B C D E F G H I J
K L M N O P Q R S T
U V W X Y Z Attack Canceled End of signal

118

Air Traffic Signals

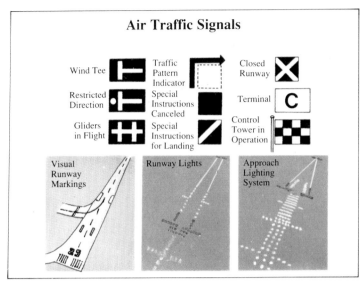

Wind Tee — Traffic Pattern Indicator — Closed Runway
Restricted Direction — Special Instructions Canceled — Terminal
Gliders in Flight — Special Instructions for Landing — Control Tower in Operation

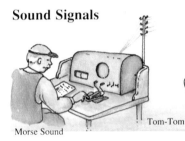

Visual Runway Markings — Runway Lights — Approach Lighting System

Light Signals

Traffic Control Signals — Lighthouse

Morse Code Signals in the Mountains

Sound Signals

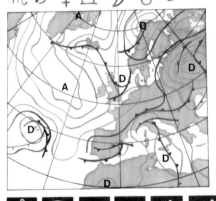

Morse Sound — Tom-Tom — Warning Siren — Intercom — Ambulance Siren

Various Symbols

Above: Signs of the Zodiac and of different planets.
Right: Symbols of Olympic Sports
Left: Weather map: A = High D = Low.

Can you identify these 26 signs?

Braille

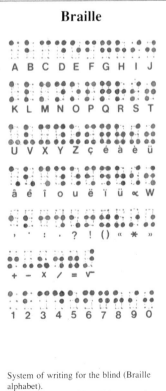

A B C D E F G H I J
K L M N O P Q R S T
U V X Y Z ç é à è ü
â ê î o u ë ï ü œ W
. ; : . ? ! ( ) « * »
+ − × / = √
1 2 3 4 5 6 7 8 9 0

System of writing for the blind (Braille alphabet).
Braille is raised writing. This system is also used for musical notes.

The English Language

cwaedon þæt he wære Wyruld-cyninga
manna mildust ond mon·þwærust,
leodum liðost ond lof-geornost.

Old English from the Poem *Beowulf*

> Translation: "It's said that of all the world's kings he was the mildest and gentlest of men, the kindest to his people, and most eager for praise."

The Beginning of English

About the year 449 A.D., bands of Anglo-Saxon warriors came from Europe to conquer the British Isles. They spoke a language called *Old English*, which was very different from the English we now speak. They used some words they learned from the Celtic people they had defeated. Some of these new words were Latin which had been taught to the Celts by the Roman soldiers who once occupied England. English is a language that grows and develops by bringing in words from other languages.

Middle English and Modern English

When the Normans from France conquered England in 1066, hundreds of words came into the language, and English continued to grow and develop into what we now call *Middle English*.

The Normans defeat the English in 1066. Note the Latin words on this Bayeux tapestry. Latin was used in the Church and for formal purposes.

The English Bible, 1611

An example of Middle English is the line:

> "Soune ys noght but eyre ybroken,"

which means: "Sound is nothing but air broken." By the year 1500, English, as we now speak it, was well established. This "Modern English" became widely used when the English Bible (the King James Version) was published in 1611. Modern spelling, of course, was not established until Dr. Samuel Johnson published his famous dictionary in 1755.

English Words from Other Languages

Like no other language in the world, English is a mixture of all languages. More than half of our words come from Latin; for example, *memorandum, orbit,* and *item.*

Here is a list of some of these English words from other languages:

French: *baton, fruit.*   German: *pretzel, wiener.*   Japanese: *ju-jitsu, samurai.*
Spanish: *barbecue, alligator.*   Hebrew: *cherub, kosher.*   Chinese: *kowtow, catchup.*
Italian: *violin, soprano.*   Persian: *caravan, bazaar.*   African: *banana, yam.*
Indian (East): *dungaree, shampoo.*   Hawaiian: *ukelele.*   Scandinavian: *muggy, ski.*

English Spoken Around the World

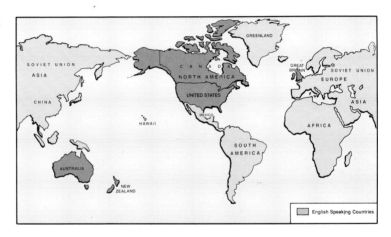

More people speak Chinese than any other language. That is because there are a billion Chinese people—one-fourth of the world's population. The next most widely spoken language is English, which is the primary language in the United States, Canada, Great Britain, Ireland, Australia, South

Countries Where the Primary Language Is English

Africa, and New Zealand. In other countries, most people who decide to learn a second language choose English. It is the official language for all aircraft controllers and is used all over the world in business.

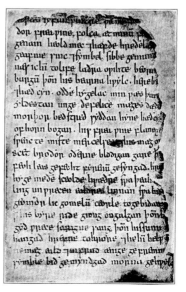

The Oldest Manuscript in English

It is the manuscript of the Old English poem, *Beowulf,* which was written about the year 1000 after having been composed in the 8th century.

A page from the only surviving manuscript of *Beowulf*

The Meaning of Words

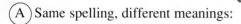

Homonyms

The English language can be troublesome because it contains many *homonyms*—words which have either the same pronunciation or the same spelling but have different meanings.

(A) Same spelling, different meanings:

- We caught a *bass* while fishing today.
- The choral director needs men with *bass* voices.

- The knight was protected by a coat of *mail*.
- Your check is in the *mail*.

- A victory would be something to *crow* over.
- The jet black *crow* flew across our path.

(B) Different spelling, same pronunciation:

- Dinner will be served at *eight* o'clock.
- She *ate* every fruit in the bowl.

- Brad handed me a *pair* of tickets.
- The painting showed a golden *pear* on a kitchen table.

- Your cupboard is completely *bare*.
- The zoo purchased a new *bear*.

> Other examples of *homographs*
> (same spelling, different meaning):
>
> state — particular condition/government
> bar — pole or rod/tavern
> boom — deep sound/business growth
> fine — excellent/punishment
> hide — conceal/animal skin

Other examples of *homophones*
(different spelling, same pronunciation):

pail (container)
pale (of little color)

meet (to encounter)
meat (animal flesh)

whole (entire)
hole (opening)

council (lawmakers)
counsel (advice)

capital (main city)
capitol (building where lawmakers meet)

Synonyms

The English language has many words which are similar in meaning. These words are called *synonyms*.

EXAMPLES

- I was *glad* to hear from you.
(You might have substituted *pleased, overjoyed, happy, delighted, thrilled.*)

- The man had a *bad* character.
(You might have substituted *wicked, evil, corrupt, vile, rotten, unpleasant.*)

Note the many possible synonyms of these words. Can you suggest others?

hungry	—	starved, famished
angry	—	enraged, upset
huge	—	big, large, enormous
strong	—	powerful, sturdy, muscular
stubborn	—	obstinate, inflexible, hard-headed
beautiful	—	attractive, lovely, delightful

As writers know, most synonyms present a different shading, a more specific way of making a point. It's one thing, for example, to say that you have a *big* job to do, but it's something else to describe that job as *immense, overwhelming, brutal, titanic, monstrous, crushing,* etc.

Antonyms

An *antonym* is a word which is opposite in meaning to another. *Tall* and *short, backwards* and *forwards, rich* and *poor, courage* and *cowardice* are all antonyms for each other.
   With the addition of a prefix, we are able to form numerous antonyms:

possible	— impossible		respect	— disrespect
inform	— misinform		similar	— dissimilar
known	— unknown		wise	— unwise
correct	— incorrect		frequent	— infrequent
equal	— unequal		accurate	— inaccurate

Writing in All Its Forms

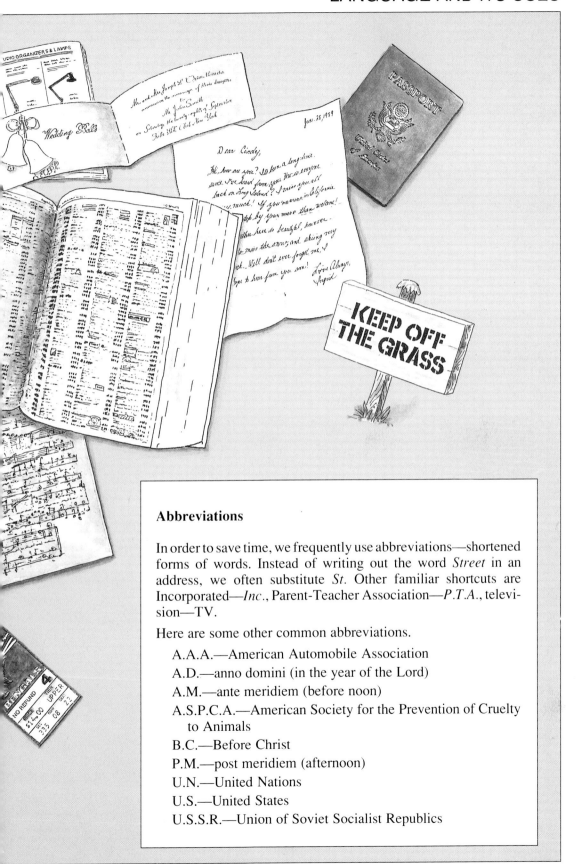

Abbreviations

In order to save time, we frequently use abbreviations—shortened forms of words. Instead of writing out the word *Street* in an address, we often substitute *St.* Other familiar shortcuts are Incorporated—*Inc.*, Parent-Teacher Association—*P.T.A.*, television—TV.

Here are some other common abbreviations.

A.A.A.—American Automobile Association

A.D.—anno domini (in the year of the Lord)

A.M.—ante meridiem (before noon)

A.S.P.C.A.—American Society for the Prevention of Cruelty to Animals

B.C.—Before Christ

P.M.—post meridiem (afternoon)

U.N.—United Nations

U.S.—United States

U.S.S.R.—Union of Soviet Socialist Republics

Playing with Words

Etymology

Etymology is the study of *word origins*. By learning the meaning of some important prefixes, suffixes, and stems you will be able to expand your vocabulary as you recognize them in unfamiliar words. For example, if you are aware that *auto* = self, *bio* = life, and *graph* = to write, you will then know that an *autobiography* is a person's story of his or her own life. Here are some useful examples:

ab (away from) — *ab*duct

able (capable of) — port*able*

agri (field) — *agri*culture

ante (before) — *ante*cedent

anthrop (man) — phil*anthrop*ist

aqua (water) — *aqua*tic

aud (to hear) — *aud*itorium

belli (war) — re*belli*on

bene (good, well) — *bene*factor

bi (two) — *bi*annual

cap (head) — de*cap*itate

contra (against) — *contra*dict

Anagrams

An anagram is a word or phrase formed from another by rearranging the letters.

devil	—	lived
charm	—	march
tea	—	eat
read	—	dear
teach	—	cheat

Exercise

What anagrams can you suggest for these words?
1. male
2. thread
3. bleat

Idioms

Idioms are phrases or expressions which cannot be understood from the ordinary meanings of their words. For example, when we say, "I'm going to catch a train," we don't mean that we are going to use a baseball glove *to catch* a train. Over the years, idioms have gained acceptance in a language, and it is almost impossible to deal with people without an understanding of the true meanings of the idioms they use. If someone gives you "the cold shoulder" or "calls you on the carpet," for example, will you be happy about those two experiences?

Here are some idioms in constant use in English:

a pig in a poke—an item you buy without having seen it; a disappointment

a flash in the pan—promising at the start but then disappointing

to pour oil on troubled waters—to make peace

a wet blanket—one who spoils your fun

crocodile tears—insincere emotion

to rule the roost—to be in charge

to pass the buck—to avoid responsibility

red-letter day—time for rejoicing

let sleeping dogs lie—let well enough alone

thumbs down—sign of rejection

an ax to grind—having a selfish motive

to cool one's heels—to be kept waiting

Crossword Puzzle

Across
1. Stream of water
5. Conjunction
6. Abbrev. for radium
7. Sloping edge
9. Poor

Down
1. red-breasted bird
2. anger
3. before
4. mass meeting
8. compete

1.	2.		3.	4.
5.		■	6.	
7.		8.		
	■		■	
9.				

Answers

Down
1. robin
2. ire
3. ere
4. rally
8. vie

Across
1. river
5. or
6. RA
7. bevel
9. needy

Find the "Bad Guys"

Somewhere in this box of letters, reading up, down, across, or diagonally, find the names of three well-known villains from children's literature.

E	A	V	E	D	C	G	I
A	S	E	K	U	A	L	N
S	T	C	E	S	P	I	J
O	L	I	R	O	T	P	U
M	B	X	N	O	H	F	N
U	R	O	Y	Q	O	T	J
T	A	I	G	U	O	G	O
T	Y	L	Z	E	K	E	E

Answers

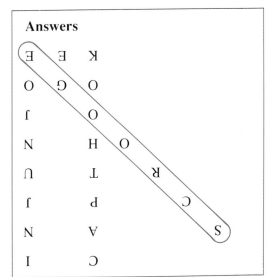

Funny Bunny Game

What's an amusing rabbit? The rhyming answer is "funny bunny." Now, solve these:

1. an improved woolen pullover
2. a stiff finger
3. the most important cot
4. an angry boy

Answers

1. better sweater   2. rigid digit   3. head bed   4. mad lad

Poetry

Poets are writers who use words in harmonious and imaginative ways to create word pictures and gain emotional responses from readers. Poets use *meaning*, *sound*, *meter*, and *rhyme* to transmit thoughts to the reader. *Prose*, unlike *poetry*, generally does not have a metrical structure.

Ancient Times

Poetry was very important in ancient Greece, where the great poet Homer sang of heroes—and the gods who interacted with them—in the long epic poems, the *Iliad* and the *Odyssey*.

The ancient Greeks loved drama, which was written in poetic meter by the great writers of tragedy: Aeschylus, Sophocles, and Euripides.

In the golden age of Roman literature (first century B.C.) Virgil wrote his epic masterpiece, the *Aeneid*, as well as the *Eclogues*, poems about the charms of nature.

The blind Greek poet Homer lived in the 9th century B.C.

The Middle Ages

Around the 12th century, wandering French troubadours wrote *chansons de geste* (songs about deeds) to praise legendary heroes. The best known of these was the *Song of Roland*, about King Charlemagne's nephew, a hero in the Crusades.

One of the world's greatest writers, Dante Alighieri, was born in the 13th century in Italy. His long poem, *The Divine Comedy*, en-compasses all the knowledge of the medieval period and dramatizes humanity's search for perfection.

Geoffrey Chaucer, in 14th century England, wrote the remarkable long work, *The Canterbury Tales*, filled with the wit and wisdom of the Middle Ages and a vast array of characters of the time.

"There came one night into that hostelry
Some nine and twenty in a company
Of sundry persons who had chanced to fall
In fellowship, and pilgrims were they all,
And toward Canterbury would they ride."

(Modern English version)

A commoner who worked in the Royal Court, Geoffrey Chaucer (c. 1343–1400) knew all of English society and described it brilliantly.

The Renaissance

In the 16th century the English poet William Shakespeare, generally acknowledged to be the greatest writer the world has ever known, began writing his extraordinary sonnets and plays, many of which were written in verse.

At this time, when new knowledge was bursting forth—the Renaissance—other English poets flourished: Edmund Spenser (c. 1552–1599), author of *The Faerie Queene*, a long allegorical poem, and Christopher Marlowe (1564–1593), who wrote great plays in verse.

William Shakespeare (1564–1616)

"Shall I compare thee to a summer's day?
Thou art more lovely and more temperate:
Rough winds do shake the darling buds of May,
And summer's lease hath all too short a date."

John Milton

The 17th Century
English poetry took a new direction when John Donne (1572–1631) composed sonnets and lyrics with startling, complex images and John Milton (1607–1674) wrote a distinctive type of epic poem, *Paradise Lost*, as well as some of the world's greatest sonnets.

[Quotation, from one of Milton's sonnets]
"How soon hath Time, the subtle thief of youth,
Stol'n on his wings my three and twentieth year!"

In France, Jean Racine (1639–1699) is universally acknowledged as that country's greatest dramatic poet.

The 18th Century
The century of the Enlightenment produced a new kind of poetry, called *Neo-classical*, which was mainly philosophical and satirical. Alexander Pope (1688–1744), who wrote profound and witty couplets in poems such as *Essay on Man* and *Essay on Criticism*, was by far the greatest poet of his age.

The 19th Century
This, the greatest century of poetry, saw the emergence of the English Romantic poets, who glorified nature and the individual—William Wordsworth (1770–1850), Samuel Taylor Coleridge (1772–1834), Lord Byron (1788–1824), Percy Shelley (1792–1822), and John Keats (1795–1821). In America there appeared such great traditional poets as Henry Wadsworth Longfellow (1807–1882) and James Russell Lowell (1819–1891). There were also two American poets who blazed new trails: Walt Whitman (1819–1891), who wrote lyrical, self-centered outbursts of song about himself and his country, and Emily Dickinson (1830–1886), a shy New England woman whose keen observation and talent for imagery transformed American poetry. In the last part of the century, the English poets Alfred Tennyson (1809–1892) and Robert Browning (1812–1899) built a new structure on Romantic poetry to form the serious Victorian school of poetry. In France at this time, Charles Baudelaire, Paul Verlaine, and Arthur Rimbaud liberated poetry by introducing a daring new style, the basis for modern poetry.

Emily Dickinson

The 20th Century
Poetry has continued to develop as an art form in this century. Some of the most acclaimed of the modern poets are William Butler Yeats (1865-1939), T.S. Eliot (1888-1965), Robert Frost (1874-1963), Carl Sandburg (1878-1967), Langston Hughes (1902-1967), and Sylvia Plath (1932-1963). Following no precise rules, this poetry plays with words, with rhythms, and with sounds.

Robert Frost

Langston Hughes

Literature

What is Literature?

Literature consists of the body of written works, in prose or verse, that expresses the ideas of a particular culture. Western literature would include·modern works as well as those that have survived from the Middle Ages and ancient Rome and Greece.

From the Spoken to the Written Word

At first, legends and stories were transmitted by word of mouth. Starting mainly in the 15th century, with the development of the printing press, literary works were put down in permanent form and widely distributed.

The Writer and Language

Not every written work is classified as literature. Only a few great writers can convey precisely, originally, and brilliantly such important ideas as those relating to life and death, love and hate, politics and society.

Every century has its great writers. Among the most famous, not including the ones mentioned among the poets, are:

Middle Ages	16th Century	17th Century
Petrarch	Sir Thomas More	Ben Jonson
Boccaccio	John Lyly	Robert Herrick
Malory	Niccolo Machiavelli	Sir Francis Bacon
Villon	François Rabelais	Sir Thomas Browne
	Michel de Montaigne	Molière
	Miguel de Cervantes	Pierre Corneille
		René Descartes
		Blaise Pascal

Types of Literature

The many different forms of literature are usually distinguished by subject and treatment:

- The *Novel*—the most popular form; a work of fiction, a product of the imagination. The author brings people to life, describing their feelings, their thoughts, and their adventures. There are detective, historical, romantic, science-fiction, and spy novels.
- The *Short Story*—a short narrative with a plot and characterization pertaining to a single set of circumstances and no sub-plots as in novels.
- The *Essay*—impressions and observations on a particular subject; non-fiction.
- *Satire*—writing that ridicules human faults, often with the intent of correcting them.
- A *Journal*—a record of daily events witnessed by the author.
- *Memoirs*—narratives of events in which the author has participated.

Other literary forms include *maxims*, *sayings*, *proverbs*, and *letters*.

World Literature

Some authors have become internationally known. Through translations, it is possible to read and appreciate the literature of *France* (Hugo, Dumas), *Russia* (Tolstoi, Dostoyevski), *Germany* (Mann, Goethe), *Italy* (Dante), and *Spain* (Cervantes). The works of *American* authors (Faulkner, Hemingway) and *British* authors (Shakespeare, Dickens) have been translated into many different languages and are read all over the world.

Reference Books

Many works such as encyclopedias, dictionaries, textbooks, or guidebooks do not "tell stories." They are mainly used to provide knowledge.

18th Century	19th Century	20th Century
Voltaire	Victor Hugo	Marcel Proust
Jean Jacques Rousseau	Alexandre Dumas	André Gide
Goethe	Honoré de Balzac	François Mauriac
Samuel Johnson	Gustave Flaubert	Albert Camus
Oliver Goldsmith	Emile Zola	Jean-Paul Sartre
William Blake	George Sand	Theodore Dreiser
Daniel Defoe	Matthew Arnold	Sinclair Lewis
	Sir Walter Scott	F. Scott Fitzgerald
	Charles Dickens	William Faulkner
	Emily Brontë	Ernest Hemingway
	Thomas Hardy	Bernard Malamud
	Nathaniel Hawthorne	Flannery O'Connor
	Herman Melville	Eugene O'Neill
	Washington Irving	James Baldwin
		Arthur Miller
		Thomas Mann

Information—Three Powerful Media

What Does "Media" Mean?

Media refers to newspapers, magazines, radio and television—all forms of mass communication and advertising that *circulate information, opinions and entertainment* all over the world. Both competing with each other, and complementing one another, media plays an important and influential role in our lives.

The Press

Over 400 million copies of thousands of *newspapers* are printed daily throughout the world. In addition, *magazines* cover almost every possible subject. Information has not always been so readily available.

The First Reporters

At first, news was circulated in the form of handwriting. Ancient Romans engraved information on wax tablets. The first printed sheets were made possible by the invention of the printing press in about 1450. The first daily newspaper, *The Daily Courant*, began publication in London in 1702. In the United States, the first newspaper, *Publick Occurrences Both Forreign and Domestick*, was published in 1690 by John Harris. This four-page newspaper was halted after one issue by the English government for being critical of government policies. Fourteen years later, a second newspaper, *The News-Letter* appeared.

Advances in print technology during the 1800s made illustrated newspapers possible. This led to the growth of print *advertising*. Soon, newspapers and magazines became not only major business operations, but were also influential in causing political and social change.

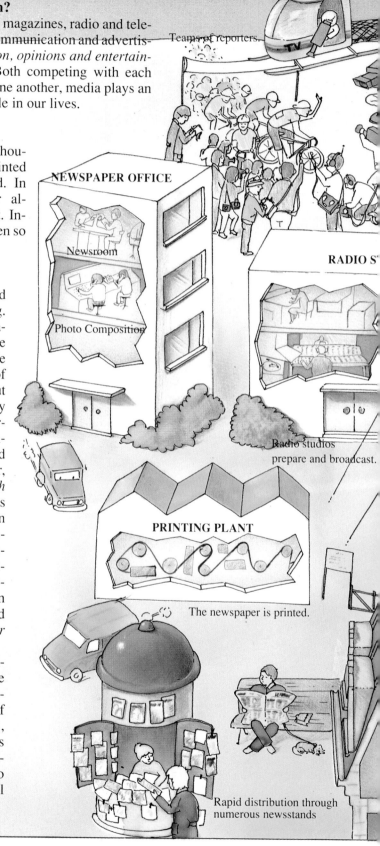

Teams of reporters.

NEWSPAPER OFFICE

Newsroom

Photo Composition

RADIO S

Radio studios prepare and broadcast.

PRINTING PLANT

The newspaper is printed.

Rapid distribution through numerous newsstands

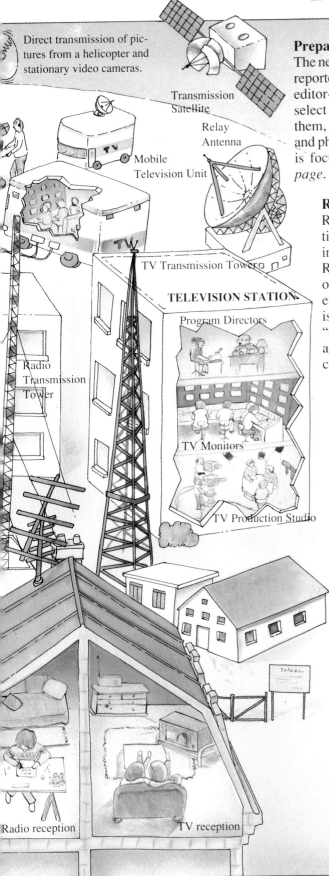

Direct transmission of pictures from a helicopter and stationary video cameras.

Transmission Satellite

Relay Antenna

Mobile Television Unit

TV Transmission Tower

TELEVISION STATION

Program Directors

TV Monitors

TV Production Studio

Radio Transmission Tower

Radio reception

TV reception

Preparing a Newspaper

The newspaper is the product of a team of reporters and editors who work under an editor-in-chief. Together they write and select articles, decide where to place them, and create headlines, illustrations, and photographs. Much of their attention is focused on the first page—the *front page*.

Radio Broadcasting

Radio is a relatively recent invention. The first broadcasts were heard in the United States in the 1920s. Radio is the most accessible means of communication and can be heard everywhere. A reporter or journalist—a special correspondent—can "cover" an event where it happens and as it happens. This coverage is called a *news flash* or *bulletin*.

Television

Television provides sight, sound, and movement. Its invention dates back to the 1920s but it was not used until after World War II. Large resources (in technique, equipment, and personnel) are needed to produce television programs. The *image*, however, seems to speak directly to the viewer in a very personal way. While radio can usually bring news of unexpected events faster, television is unequaled for live transmission of planned events, close or far away (sports competitions, the walk on the moon, political debates, etc.). The camera sometimes transforms a televised event into recorded history. The televised assassination of President John F. Kennedy and the explosion of the space shuttle *Challenger* shocked and moved viewers who saw these events. Today, new techniques in broadcasting (satellites, cable television) pave the way for even greater means of communication.

The World of Pictures

The Language of Pictures

All around us, pictures, either *animated* (movie, television) or *still* (photograph, cartoon, illustration), show and tell, describe, and talk to our imagination. This language is universal.

Talking and Communicating through Photographs

Understood by everyone, a photograph has various characteristics, depending upon its purpose.

A *family picture* or a *souvenir picture* has sentimental value and records a certain time in life.

An *artistic picture*, taken to communicate a thought or feeling, uses light, color, frame and perspective to achieve its purpose.

Newspaper photos illustrate printed text.

An *impact picture* captures our attention and forces us to think and read.

Cartoons—A Story in Pictures

Considered popular art, cartoons (comic strips) are a form of entertainment. They may be dramatic, humorous, or satirical. Like the words of a text, successive pictures (text illustrations or small scenes) show action and build a story.

The story may be *silent*—the picture by itself presents the meaning. It may be *spoken*—some text, often a conversation, is included along with the picture.

Cartoon text is written according to very specific rules.

"Balloons," which contain the text, vary in

their placement and shape in order to produce different emotions—fear, excitement, love, sadness, anger, humor.

The *way letters are printed*, their size and shape, indicate variations in voice—intonation, hesitation, stuttering, yelling, whispering.

Color also contributes to a better understanding of the cartoon by expressing moods such as happiness or fear.

Cartoon Heroes

The cartoon hero is the main character in the story. He or she is meant to represent the reader's desires, ambitions or dreams and is often likeable—a model of honesty, courage, and justice, from Mighty Mouse to Superman to Wonder Woman.

Advertising Pictures Arouse Interest and Desire

These pictures are meant to grab our attention and strike our imagination. Their goal is to *sell* a product, service or idea. Advertisements use *esthetic* means (settings, colors, space, attractive people), *technical effects* (props), and *psychological* means (types of motivations) in order to attract and keep our attention. They are designed to appeal to our dreams, our emotions and our needs. They are "*manipulated*" pictures—they make us react without even thinking.

Advertising pictures are often enhanced by *slogans* or catchwords—short sentences that can be quickly understood and easily remembered. For example, Pepsi's "choice of a new generation."

Motion Pictures

The "Seventh Art"
Motion pictures (movies) were invented by William K.L. Dickson in 1895. This invention, capable of capturing real life images, was at first considered merely an amusement. However, motion pictures, like the theater, have developed into an art form including many cultural masterpieces.

The "wheel of life." Bands of drawings were brought to life when viewed through the openings in a rotating cylinder. You can create this effect by flipping through a stack of 3×5 cards with drawings.

The Impossible Became Possible
Motion pictures were silent until 1926. The actors used exaggerated gestures and facial expressions to communicate their feelings. Written dialogue was projected onto the screen. An organist in the movie theater provided background music.

Even without sound, motion pictures were exciting and a powerful means of communicating. Filmmakers used every available means, including trick-lighting and special effects, artificial sets, unusual camera angles and editing to make the unreal seem real. Sound was first used in the film, *The Jazz Singer* (1927). Later, as sound tracks improved and color was used, movie images became even more alive.

A Social Role
Finding sources of inspiration in all aspects of life, films entertain us, make us laugh, cry and dream, and increase our understanding of ourselves and of the world. Therefore, they have an important social function. Many of our heroes, fashions and phrases come from the movies.

Many fine novels and plays have been made into movies. Among these were *Treasure Island* (1935) by Robert Louis Stevenson, *Gone With the Wind* (1939) by Margaret Mitchell, and *The Wizard of Oz* (1939) by L. Frank Baum.

Here is a list of some popular American films:

Title and Year	Stars
King Kong (1932)	Fay Wray Robert Armstrong
Gone With the Wind (1939)	Clark Gable Vivien Leigh
An American in Paris (1951)	Gene Kelly
The Sound of Music (1965)	Julie Andrews Christopher Plummer
The Godfather (1972)	Marlon Brando Al Pacino
Jaws (1975)	Richard Dreyfuss Roy Scheider
Star Wars (1977)	Mark Hamill Carrie Fisher
E.T.: The Extra-Terrestrial (1982)	Henry Thomas

Shooting a Scene in a Studio

Spotlights

Boom Operat

Set Assistant

Actors

Script C

Recording Engineers

Film Editor

1-4 Sound and Film Editing

The Director

The director is the creative head of the team that makes the movie. He or she determines how to use actors, special effects, sets, sound, cameras and film editing to produce his or her interpretation of the script or story line. Some directors have achieved world fame: Frank Capra (United States), Steven Spielberg (United States), Alfred Hitchcock (Great Britain), Federico Fellini (Italy), Ingmar Bergman (Sweden), Jean Cocteau, François Truffaut (France).

Below is a list of some important U.S. directors and their films.

Film Directors	Movies	Leading Actors
Frank Capra (1897-)	*Mr. Smith Goes to Washington* (1939)	James Stewart
John Ford (1895-1973)	*The Grapes of Wrath* (1940)	Henry Fonda Jane Darwell
Alfred Hitchcock (1899-1980)	*Rear Window* (1954)	James Stewart Grace Kelly
John Huston (1906-(1988)	*The African Queen* (1951)	Humphrey Bogart Katharine Hepburn
Steven Spielberg (1946-)	*Close Encounters of the Third Kind* (1977)	Richard Dreyfuss
Orson Welles (1915-1985)	*Citizen Kane* (1941)	Orson Welles

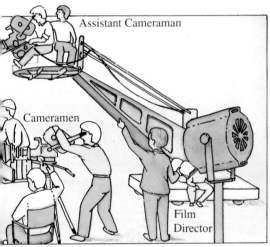

Assistant Cameraman

Cameramen

Film Director

Movie Theater

Projection Booth

Screen

Awards and Festivals

Beginning in 1927, the Academy of Motion Picture Arts and Sciences in Hollywood has presented annual awards, or "Oscars," for the best picture, actor, actress, supporting actor and actress, producer, director, cinematographer, set designer, screenplay, costume designer, and many other categories. There are awards from other organizations but the Oscar is the most prestigious.

Film festivals are held in many parts of the world. New movies are often premiered (first shown) at these festivals. Some festivals involve a theme such as the films of a particular director or actor. Perhaps the best known is the Cannes Film Festival in France, at which top films from all over the world are presented every year.

Rating System

Since 1968, the Motion Picture Association of America has assigned ratings to movies based upon content. Its objective is to advise parents of the suitability of a film for young audiences. Excessively violent or pornographic movies receive an **X** rating, indicating only persons over 17 will be admitted. Other ratings include **G** (general audiences), **PG** (parental guidance), **PG-13** (PG rating but some inappropriate violence), **R** (children under 17 not admitted without a parent or guardian).

Theater

Origin

In ancient times, the Greeks enjoyed the theater. Sitting on wooden or stone benches in the open air, spectators watched *comedies* and *tragedies* about legendary heroes. Actors wore elaborate masks and costumes.

The Mystery Plays of the Middle Ages

In the marketplace or in front of the cathedral, actors played out religious scenes based on the Old and New Testaments. These plays attracted large crowds who participated actively along with the actors.

The Commedia dell'Arte

This form of *theater of comedy* started in the 16th Century in Italy where actors were also singers, musicians, dancers and acrobats.

Troupes played in castles for the nobles and in the street for others. They often played the same character in different plays much like modern day actors in movie sequels. In these plays, much fun was made of human weaknesses. The actors used a bare outline of a plot and no script, making up the dialogue as they acted out the play.

1. The theater in ancient times—performance of a Greek tragedy.

2. Middle Ages—a mystery play performed in front of a cathedral.

3. 16th Century—a clown in an Italian comedy.

A Brilliant Period

Writers from the European theater produced plays of great artistic merit in the 17th century. It is called the *Classical Period*, during which theater became art. Plays were often written in verse. They were addressed only to the educated few.

William Shakespeare in England wrote some of the greatest plays of all time. Many plays written since that time borrow some part of their plot from Shakespeare.

The American theater was founded by the Hallam Family who brought a troupe of actors from England to America in 1752. Their "American Company" performed *The Prince of Parthia* in 1767. This was the first American play to be presented professionally. Since

4

5

6

The Romantic Theater

This was the theater of the 1800s. Playwrights gave up the rules of the classical theater and showed human nature more realistically. The various types of drama were no longer separated. Tragedy and comedy were combined within a play to better illustrate all aspects of humans, their emotions and experiences. Prose became more commonly used than verse because it better represented real life. These changes in the theater stirred emotional debates.

The 20th Century

Theater is still an important means of artistic expression. All sorts of subjects are used as topics for plays. Among the many great American playwrights are the dramatists Eugene O'Neill, Arthur Miller and Tennessee Williams. Richard Rodgers, Oscar Hammerstein II, Ira Gershwin and George Gershwin wrote some of the best loved musicals of all time.

The "*new theater*" involves direct contact with the audience, encouraging its participation. In *Tony and Tina's Wedding*, the audience plays the part of wedding guests, dancing and eating with the actors. This part of the theater has returned to its earliest form of street play.

4. 17th Century—theater performance before a royal court.

5. 19th Century—Romantic theater. Drama played in a formal theater.

6. 20th Century—Abstract stage of the modern theater.

then, England and America have continued to share their theatrical talents, for example, the production of *Phantom of the Opera*, a huge success in London as well as in New York in the 1980s.

A Summary

- *Comedy* makes us laugh through amusing situations or characters.

- *Tragedy* describes the passions and the weaknesses of human beings and the unhappy, sometimes disastrous, consequences of these passions or weaknesses.

- *Tragicomedy* combines elements from both tragedy and comedy.

- *Drama* depicts violent actions or serious conflicts between people.

- *Melodrama* exaggerates emotions and conflicts in extreme and tries to stir our simplest emotions such as fear and love.

Painting and Sculpture

The First Artists

In prehistoric times, human beings expressed themselves by drawings and paintings on the walls of caves.

About 3000 years B.C., the *Egyptians* decorated their tombs, temples, and palaces with scenes of daily life. The *Greeks* and *Romans*, became in turn sculptors and painters.

Painting and Religion

For a very long time, painting like music and theater expressed and evoked *religious devotion*. Many medieval works—stained glass, sculpture, illuminations—show this influence.

Art Became More Expressive

Slowly, under the Italian influence, painting changed. Renaissance artists searched for a more human and more realistic expression. They studied *anatomy*, *perspective*, and *proportions*. Religion was no longer the only source for their art. The artist was motivated by everything that excites, astonishes, causes anxiety or enthusiasm. Landscapes, portraits, battles, still lives, and scenes of daily life were now common and represented the artist's country, his time, and his contemporaries. In the 1700s, American artists portrayed their land and people in the style of English painting.

Great Changes

During the second half of the 1800s, artists called *Impressionists* painted directly from nature with an emphasis on movement, rich colors, and intense light. That is why they painted with small touches of color (*Impression of the Rising Sun* by Claude Monet).

In the 1900s *Cubist* painters such as Picasso went further away from reality by using geometric shapes. Thereafter, painting became *abstract*.

Today, painters sometimes avoid traditional materials and use *collages* or even additional material stuck on the canvas. They may even replace the canvas with metal, wood, or plastic.

Expression in Three Dimensions: Sculpture

The first sculptures were made *35,000 years ago*. For quite some time it remained a *religious art* associated with architecture. During the Renaissance, sculpture became *secular*, stressing the beauty of the human body. Since the late 1800s, sculptors have been using materials ranging from steel, aluminum and copper to glass and fluorescent lights.

FAMOUS ARTISTS AND SCULPTORS

	France and Belgium	Germany and Switzerland	Italy	Spain	Holland	England	United States
1400s	Froment, Le Maitre de Moulins		Fra Angelico, Botticelli , Della Francesca, Donatello (sculptor),		Van Eyck Brothers Bosch		
1500s	Clouet	Dürer, Grunewald, Holbein, Cranach	Da Vinci, Michelangelo, Raphael, Titian, Cellini (sculptor),		Brueghel		
1600s	Poussin, Le Lorrain		Carravaggio, Bernini (sculptor),	El Greco, Velázquez	Rembrandt, Hals, Vermeer, Rubens		
1700s	Watteau, Fragonard, Moudon (sculptor),	Fuseli	Canaletto, Guardi, Longhi, Tieplol	Goya		Hogarth, Reynolds Gainsborough	Copely, Stuart
1800s	David, Ingres, Delacroix, Daumier, Courbet, Manet , Monet, Degas, Cézanne, Gauguin, Toulouse-Lautrec Rodin (sculptor)	Friedrich, Liebermann Bocklin			Van Gogh	Turner, Constable	Homer, Trumbull, Harnett, Greenough (sculptor), French (sculptor)
1900s	Braque, Matisse Chagall, Maillol (sculptor),	Ernst, Grosz, Klee	Modigliani, De Chirico, Giacometti (sculptor)	Picasso, Dali, Miró	Mondrian	Bacon, Hockney, Moore (sculptor), Hepworth (sculptor)	Sargent, Bellow, Pollock, De Kooning, Wyeth, Rothko, Warhol, Calder (sculptor)

Music and Dance

Magical Power

Primitive people believed that music had power to cure diseases, cause the rain to fall, or calm the anger of the gods. Many legends are told about the good effects of music on humans, animals, and nature.

A troubadour plays the lute.

Today, almost everyone enjoys the music that is all around us in various forms—modern, classical, folk, jazz, and rock.

An ancient Greek musician plays the lyre.

Always Changing

From ancient times to the present day, music has never stopped developing. At first it was mainly religious, but in the Middle Ages *troubadours* (traveling poets) began singing about love and nature. Later, music was used for entertainment and dancing.

Great composers like Bach, Mozart, Beethoven, and Chopin expressed in music many emotions, such as happiness, patriotism, and hope.

Today, music is often composed on *computers* and played on *synthesizers*, which can reproduce the sounds of all instruments.

Chopin
Bach
Mozart
Beethoven

Necessary Instruments

A modern symphony orchestra uses 100 instruments, half of them *stringed instruments* (violins, violas, cellos, and double-basses). There are also *woodwinds* (clarinets, oboes, flutes, and bassoons), *brass instruments* (trumpets, French horns, trombones, tubas), and *percussion instruments* (drums and cymbals). To learn the special sounds of these instruments, listen to Prokofiev's musical fairy tale, *Peter and the Wolf*, where a cat is represented by a clarinet, a bird by a flute, Peter by a string quartet, and the wolf by horns.

A modern rock band is made up of guitars, a string bass, a keyboard synthesizer, and drums.

1. Bass   2. Drums   3. Harp   4. Bassoon
5. Flute   6. Harmonica   7. Trumpet

Body Language

Even before music existed, human beings used dancing to express their emotions. Every civilization has used dance to celebrate great events such as birth and death. Like music, dancing was at first a religious expression, and this is still true in African and Asian countries.

African Dance

From Folk Dancing to Ballroom

Dancing is also used for entertainment and fun. In Europe and America, ballroom dances include the *tango*, *waltz* and *foxtrot*. Folk dances include the *morris dances* of England, the *flamenco* of Spain, the *square dances* of rural America, and the *polkas* of eastern Europe. People also dance to rock bands and to jazz, which is a special form of music invented by African Americans.

Flamenco

American Square Dancing

Ballet

In 1661, King Louis XIV of France founded the Royal Academy of Dance to train dancers according to precise rules. From that time, dancing became a theatrical performance called *ballet*, in which stories are told by dance movements.

In the 1900s, ballet began to change. Today, although stories are still told through dance, the movements are more realistic and communicate more directly with the audience. Modern ballet does not follow the rules of classical ballet or use the classical costumes.

Classical Ballet

Modern Ballet

The History of Mathematics

Necessary to the social and economic life of human beings, mathematics remained purely an applied subject for a long time (a means of counting goods or of measuring lengths and volumes) before it became a science and achieved extraordinary theoretical development.

These primitive sticks with notches were delivered by a messenger who, upon his arrival, read aloud the number of objects or persons written on the stick.

On this Babylonian clay tablet, a scribe practices writing the sign for *one*.

The Oldest Way of Counting
It was found in Czechoslovakia engraved on a bone from a young wolf and dates from about *30,000 B.C.!* This bone is engraved with 55 lines divided into two sequences representing groups of 5 lines.

The Difference Between *One* and *Several*
This difference is the basis of the number system. Early human beings established this difference by observing the world around them. The ancient Hindus, for example, considered the moon and the earth the number *one*; the wings of a bird, *two*; the leaves of a clover, *three*; the legs of a dog, *four*; and the fingers of a hand, *five*. Ultimately, the use of *ten* fingers, to which were sometimes added

ten toes, became the most frequently used system of counting.

Mesopotamia
In 2500 B.C., Babylon was a great cultural center. Many clay tablets have been found that show the mathematical knowledge of

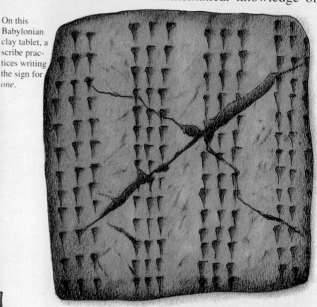

that time. These tablets are marked with a series of numbers, with statements of problems and their solutions, and with operations, calculations of surface areas, volumes, and algebraic calculations.

India
Mathematics was characterized by the development of numerical and algebraic calculations. Our decimal system, with symbols for the numerals 1 through 9, was developed in India and transmitted by the Arabs.

Arabia
Greek and Indian discoveries in mathematics were preserved and improved by the Arabs from whom we obtained this ancient knowledge. The Arabs were especially clever in perfecting new methods of calculation.

Egypt
A papyrus (*the papyrus of Rhind*) written by a scribe in *1650 B.C.* shows that the Egyptians

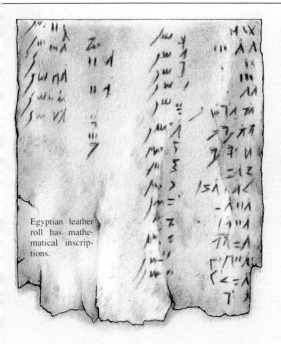

Egyptian leather roll has mathematical inscriptions.

Bead Abacus

used today, helps to perform many kinds of mathematical calculations.

America
The *Incas* of Peru had their own number system—knots of *quipu* (cord) represented values in a decimal system. The *Mayas* in

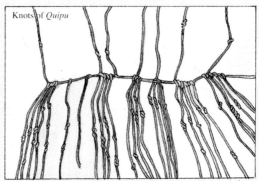

Knots of *Quipu*

Guatemala used the calendar and employed the zero in their number system.

Rome
The Romans began the number system that we still use today.

Europe
After the barbarian invasions of Europe that began about 400 A.D., the science of mathematics was not taken up again until the Middle Ages. The Renaissance was an important time for the development of algebra, trigonometry, and geometry.

Later on, developments in mathematics increased and knowledge spread rapidly. Today, it is no longer possible, even for a scientist, to be an expert in all fields.

had a good knowledge of mathematics which they used in their daily life for agriculture, land measurement, accounting, and architecture (the pyramids).

Greece
The Greeks took advantage of Babylonian and Egyptian contributions and turned mathematics into a real *science*—an activity where research is done for its own sake. Besides finding better methods of calculation, Greek mathematicians also stated, defined, and demonstrated important mathematical *laws* and *principles*. These included the theory of numbers, the theory of propor-

Pythagoras   Archimedes

tions, the calculation of areas and surfaces, and geometry and algebra. *Thales of Miletus*, *Pythagoras*, and later, *Archimedes*,were responsible for these important developments.

The Far East
The Chinese and Japanese developed their own number system. The *bead abacus*, still

Early Methods of Counting

We have seen that learning how to count was the first mathematical problem to occupy the attention of human beings. Through time and various civilizations, different systems of numeration (of counting and numbering) were invented and developed.

Primitive Human Beings

They used *oral numeration*. For example, the ancient Sumerians used the words:
"man" for 1,
"woman" for 2,
"several" for 3.

The Mesopotamians

Written signs were carved into a wet clay tablet which was later baked.

▼ the value of **1**   ◄ the value of **10**   ▼ the value of **60**

45 was written

62 was written

The Egyptians

They used a system of written symbols called *hieroglyphics*.

| | = **1** (one line)

| | | / | | = **5** (five lines)

∩ = **10** (an arch)

℮ = **100** (a manuscript roll)

= **1,000** (lotus flower)

(= **10,000** (pointing finger)

= **100,000** (tadpole)

= **1,000,000** (astonished man)

The Greeks

They used two principal systems—the "Attic" and the "Herodianic" systems. These were used often in Athenian inscriptions. Later, in the 5th century B.C., they also used the "Ionic" or "alphabetical" system.

Attic Numerals

| = 1

| | = 2

| | | = 3

| | | | = 4

Γ = 5

Δ = 10

Η = 100

Χ = 1,000

Μ = 10,000

Ionic Numeral System

Units

A α 1	B β 2	Γ γ 3	Δ δ 4	E ε 5	Ϛ ς 6	Z ζ 7	H η 8	Θ θ 9

Tens

I ι 10	K κ 20	Λ λ 30	M μ 40	N ν 50	Ξ ξ 60	O o 70	Π π 80	Ϟ ς 90

Hundreds

P ρ 100	Σ σ 200	T τ 300	Y υ 400	Φ φ 500	X χ 600	Ψ ψ 700	Ω ω 800	ϡ 900

The Romans

They used a numeration system that is additive and repetitive.

I = 1　　　II = 2　　　III = 3　　　IV = 4　　(The sign placed to the left of a higher sign is subtracted from it.)

V = 5　　　VI = 6　　　X = 10　　　L = 50

C = 100　　D = 500　　M = 1,000　　$\overline{V}$ = 5,000　　(One line above a letter indicates thousands.)

$\overline{\overline{V}}$ = 5,000,000　(Two lines above a letter indicate millions.)

The Mayas

They used a numeration system with a base of 20 and with vertical writing.

• = 1　　　⎯ = 5　　　☰ = 10　　　(••• over ☰) = 13

The Chinese

They used a base 10 multiplication system.

一	二	三	四	五	六	七	八	九	十
= 1	= 2	= 3	= 4	= 5	= 6	= 7	= 8	= 9	= 10

百 = 100 (10^2)　千 = 1,000 (10^3)　万 = 10,000 (10^4)　十万 = 100,000 (10^5)　百万 = 1,000,000 (10^6)　千万 = 10,000,000 (10^7)

A Few Comparisons

	Mesopotamia	Egypt	Greece	Rome	Mayas	China
1	▼	I	α′	I	•	一
5	▼▼▼▼▼	¦¦¦	ε′	V	⎯	五
10	◄	∩	ι′	X	=	十
15	◄▼▼▼▼▼	∩¦¦¦	ιε′	XV	☰	十五
18	◄▼▼▼▼▼▼▼	∩¦¦¦¦	ιη′	XVIII	(••• over ☰)	十八
100	▼◄◄◄◄	ℓ	ρ′	C	(⎯ over •)	百

Actually, two types of numeration systems exist.

A System of Juxtaposition
Additive Type

This system is not very practical because many signs had to be used to write larger numbers (Mesopotamian and Egyptian systems).

A System of Position
Practical Type

It is the position of the number which determines its value. (An example is our decimal system.)

Modern Methods of Counting

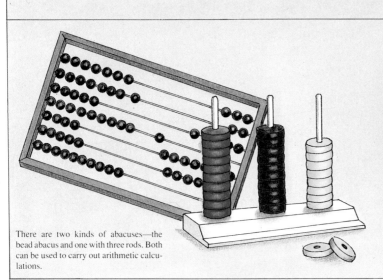

Muslim scholars from the Arab world transmitted the decimal numeral system to the Western world. Slowly, it replaced the former Roman numeral system. The decimal numerals (1-9) were first used to count tokens on the abacus (calculation table).

There are two kinds of abacuses—the bead abacus and one with three rods. Both can be used to carry out arithmetic calculations.

Numeral, Digit and Number

A numeral is a symbol for a number. XVI is a Roman numeral; 16 is a decimal numeral; both are symbols for the number sixteen.

A digit is one of the symbols 0, 1, 2, 3, 4, 5, 6, 7, 8, 9 in the decimal system.

Base 10

$9 + 1 = 10$ $99 + 1 = 100$ $999 + 1 = 1,000$

This base of numeration allows us to represent any number by using only ten digits:

0, 1, 2, 3, 4, 5, 6, 7, 8, 9.

According to its *position*, from left to right, each digit corresponds to a specific unit ten times greater than the one before it.

3	2	5	4	8
Tens of Thousands	Thousands	Hundreds	Tens	Units

Whole Numbers (or Integers)

125 pages, 12 eggs, 3,585 inhabitants: 125, 12, 3,585 are natural whole numbers.

These numbers that we commonly use for counting form an *infinite sequence*:

$\mathbb{N} = \ldots 0, 1, 2, 3, \ldots 15 \ldots 170 \ldots 4,624 \ldots$

because it is always possible to add 1 to any number to get the next one in the sequence.

Positive Numbers, Negative Numbers

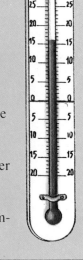

$\ldots, -4, -3, -2, -1$
1 is subtracted each time we move left.

$0, 1, 2, 3, 4, \ldots$
1 is added each time we move right.

This morning, the thermometer showed $-10°$F.

The sequence of negative numbers is also *infinite*.

Decimal Numbers

They are used to account for values between two whole numbers.

$2   **$2.50** $3   14 in.   **14.25 in.**   15 in   1 lb.   **1.250 lb.**   2 lb.

A period (called the decimal point) separates a whole number from the decimal fraction.

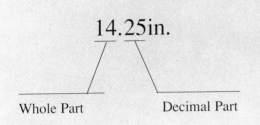

14.25in.

Whole Part   Decimal Part

On the right of the decimal point, the numbers represent successive units smaller than the inch by a factor of 10.

the 2 represents *tenths* of an inch: $\dfrac{2}{10}$

the 5 represents *hundredths* of an inch: $\dfrac{5}{100}$

One goes from a decimal number to a whole number by a change of unit.

Hence, $2.50 → 250 cents; 1.25 ft. → 15 in.

1.2→12 tenths; 0.85→85 hundredths.

Fractions

 1      $\dfrac{1}{2}$ $\dfrac{1}{3}$ $\dfrac{1}{4}$ $\dfrac{2}{3}$ $\dfrac{3}{4}$

They represent parts of a whole.

$\dfrac{1}{3}$ means that a whole was divided into *3 parts* and that *one* of these parts is being considered.

$\dfrac{2}{3}$ means that *two* are being considered, etc.

2 is the numerator.

3 is the denominator.

(from $\dfrac{2}{3}$)

Decimal value of fractions

To transform a fraction into a decimal number, the numerator is divided by the denominator.

The fraction $\dfrac{1}{2}$ equals **0.5**.

The fraction $\dfrac{1}{4}$ equals **0.25**.

$\dfrac{5}{10} = 0.5$ $\dfrac{5}{100} = 0.05$ $\dfrac{5}{1,000} = 0.005$

All fractions do not have a value that can be expressed precisely as a decimal.

$\dfrac{1}{3}$ has an infinite decimal value of 0.3333 . . .

Whole numbers expressed in fractions:

$1 = \dfrac{2}{2} ; \dfrac{3}{3} ; \dfrac{4}{4} ; \cdots$

$2 = \dfrac{4}{2} ; \dfrac{6}{3} ; \dfrac{8}{4} ; \dfrac{10}{5} ; \cdots$

$5 = \dfrac{10}{2} ; \dfrac{15}{3} ; \dfrac{20}{4} ; \cdots$

Other Counting Bases

A Choice of Numeration System

We count with a base of 10. The Babylonians counted mainly with a base of 60, a base which we use today to measure time.

The Mayas counted with a base of 20. It is possible to use any whole number starting with 2 as a base of numeration:

Base 2

To write a number in base 2, only two digits are used: **0** and **1**. This is the *binary system*. It is used for computers.

Thus, 7 (base 10) is written **111** (read one, one, one) in base 2.

One way to write the number in base 2 is to form possible groups of 2 and powers of 2, that is, of 2, 4, 8, 16, . . .

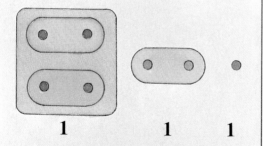

Successive division by 2 is faster.

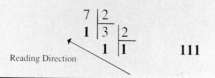

Reading Direction

Base 4

To write a number in base 4, only 4 digits are used: **0, 1, 2, 3.**

Thus, 12 (base 10) is written **30** (read three, zero) in base 4.

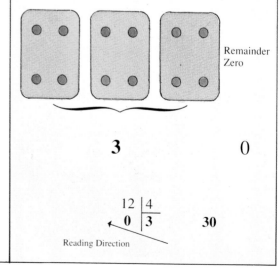

Reading Direction

150

Base 6

To write a number in base 6, the digits **0, 1, 2, 3, 4, 5** are used. 21 (base 10) is written **33** (read three, three) in base 6.

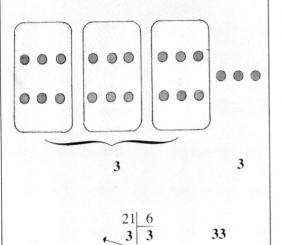

3   3

$$\frac{21\ \vert\ 6}{3\ \vert\ 3}$$ 33

Reading Direction

Base 12

To write a number in base 12, 12 digits are used: **0, 1, 2, 3, 4, 5, 6, 7, 8, 9, X, E.** (X = 10; E = 11.) 32 (base 10) is written **28** (read two, eight) in base 12. 126 (base 10) is written **X6** (read ten, six) in base 12.

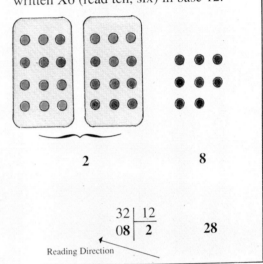

2   8

$$\frac{32\ \vert\ 12}{08\ \vert\ 2}$$ 28

Reading Direction

To Change Base

Value of each column (base 2)

101 (base 2) →

2^3	2^2	2^1	1
8	4	2	1
	1	0	1

$= (4 \times 1) + (0 \times 2) + 1 = 5$ (base 10)

Value of each column (base 4)

131 (base 4) →

4^3	4^2	4^1	1
64	16	4	1
	1	3	1

$= (16 \times 1) + (4 \times 3) + 1$
$= 16 + 12 + 1 = 29$ (base 10)

From One Base to the Other
Table of Equivalence

Base 10	0	1	2	3	4	5	10	20	50	60
Base 2	0	1	10	11	100	101	1,010	10,100	110,010	111,100
Base 4	0	1	2	3	10	11	22	110	302	330
Base 6	0	1	2	3	4	5	14	32	122	140
Base 12	0	1	2	3	4	5	10	18	42	50
Base 60	0	1	2	3	4	5	10	20	50	10

Computers

What Is a Computer?

It is an electronic device that stores instructions (words, numbers, drawings, music) for processing data and then follows these instructions at high speed when requested.

A computer is not intelligent. It processes data only according to the instructions it is given.

The first computers, built around 1950, were very large, took up a great deal of space, and were very expensive. Today, computers are small in size, relatively inexpensive, and a thousand times faster, such as *minicomputers* or *P.C.s* (personal computers).

A Very Helpful Machine

With the help of computers, great technical progress became possible in various fields.

Now, one can:
· control the flight of a rocket or a plane or the movement of a train
· operate a robot
· diagnose and treat patients
· produce pictures
· compose music
· teach

Computers can also be used to create and operate military weapons.

Pictures

Medical Treatment   Controls

How Do They Work?

All computers do four things: input, store information in a memory, process, and output.

During *input*, data is entered and stored in a *memory*. The data is then *processed* according to instructions in the *central processing unit*, the brain of the machine. During *output*, processed data, or information that results from the computer's calculations, is displayed on a screen and can be printed.

Communication between the different elements is done by *electric currents*.

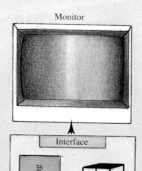
Monitor

Interface

Central Processing Unit

Memories

Interface

Keyboard

The Conductor

It is a tiny *microprocessor* or *chip* within the computer that handles the flow of data and is capable of processing several million operations per second.

Microprocessor

It is surrounded by aids called "memories."

Main Unit and Other Devices
It is possible to connect the main unit with devices other than the keyboard and the screen.

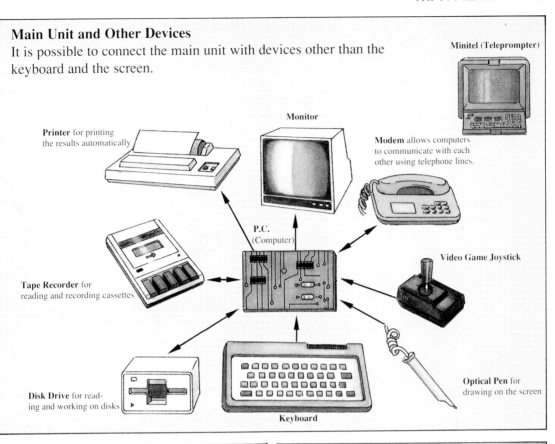

Minitel (Teleprompter)

Printer for printing the results automatically

Monitor

Modem allows computers to communicate with each other using telephone lines.

P.C. (Computer)

Video Game Joystick

Tape Recorder for reading and recording cassettes

Disk Drive for reading and working on disks

Keyboard

Optical Pen for drawing on the screen

Computer Language
The computer does not understand human language and uses only a machine language—electrical impulses flowing through the different circuits. This language is coded by means of two digits, 0 and 1

0: the current does not pass.
1: the current passes.

This is called the *binary code*. All information received is translated into this language.

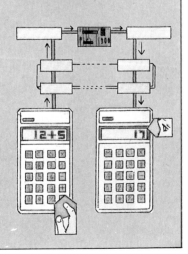

Computer Programming
This means to give a list of instructions to the computer for processing.

Various *computer language programs* have been invented. With the help of a *compiler*, a kind of interpreter, the program translates words of high-level languages into binary numbers 0 and 1.

To understand a computer language program, one has to learn its words and grammar.

The most often used language is *BASIC*. The easiest to learn is LOGO.

Other computer languages are

FORTRAN

ALGOL

APL

PASCAL

ASSEMBLY

FORTH

Large Numbers—Powers

Texas has a surface area of about 267,000 square miles.
The sun is about 93,000,000 miles away from the earth.
The earth will soon number 6,000,000,000 inhabitants.

Thousands, Millions, Billions

It is easy to read whole numbers of 4, 5, or 6 digits (**2,965, 34,254, 987,672 . . .**), but that is not the case for larger numbers.

The reading and writing of these large numbers follows certain rules.

The number **234597643275** written like this is not written correctly and it is therefore difficult to read.

It is much easier to read **234,597,643,275** written like this.

Starting from the right, the number is divided by commas into segments that consist of three digits and indicate units, thousands, millions, and billions.

234597643275 reads: **234** billion, **597** million, **643** thousand, **275**.

How Are These Large Numbers Read?

128 534 217 000   **24 609 240 000 000**   **398 215 132 024 013**

Answers

128 billion, 534 million, 217 thousand
24,609 billion, 240 million
398,215 billion, 132 million, 124 thousand, and 13

Eliminating Zeros

To make calculations easier, mathematicians do not write:

1,000 but 10^3 (which reads *ten raised to the third power*), that is
$10 \times 10 \times 10$, namely 1 thousand.

1,000,000 but 10^6 (which reads *ten raised to the 6th power*), that is
$10 \times 10 \times 10 \times 10 \times 10 \times 10$, namely 1 million.

1,000,000,000 but 10^9 (which reads *ten raised to the 9th power*), that is
$10 \times 10 \times 10 \times 10 \times 10 \times 10 \times 10 \times 10 \times 10$, namely 1 billion.

3, 6, 9, are *exponents*. They indicate the number of zeros that must be written after the 1.

Going back to the above examples, one can write:

Texas has (267×10^3) miles of surface area.
The sun is at a distance of (93×10^6) miles from the earth.
The earth will soon number (6×10^9) inhabitants.

The Advantage of Exponents

When multiplying a number several times by itself, exponents can be used.

Instead of writing $4 \times 4 \times 4 \times 4 \times 4$, one writes 4^5
$$2^4 = 2 \times 2 \times 2 \times 2$$

To write large numbers with the help of exponents
$$4,585,278,000 = 4,000,000,000 + 585,000,000 + 278,000$$
$$= 4 \times 10^9 + 585 \times 10^6 + 278 \times 10^3$$

Thus 4,585,278,000 can be written: $(4 \times 10^9) + (585 \times 10^6) + (278 \times 10^3)$

What Number Is This?

$$(275 \times 10^9) + (834 \times 10^6) + (173 \times 10^3)$$

Answer

275 billion, 834 million, 173 thousand

Romans and Large Numbers

To write large numbers, the Romans introduced the symbol ‾ and ▯ which have the respective value of 1,000 and 100,000.
Here are some large numbers written:

$\overline{\text{VII}} = 7{,}000$ $\boxed{\text{III}} = 300{,}000$ $\overline{\text{L}} = 50{,}000$ $\boxed{\text{XV}} = 1{,}500{,}000$

What are these numbers?

$\overline{\text{C}};$ $\boxed{\text{IV}};$ $\overline{\text{CX}};$ $\boxed{\text{X}};$ $\boxed{\text{LV}}$

In Roman writing, how did one write?

6,000;   900,000;   12,000;   10,010;   511,000

Answers

1) $\overline{\text{C}} = 100{,}000.$ $\boxed{\text{IV}} = 400{,}000.$ $\overline{\text{CX}} = 110{,}000.$ $\boxed{\text{X}} = 1{,}000{,}000.$ $\boxed{\text{LV}} = 5{,}500{,}000.$

2) $6{,}000 = \overline{\text{VI}}.$ $900{,}000 = \boxed{\text{IX}}.$ $12{,}000 = \overline{\text{XII}}.$ $10{,}010 = \overline{\text{XX}}.$ $511{,}000 = \boxed{\text{V}} \overline{\text{XI}}.$

Game

Which is the largest number that one can write with 3 digits?

Answer

It is a number composed of three 9s written as follows: 9(9⁹).
This number includes 369,693,101 *digits!* The first 7 are
9,431,549 . . . the last digit is 9.

From Coins to Credit Cards

Money

The dollar is the basic currency of the United States. It has a value of *100 cents*. Bank notes and coins together are called *legal tender*. To pay with money is to *pay cash*.

Coins in Circulation

Penny (1¢)   Nickel (5¢)

Dime (10¢)   Quarter (25¢)

Half-Dollar (50¢)

Bills (Paper Money)

Paying with a Check

To pay large amounts, checks are commonly used.

Checkbooks are issued to persons who open a *bank account*, called a checking account, and deposit money in the bank. *Money orders* can also be bought in banks, U.S. post offices, etc., and used like checks.

On the check, the amount to be paid is written in numbers and in letters, and the words *to the order of* are followed by the name of the person or company to whom the check is written. The check is dated and signed by the owner of the checking account.

Bank Check

Money Order

Credit Cards

Credit cards have become popular all over the world. They are used instead of cash or checks to pay for many goods or services.

The bill is sent monthly to the owner of the card.

There are many issuers of credit cards: Visa, MasterCard, American Express,

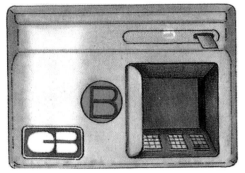

department stores, and gasoline companies, to name the most common ones.

A bank checking card can be used to *withdraw* or *deposit money* at automated teller machines.

Magnetic Card

This card contains a *microprocessor* (a chip) which automatically records all transactions and transmits them directly to the bank.

ECU (European Currency Unit)

This is the currency of the countries belonging to the European Community. It came into effect on March 13, 1979. Ten currencies determine its value: the Belgian and Luxembourgian franc, the Deutsche mark, the Dutch guilder, the Danish krone, the French franc, the Italian lira, the Irish pound, and the Greek drachma.

Federal Reserve Banks

They are the bankers for the United States government. These 12 banks cooperate closely with the Treasury Department to help establish money and banking conditions that will make the country prosperous. The Secretary of the Treasury deposits the funds of the U.S. in these banks.

The Dollar and Foreign Currencies

When you go to a foreign country, you must buy the *currency* (money) of that country to use in paying for purchases and services.

The value in dollars of each country's currency is different. The *rate of exchange* varies frequently.

A few examples as of November 18, 1988:
   You need:
$1.83 for *1 pound* (Great Britain)
$ .81 for *1 Canadian dollar* (Canada)
$ .17 for *1 French franc* (France)
$ .69 for *1 Swiss franc* (Switzerland)
$ .08 for *100 Italian lire* (Italy)
$ .08 for *10 Japanese yen* (Japan)
$ .09 for *10 Spanish pesetas* (Spain)

Amazing!

One billion dollars stacked up in banknotes of $100 would form a tower over $\frac{9}{10}$ of a mile high!

Measuring Lengths

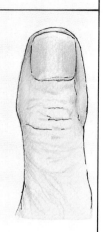
The English System of Measures

In the United States, the English system of weights and measures is the most commonly used system for measuring lengths, weights, areas and volumes. The system consists of standard units of measure that are defined by samples, or models, that are carefully preserved in the Bureau of Standards in Washington, D.C.

The standard units of length in the English system are the inch, foot, yard, and mile.

The **inch** (in.) is used to measure small lengths such as a person's height, or the diameter of a pipe, or a dinner plate.

The **foot** (ft.) is used to measure such lengths as the height of buildings, dimensions of rooms, and land plots. 1 ft. = 12 in.

The **yard** (yd.) is used for larger lengths such as the runs or passes in a football game, or the lengths of pieces of cloth. 1 yd. = 3 ft. or 36 in.

The **mile** (mi.) is used for describing very large distances such as those between cities, or journeys by airplane, automobile or train. 1 mi. = 5,280 ft. or 1,760 yd.

The symbol, ', is often used to represent feet, as in 8', meaning 8 ft.

The symbol, ", is used to represent inches as in 5", meaning 5 in. Thus, 2'6" means a length of 2 feet and 6 inches.

Changing from One Unit to Another

Since it takes 12 in. to equal 1 ft., a measurement in inches can be changed to feet by dividing by 12. Example: 72 in. = $\frac{72}{12}$ ft. or 6 ft.; 42 in. = $\frac{42}{12}$ ft. or 3½ ft.

A measurement in feet can be changed to inches by multiplying by 12. Example: 4 ft. = 4 × 12 in. or 48 in.; 2⅓ ft. = 2⅓ × 12 in. or 28 in.

Since it takes 3 ft. to equal 1 yd., a measurement in feet can be changed to yards by dividing by 3. Example: 27 ft. = $\frac{27}{3}$ yd. = 9 yd.; 16 ft. = $\frac{16}{3}$ yd. or 5⅓ yd.

A measurement in yards can be changed to feet by multiplying by 3. Example: 4 yd. = 4 × 3 ft. = 12 ft.; 5½ yd. = 5½ × 3 ft. = 16½ ft.

Expressing Measurements

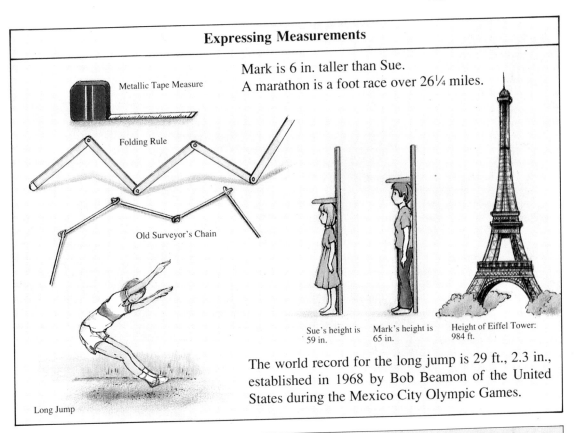

Metallic Tape Measure

Folding Rule

Old Surveyor's Chain

Long Jump

Mark is 6 in. taller than Sue.
A marathon is a foot race over 26¼ miles.

Sue's height is 59 in.   Mark's height is 65 in.   Height of Eiffel Tower: 984 ft.

The world record for the long jump is 29 ft., 2.3 in., established in 1968 by Bob Beamon of the United States during the Mexico City Olympic Games.

Adding and Subtracting Lengths

Suppose we wish to find the total length spanned by two sticks placed end-to-end if one is 3'8" long and the other is 4'6" long. Add the lengths:

$$
\begin{array}{r}
3' \quad 8" \\
+ \quad 4' \quad 6" \\
\hline
7' \quad 14"
\end{array}
$$

But since 12" = 1', 14" = 1'2"; therefore, 7'14" is 8'2".

We might wish to know how many yards are included in a length of 8'2". Since 3' = 1 yd., 8' = 2 yd. (that is, 6') plus 2 more feet. Thus, 8'2" = 2 yd., 2 ft., 2 in.

Suppose we wish to find the length remaining from a board 9'3" long if we saw off a piece that is 6'8" long. Subtract the lengths:

$$
\begin{array}{r}
9' \quad 3" \\
- \quad 6' \quad 8"
\end{array}
$$

But since 8" cannot be subtracted from 3", we borrow 1' (or 12") from the 9' and add it (as 12") to the 3":

$$
\begin{array}{r}
8' \quad 15" \\
- \quad 6' \quad 8" \\
\hline
2' \quad 7"
\end{array}
$$

The remaining length is:

Measuring Masses

Weights or Masses?

Because of the earth's attraction, each body presses upon whatever supports it from below. This pressure is the *weight* of the body.

This weight varies according to the location of the body. When the body is located at a *higher* elevation, the attraction of the earth *decreases* and the body weighs *less*.

On the other hand, the *mass* of a body does not change according to its location. Mass depends upon the quantity and the nature of materials which form the body, and thus the mass of a body is *constant*. Nevertheless, the distinction between mass and weight is not usually made.

180 lb.

Earth

30 lb.

Moon

The moon attracts bodies less than the earth (⅙ as much). An astronaut weighs only 30 lb. on the moon although his mass has not changed.

The English System of Weights

The **ounce** (abbreviated as **oz.**) is used for weights of small quantities such as the contents of a medicine bottle.

The **pound** (abbreviated as **lb.**) is used to measure larger weights as in the purchase of meats, fruits or vegetables at the supermarket. 1 lb. = 16 oz.

The **ton** is used for very large weights as in truckloads or railroad car loads. 1 ton = 2,000 lb.

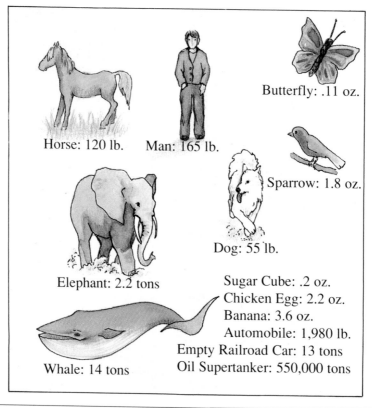

Horse: 120 lb. Man: 165 lb.

Butterfly: .11 oz.

Sparrow: 1.8 oz.

Dog: 55 lb.

Elephant: 2.2 tons

Sugar Cube: .2 oz.
Chicken Egg: 2.2 oz.
Banana: 3.6 oz.
Automobile: 1,980 lb.
Empty Railroad Car: 13 tons
Oil Supertanker: 550,000 tons

Whale: 14 tons

Changing Units of Weight

How many pounds of peanuts will be required to fill 10 small bags each containing 8 ounces of peanuts?

The 10 bags will contain 10×8 oz. or 80 oz.

Since 16 oz. = 1 lb., 80 oz. = $\dfrac{80}{16}$ lb. or 5 lb.

Large Masses

Mass: 385 tons or 770,000 lb.

G.W. = Gross Weight: 6,600 lb.
C.W. = Cargo Weight: 5,500 lb.
M.G.W. = Maximum Gross Weight: 12,100 lb.

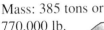

A bag of potatoes weighing 20 lb.

Adding Weights

Butter: 8.8 oz.

Chocolate: 3.5 oz.

If the contents of a can containing 2 lb., 11 oz. of a substance is mixed with the contents of another can weighing 4 lb., 9 oz., what is the weight of the mixture?

Coffee: 1 lb.

Tea: 7 oz.

Butter: 5 oz.

Add the weights:

$$
\begin{array}{r}
2 \text{ lb., } 11 \text{ oz.} \\
+ \ 4 \text{ lb., } \ \ 9 \text{ oz.} \\
\hline
6 \text{ lb., } 20 \text{ oz.}
\end{array}
$$

Candy: 10.6 oz.

But 20 oz. = 16 oz. (or 1 lb.) plus 4 oz.:   7 lb.,   4 oz.

Michael weighs 93 lb.

Units of Volume

The English System of Volume Measure

In the United States, there are two measuring systems for volume. One is used for measuring liquid volumes and the other for dry measure of volumes.

LIQUID MEASURE
The basic unit is the liquid **pint** (pt.)

2 pt. = 1 **quart** (qt.)

4 pt. = 1 **gallon** (gal.)

DRY MEASURE
The basic unit is the dry **pint** (pt.)

2 pt. = 1 **quart** (qt.)

8 qt. = 1 **peck** (pk.)

4 pk. = 1 **bushel** (bu.)

Great Britain and Canada use a measure called the Imperial gallon that is ⅙ larger than the American gallon.

Changing Units of Volume

How many pints of milk are there in 9 gallons?

Each gallon = 4 qt., so 9 gal. = 9 × 4 qt. or 36 qt.

Each qt. = 2 pt., so 36 qt. = 36 × 2 or 72 pt.

For Very Large Quantities

Tank Trucks. They can carry 8,000 gal.

Large barrels called *tuns* may contain between 1,300 and 8,000 gal.

Tank Cars. Their capacity is also very large: on the average, 13,000 gals.

All Kinds of Containers

For Small Quantities

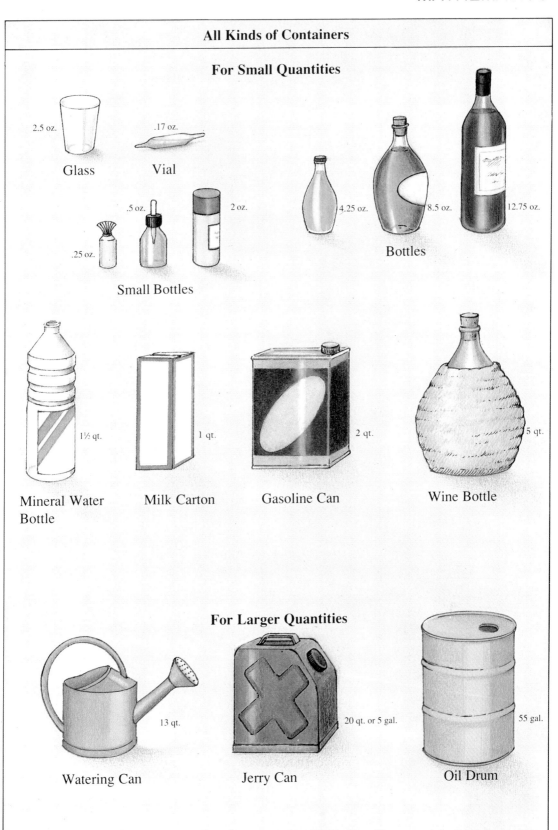

2.5 oz. — Glass

.17 oz. — Vial

.25 oz.

.5 oz.

2 oz.

Small Bottles

4.25 oz.

8.5 oz.

12.75 oz.

Bottles

1½ qt. — Mineral Water Bottle

1 qt. — Milk Carton

2 qt. — Gasoline Can

5 qt. — Wine Bottle

For Larger Quantities

13 qt. — Watering Can

20 qt. or 5 gal. — Jerry Can

55 gal. — Oil Drum

The Metric System

The metric system is a different system of measuring units from the English system used in the United States. It is used in most other countries of the world and also for certain measurements in the United States such as in scientific work.

Metric Measures of Length

The basic unit of length in the metric system is the **meter**, which is a bit longer than the U.S. yard. All the other units of measure are either 10, 100, or 1,000 times as large as the meter, or $\frac{1}{10}$, $\frac{1}{100}$, or $\frac{1}{1,000}$ of the size of the meter. The names of these other units are made up by attaching special prefixes to the front of the word "meter" to show how many times its size they are. These prefixes are:

milli for $\frac{1}{1,000}$	**deka** for 10 times
centi for $\frac{1}{100}$	**hecto** for 100 times
deci for $\frac{1}{10}$	**kilo** for 1,000 times

Thus, a **millimeter** (mm) is $\frac{1}{1,000}$ of a meter   a **dekameter** (dkm) is 10 times the size of a meter

a **centimeter** (cm) is $\frac{1}{100}$ of a meter   a **hectometer** (hm) is 100 times the size of a meter

a **decimeter** (dm) is $\frac{1}{10}$ of a meter   a **kilometer** (km) is 1,000 times the size of a meter

Since we multiply by 10 by moving a decimal point one place to the right and divide by 10 by moving a decimal point one place to the left, the metric system makes it very easy to change from one unit to another by simply moving the decimal point. For example, 483 meters = 48.3 dekameters or 4.83 hectometers or 0.483 kilometers or 4,830 decimeters or 48,300 centimeters or 483,000 millimeters.

The Meter and Its Multiples (measures smaller than a meter)

This line measures 1 **dm** (decimeter) or 10 **cm** (centimeter) or 100 **mm** (millimeter)

The double-decimeter = 2 dm
2 **dm** or 20 **cm** or 200 **mm**

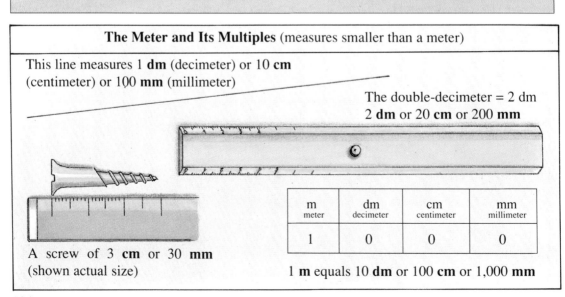

A screw of 3 **cm** or 30 **mm** (shown actual size)

m meter	dm decimeter	cm centimeter	mm millimeter
1	0	0	0

1 **m** equals 10 **dm** or 100 **cm** or 1,000 **mm**

Metric Measures of Volume

The basic metric measure of volume is the **liter** (abbreviated **l.**) A liter is slightly larger than our liquid quart. In Europe, milk and bottles of soda are sold by the liter instead of by the quart and gasoline is priced by the liter instead of by the gallon. A **milliliter** (**ml**) ($\frac{1}{1,000}$ of a liter) is about a $\frac{1}{30}$ of an ounce; a **centiliter** (**cl**) ($\frac{1}{100}$ of a liter) is about $\frac{1}{3}$ of an ounce.

Metric Measures of Weight

The basic metric measure of weight is the **gram** (**g**). A gram is only about 0.035 ounces, so a **kilogram** (equal to 1,000 grams) is more commonly used for weights such as purchases of meats and vegetables or weights of people or even automobiles.

A **kilogram** (**kg**) is a bit more than 2 lb. **Centigrams** (**cg**) (equal to $\frac{1}{100}$ of a gram) and **milligrams** (**mg**) (equal to $\frac{1}{1,000}$ of a gram) are used for very small weights such as those of substances which a druggist uses in mixing a prescription.

Other units of weight are made from the gram by using the same prefixes described under measuring lengths in the metric system.

Tables of Conversion Between English and Metric Systems of Measure

Converting from English to Metric System			Converting from Metric to English System		
1 in.	=	25.4 mm	1 mm	=	0.039 in.
1 in.	=	2.54 cm	1 cm	=	0.39 in.
1 ft.	=	0.3 m	1 m	=	3.28 ft.
1 yd.	=	0.91 m	1 m	=	1.09 yd.
1 mi.	=	1.61 km	1 km	=	0.62 mi.
1 liquid oz.	=	29.6 ml	1 l	=	1.06 qt.
1 liquid qt.	=	0.95 l	1 l	=	0.26 gal.
1 gal.	=	3.79 l	1 g	=	0.04 oz.
1 oz. (weight)	=	28.3 g	1 kg	=	2.2 lb.
1 lb.	=	0.45 kg			

The table on the left permits changes from an English system measure to an equivalent metric measure. For example, suppose you know a distance is 5 mi. and want to convert it to kilometers. The table shows that 1 mi. = 1.61 km. Therefore, 5 mi. = 5 × 1.61 km or 8.05 km.

The table on the right permits changes from measurements in the metric system to an equivalent English system measure. For example, suppose you know that a line is 6 centimeters long and you wish to find its length in inches. The table shows that 1 cm = 0.39 in. Therefore, 6 cm = 6 × 0.39 in. or 2.34 in.

To Construct Figures

Parallel and Perpendicular Straight Lines

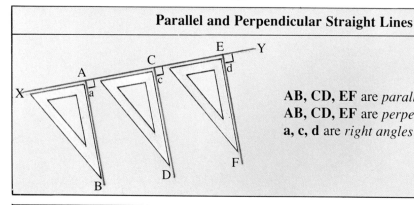

AB, CD, EF are *parallel* to each other.
AB, CD, EF are *perpendicular* to XY.
a, c, d are *right angles*.

Perpendicular Bisector of a Segment

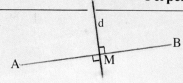

The straight line **d** is *perpendicular* to the segment **AB**.
It cuts this segment in the middle.

The straight line **d** is the perpendicular *bisector* of the segment **AB**.

The Bisector of an Angle

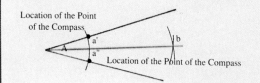

Location of the Point of the Compass

Location of the Point of the Compass

The *bisector* of an angle divides this angle into two equal angles.

Angle **A = a' + a"**

Triangles (3 sides)

h is the *altitude* of the triangles.

 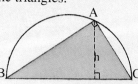 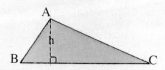

The *equilateral* triangle has three equal sides. **AB = AC = BC**.

The *right* triangle. Two of its sides form a right angle.

The *isosceles* triangle has two equal sides. **AB = AC**.

The *scalene* triangle has all its sides unequal. The joining of 3 non-aligned points forms a triangle.

Trapezoids (4 sides)

h is the *altitude* of the trapezoids.

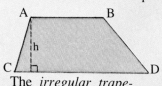 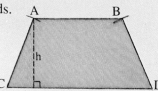 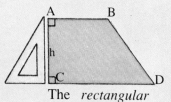

The *irregular* trapezoid. **AB** (its small base) is parallel to **CD** (its large base).

The *isosceles* trapezoid has two equal legs: **AC** and **BD** (the non-parallel sides).

The *rectangular* trapezoid has two right angles.

Parallelograms (4 sides)

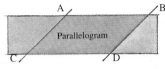

Non-perpendicular crossing of two bands, each of uniform width, but not necessarily the same width.

The opposite sides are equal and parallel.

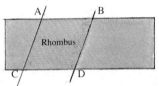

Non-perpendicular crossing of two bands of the same width.

4 sides equal, parallel two by two.

4 sides equal, parallel two by two.
4 right angles.

Perpendicular crossing of two bands, each of uniform width but not necessarily the same width.

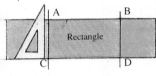

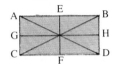

The diagonals **AD** and **BC** are equal. The median lines **EF** and **GH** are perpendicular.

Perpendicular crossing of two bands of *same width*.

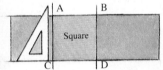

4 equal sides.
4 right angles.
The *diagonals* are equal and perpendicular. The *median lines* are equal and perpendicular.

Circle

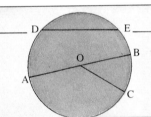

AB is a diameter.
OC is a radius (half of the diameter).
DE is an arc of the circle.
DE is a chord.

Irregular Polygons (figures with several sides, not all of which are equal)

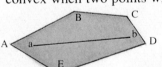

Convex polygon with 5 sides. A polygon is convex when two points within the polygon can be connected to each other by a segment lying entirely *inside* the polygon (a,b).

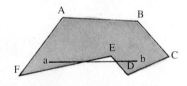

Non-convex polygon. The segment of the straight line (a,b) is *not entirely inside* the surface of the polygon.

Regular Polygons (all sides equal)

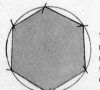

With a compass, the length of the radius is traced six times on the circle.

4 diameters perpendicular two by two.

The regular *pentagon* has 5 equal sides.
The regular *decagon* has 10 equal sides.
The regular *dodecagon* has 12 equal sides.

The Regular Hexagon
Polygon with 6 equal sides.

The Regular Octagon
Polygon with 8 equal sides.

Measuring Areas and Volumes

Area Units

1 in.

1 in.² | 1 in.

A square inch (in.²) is a unit of area measurement equal to a square measuring 1 in. on each side.

In the English system of measures, some areas are measured in **square inches** (in.²) such as the size of a printed page. Some

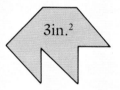

3 in.²

The area of this surface is 3 in.² It occupies the same space as three squares measuring 1 in. on each side.

are measured in **square feet** (ft.²) such as the floor area of rented office or store space. Carpeting is sold by the **square yard** (yd.²) and the areas of states are given in **square miles** (mi.²). The **acre** is a measure used to denote land areas; an acre = 43,560 ft.² or $\frac{1}{640}$ of a mi.²

Calculation of Surface Areas

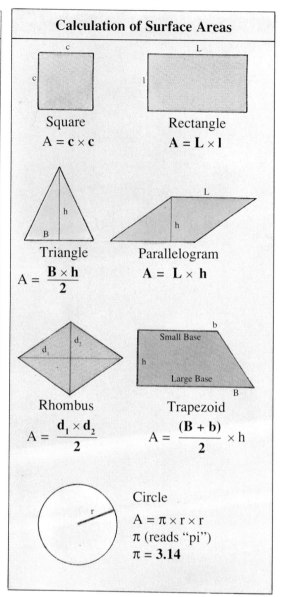

Square
$$A = c \times c$$

Rectangle
$$A = L \times l$$

Triangle
$$A = \frac{B \times h}{2}$$

Parallelogram
$$A = L \times h$$

Rhombus
$$A = \frac{d_1 \times d_2}{2}$$

Trapezoid
$$A = \frac{(B + b)}{2} \times h$$

Circle
$$A = \pi \times r \times r$$
π (reads "pi")
$$\pi = 3.14$$

Area Measure

In the metric system, a square centimeter (cm²) is the area of a square measuring 1 cm on each side. Similarly, a square millimeter (mm²) is equivalent to the area of a square measuring 1 mm on a side.

A physician would describe the size of a skin blemish by giving its area in mm².

On the other hand, an encyclopedia would give the area of a country in square kilometers (km²).

Area Measure

1 square meter (m²) equals a square measuring one meter on each side.

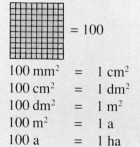

= 100

100 mm²	=	1 cm²
100 cm²	=	1 dm²
100 dm²	=	1 m²
100 m²	=	1 a
100 a	=	1 ha
100 ha	=	1 km²

English System Volume Units

In the English system of measure, volumes may be expressed in **cubic inches** (in.^{3}), **cubic feet** (ft.^{3}), or **cubic yards** (yd.^{3}).

The cubic inch is a unit which corresponds to the volume occupied by a cube of 1 in. edge length.

Calculation of Volumes

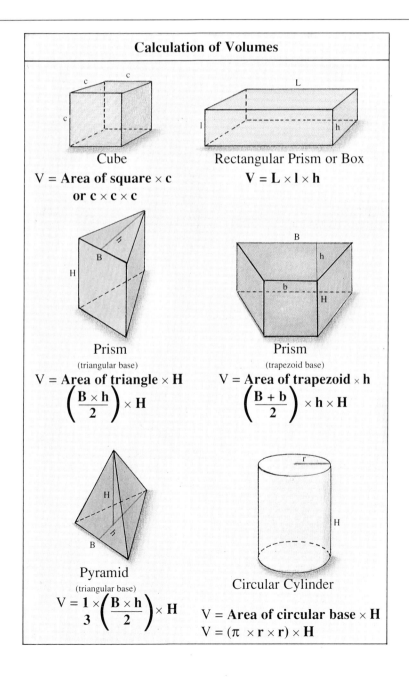

Cube

$V = $ **Area of square** $\times$ **c**

or c $\times$ c $\times$ c

Rectangular Prism or Box

$V = $ **L $\times$ l $\times$ h**

Prism
(triangular base)

$V = $ **Area of triangle** $\times$ **H**

$$\left(\frac{B \times h}{2}\right) \times H$$

Prism
(trapezoid base)

$V = $ **Area of trapezoid** $\times$ **h**

$$\left(\frac{B + b}{2}\right) \times h \times H$$

Pyramid
(triangular base)

$$V = \frac{1}{3} \times \left(\frac{B \times h}{2}\right) \times H$$

Circular Cylinder

$V = $ **Area of circular base** $\times$ **H**

$V = (\pi \times r \times r) \times H$

Constructing Solids

Polyhedrons are solids bounded by *faces*. The lines limiting these faces are edges. The intersection of one or several edges forms a *vertex*.

The Cube

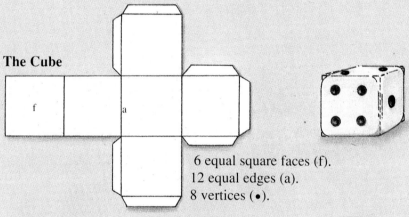

6 equal square faces (f).
12 equal edges (a).
8 vertices (•).

The Rectangular Parallelipiped or Rectangular Solid

6 rectangular faces equal two by two.
12 edges. 8 vertices.

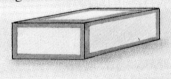

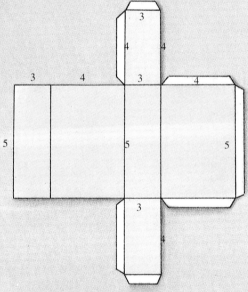

The Right Prism (triangular bases)

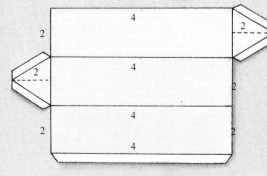

5 faces. 9 edges. 6 vertices.
The 3 rectangular faces are the *lateral faces* of the prism.
The 2 triangular faces are the *bases* of the prism.

170

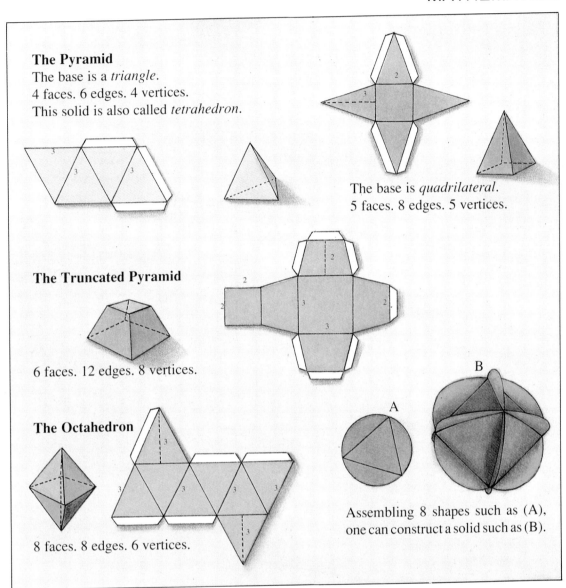

The Pyramid

The base is a *triangle*.
4 faces. 6 edges. 4 vertices.
This solid is also called *tetrahedron*.

The base is *quadrilateral*.
5 faces. 8 edges. 5 vertices.

The Truncated Pyramid

6 faces. 12 edges. 8 vertices.

The Octahedron

8 faces. 8 edges. 6 vertices.

Assembling 8 shapes such as (A), one can construct a solid such as (B).

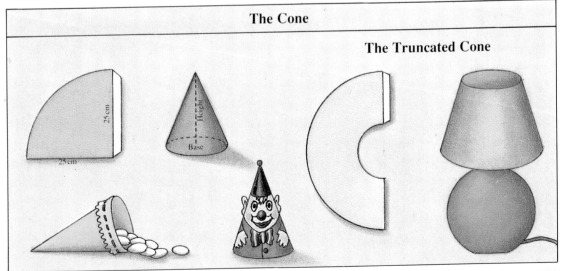

The Cone

The Truncated Cone

Plans, Maps, and Scales

The *scale model*, the *plan*, and the *map*
are representations of objects or sections of land
at different reduced scales.

In the case of large-sized objects and sections of land, the amount of reduction is very
important since details disappear with greater reduction.

Eiffel Tower: actual height 984 ft.

 Eiffel Tower
1 in. = 500 ft.
1/6,000

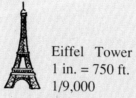 Eiffel Tower
1 in. = 750 ft.
1/9,000

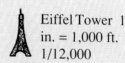 Eiffel Tower 1
in. = 1,000 ft.
1/12,000

1/6,000, 1/9,000, 1/12,000 are the *scales* of the sketches of the Eiffel Tower. They mean
1 in. represents 500 ft., 1 in. represents 750 ft., 1 in. represents 1,000 ft.

Plans

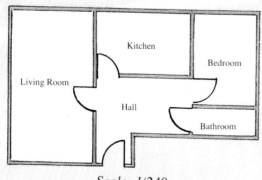

Scale: 1/240

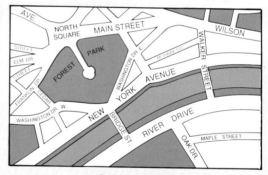

Scale 1:3,600

1 inch on the floor plan represents 20 feet in
the apartment. 1 in. = 20 ft. or 240 in.

1 in. on the city plan represents 100 yards
in the city. 1 in. = 100 yd. or 3,600 in.

Graphic Scale

It is a different representation of the scale which is generally indicated at the bottom of plans
and maps.

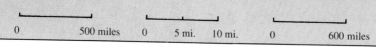

Maps

In order to be accurate, a map must be drawn to scale. The scale of a map shows how much of the earth's surface is represented by a given measurement on the map. The scale on the map enables you to measure the distances on the map so that you can figure out the real distance on the earth's surface.

Maps show places in different sizes. A map the size of this page could show the whole world or only one country. The map scale on each of these maps would obviously be different. Thus, an inch on each map would stand for a different distance. For example, an inch on a map of a city could stand for a mile or even less. But an inch on a map of the world could stand for 50,000 miles. To find out how many miles an inch stands for, you must find the map scale on the map.

The scale may be expressed in three different ways. Many maps use a *graphic scale*. The scale consists of a straight line on which distances are marked off. The marks stand for a certain number of miles on the earth's surface. For example,

 This means that one inch on the map stands for 300 miles on the earth's surface.

The map scale may be *written in words*: one-inch-to-one-mile, or 1 inch = 1 mile.

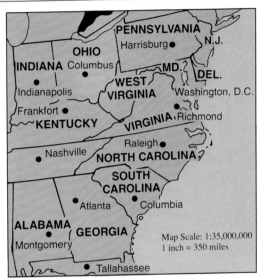

This means that 1 inch on the map equals 1 mile on the surface of the earth.

The map scale is often expressed by a *fraction* or a *proportion*: 1/36,000 or 1:36,000. This means that one unit of measurement on the map represents 36,000 of the same units on the surface of the map. Thus, one inch on the map could equal 36,000 inches or centimeters. The larger the scale's denominator, the smaller the scale of the map. Thus, 1:1,000,000 is a smaller scale than 1:100,000. Moreover, the larger the scale, the more detailed the map: 1:25,000 is a large scale; 1:1,000,000 is a small scale.

How to Find the Scale

5 in. on the plan represents 100 yd. on the

![soccer field diagram with 50 yd. and 100 yd. labels]

soccer field. 1 in. is therefore 100/5 = 20 yd. or 20 × 36 in. or 720 in.

Answer
Scale: 1:720

What Scale Has Been Used?

A. Actual length: 40 yd.; Length on the plan: 4 in.

B. Actual dimensions: 80 ft. × 40 ft.; Dimensions on the plan: 4 in. × 2 in.

C. Actual distance: 3,000 mi. Length on the plan: 6 ft.

Answers:
C: 1:2,640,000
B: 1:240
A: 1:360

Percentages and Graphic Representations

Ed Meese, opening a news conference in Chicago

Americans poll, 69 percent of respondents would return to Washington

25%

$950
OFF THE
MARKED
PRICE

25%

REIMBURSED 8% STATE TAX

70%
OF AMERICANS

8% INFLATION

33% MORE IN CANS

CREDIT
15.75%

Understanding and Calculating Percentages

25% reads 25 percent and can be written 25/100 or $\dfrac{25}{100}$

A reduction of 25% means that for $100 worth of goods, the amount reduced is $25. $100 worth of goods therefore cost $100 − $25 = $75.

For a coat costing $950, the reduction is $950 × 25/100 or $950 × 0.25 = $237.50. The coat on sale thus costs: $950 − $237.50 = $712.50.

One Operation Can Be Omitted!

25% reduction means that one has to pay 75% of the marked price.

Therefore, 75% of $950 equals $950 × 75/100 or $950 × 0.75 = $712.50.

The Meaning

An increase of 5% after April 1.

This means that for $100, the increase is $5 ($100 → $105).

For $3.50, the increase is $3.50 × 0.05 = $0.175.
The new price of the magazine: $3.50 + $0.175 = $3.67
or directly: $3.50 × 105/100 or $3.50 × 1.05 = $3.67.

What Is the Percentage of the Discount?

① The amount of the reduction is:
$1.80 – $1.44 = $.36.

The amount of the reduction for $1 is
.36/1.80 = $0.20.

The reduction *for $100*:
0.20 × 100 = $20, thus
20%.

Answers ③ = 12% ② = 30%

Percentages and Graphic Representations

Graphic representations provide easier and often more dramatically revealing presentations of comparative information. Several types of graphic representations can be used.

Among the most common:

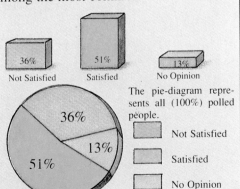

The pie-diagram represents all (100%) polled people.

☐ Not Satisfied
☐ Satisfied
☐ No Opinion

Poll of Public Opinion

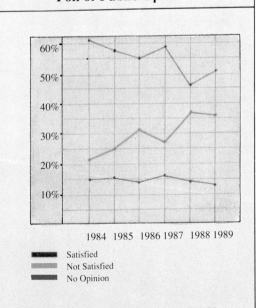

1984 1985 1986 1987 1988 1989

▬ Satisfied
▬ Not Satisfied
▬ No Opinion

On this chart the development of different trends over a 5 year period can be seen.

Logical Games

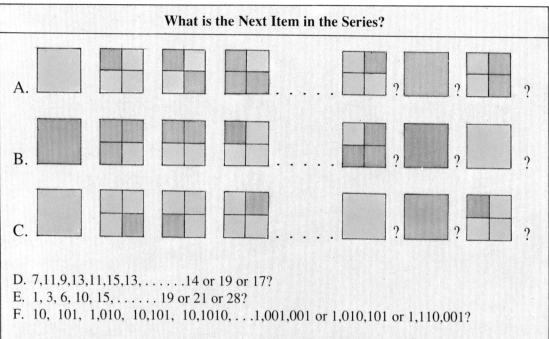

D. 7,11,9,13,11,15,13,......14 or 19 or 17?
E. 1, 3, 6, 10, 15,......19 or 21 or 28?
F. 10, 101, 1,010, 10,101, 10,1010,...1,001,001 or 1,010,101 or 1,110,001?

Missing Letters

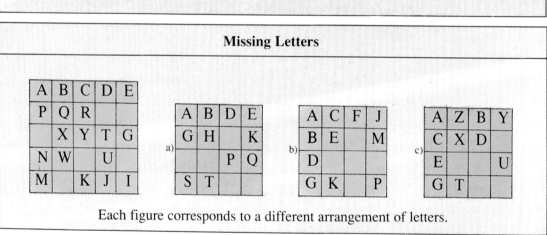

Each figure corresponds to a different arrangement of letters.

Logic

To complete:

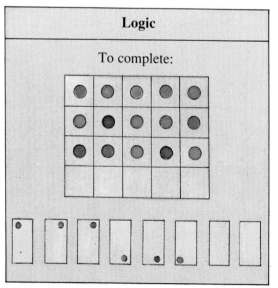

The Hidden Sides

How many spots are on the side of the dice opposite to the side shown?

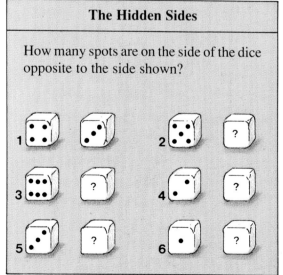

176

Missing Pieces

Which is the missing part?

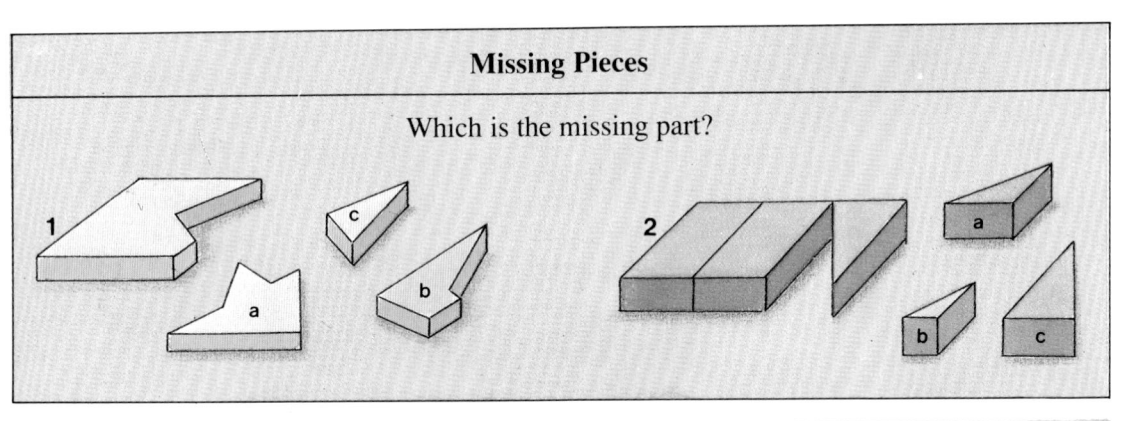

Puzzles

The tangram square (Chinese puzzle)
To construct the tangram, enlarge and cut this diagram following the heavier lines. The result: 7 pieces.

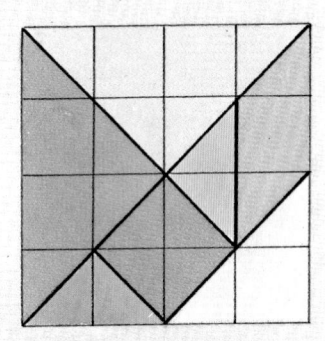

With these 7 pieces of the tangram, compose the following figures:

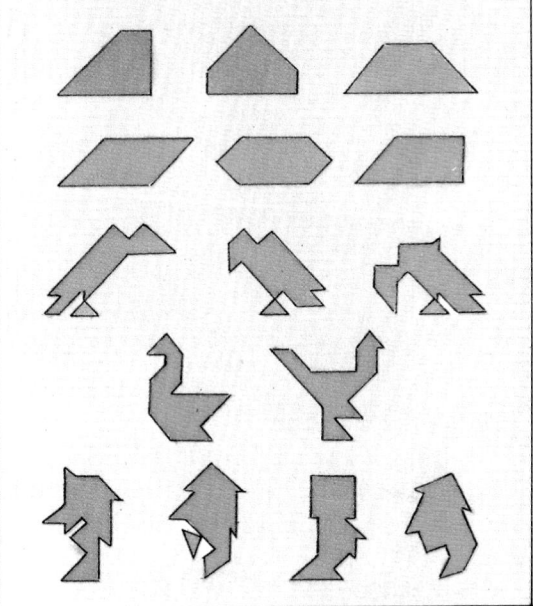

Guessing Games

A mountaineer snail!

A snail is at the bottom of a 30 ft. high wall. It climbs 2 ft. during the day and descends 1 ft. during the night. How much time does it need to reach the top of the wall?

Answers to the Games

(The answers section is printed upside-down.)

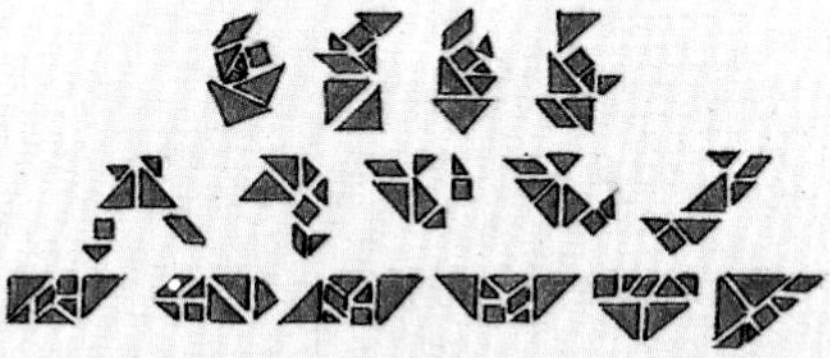

Guessing Games
The mountaineer snail:
29 days. (At the beginning of the 29th day, it will have reached 28 ft. and on this day it will climb the last 2 ft.)

Tangram

The Hidden Sides

Logic — **Missing Pieces** 1) c 2) c

Missing Letters
a) A letter omitted every two letters
b) Diagonal alphabetical order
c) Increasing and decreasing alphabetical order

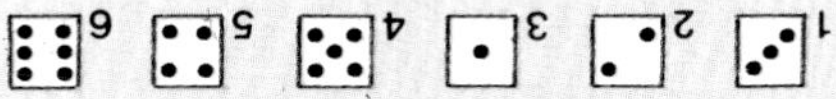

What is the Next in the Series?
A B C
D = 17 (+4) E = 21 (+6)
F = 1,010,101

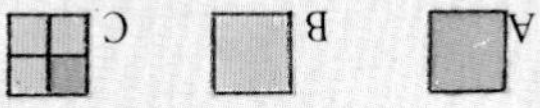

Mathematical Games

4	9	2
3	5	7
8	1	6

The sum of the numbers in any row, column, or diagonal, is 15. 15 is said to be the *constant* of the square.

The players are asked to complete the boxes to make the squares "magic."

6		4
	3	8

Constant: 21

7		
		10
11		

Constant: 24

1	15	14	
12	6		
	10	5	
			16

Constant: 34

	17	16	6
		9	
10			7
15			18

Constant: 42

Games with Matches

Arrange the matches to obtain the *double* of the present number.

Remove two matches to form two squares.

Now obtain the *triple*.

6 + 1 = 8! Is this possible?

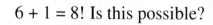

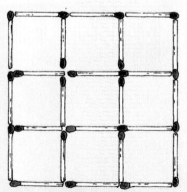

Remove 4 matches to form 5 squares.

Remove 6 matches to form 3 squares.

Remove 8 matches to form 2 squares.

A Game with Two Players

17 matches are given to 2 players. In turn, each player removes one, two, or three matches. The winner is the one who takes away the last match. (To be sure to win, he or she must remove the 13th match.)

Tricks

How is the number 23 written by using only the digit 2?
How is the number 45 written by using only the digit 4?
How is the number 1,000 written by using only the digit 9?

A Shortcut

How can all these dots be connected in the shortest way?

The starting point is anywhere.

The same dot is used only once.

Crosses and Dots

Try to draw a cross consisting of straight lines which connect *12 dots* so that *5 dots* are inside the cross and *8 dots* outside. The cross must be *symmetrical* and *regular*.

Division

Peter shares his apples with three friends. To the first he gives half of his apples plus half an apple. To the second he gives half of the remaining apples plus half an apple. To the third he gives half of what he still possesses plus half an apple. He still has an apple left.

How many apples did he have in the beginning?

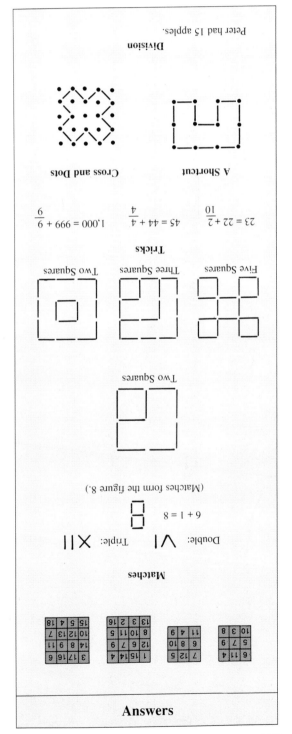

Answers

Division

Peter had 15 apples.

Cross and Dots

A Shortcut

$$23 = 22 + \frac{2}{10}$$

$$45 = 44 + \frac{4}{4}$$

$$1,000 = 999 + \frac{9}{9}$$

Tricks

Five Squares   Three Squares   Two Squares

Two Squares

(Matches form the figure 8.)

$$9 + 1 = 8$$

Double: VI   Triple: XII

Matches

Water

Water covers three-quarters of the earth's surface.
It is essential for life. Our own body consists of 61% water (92 lbs of water for an adult weighing 150 lbs)!

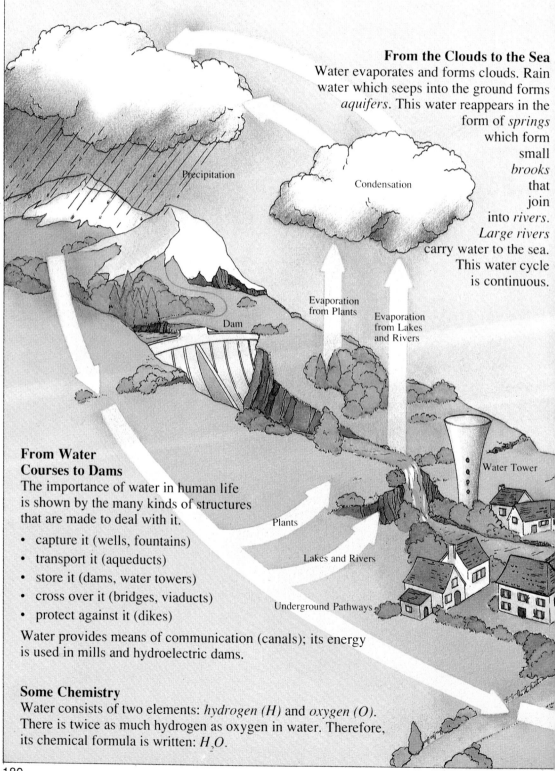

From the Clouds to the Sea

Water evaporates and forms clouds. Rain water which seeps into the ground forms *aquifers*. This water reappears in the form of *springs* which form small *brooks* that join into *rivers*. *Large rivers* carry water to the sea. This water cycle is continuous.

Precipitation

Condensation

Evaporation from Plants

Evaporation from Lakes and Rivers

Dam

Water Tower

From Water Courses to Dams

The importance of water in human life is shown by the many kinds of structures that are made to deal with it.

- capture it (wells, fountains)
- transport it (aqueducts)
- store it (dams, water towers)
- cross over it (bridges, viaducts)
- protect against it (dikes)

Plants

Lakes and Rivers

Underground Pathways

Water provides means of communication (canals); its energy is used in mills and hydroelectric dams.

Some Chemistry

Water consists of two elements: *hydrogen (H)* and *oxygen (O)*.
There is twice as much hydrogen as oxygen in water. Therefore, its chemical formula is written: H_2O.

Water That Does Not Flow!

When cooling, water becomes solid. This transformation starts at *zero degrees C.,* which is 32 degrees F.

Solid water takes up more space than liquid water. This is why the glass of a bottle filled with water shatters when the water freezes.

Some very cold regions in the world are completely covered with ice (Arctic, Antarctic). The layer of ice may reach a thickness of two and one half miles.

When tiny droplets of water in the form of clouds meet currents of cold air, these droplets change into solid water: snow (flakes) or ice (hail).

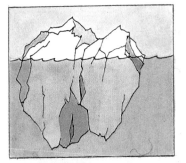

Water Which Floats on Water

The submerged part (under water) of an iceberg is much larger than the visible part.

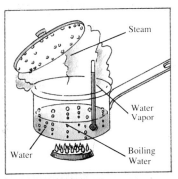

Steam

Water Vapor

Water

Boiling Water

Invisible Water!

When laundry dries, the water seems to disappear.It evaporates.

Water vapor is an invisible gas which mixes with the air.

Heat and wind speed evaporation. Every second, *millions of tons of water evaporate* at the surface of the earth! When water vapor meets cold surfaces or currents of cold air, it condenses into droplets and becomes visible: *clouds, fog, dew.*

How to Make a Cloud
Metal tray with ice cubes. Container with hot water.

Observation in the dark with a flashlight.

What is the weight of a pint of water?

At sea level, one pint of water weighs exactly 1 pound.

Water changes into ice at 0 C, which is 32 F.

At what temperature does water boil?

At sea level, water boils at 100 C., which is 212 F.

At an altitude of 3 miles, it boils at 80 C, or 176 F.

Is it true that bodies are lighter in water?

They seem lighter because the water helps to lift them.

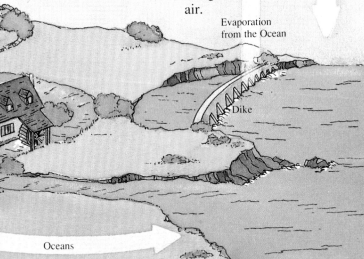

Evaporation from the Ocean

Dike

Oceans

Air

Air Everywhere

Air is an invisible gas with no color or odor, but we always know it is there.

The earth is surrounded by a layer of air, 60 miles thick, called the *atmosphere*. This atmosphere protects the earth against the strong rays of the sun. It acts as a screen.

Without Air, Life Would Be Impossible

Most living things die when they are without air because they stop breathing. Without air, fire does not burn and sounds cannot be heard.

A Bottle Is Never Empty

Air spreads out to fill all spaces. When you pour liquid from a bottle, air rushes in. The bottle which seems to be "empty" is really full of air. Here are three experiments which can prove it:

1. Air in a bottle offers resistance that prevents a balloon from being blown up.

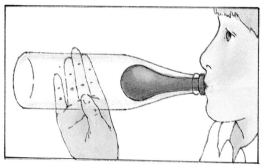

3. Under water, air from a bottle can be transferred into another container.

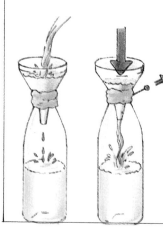

2. Put a funnel in a bottle which is two-thirds filled with water.

Seal the space between the lower part of the funnel and the neck of the bottle with modeling clay. Pour water into the funnel. Almost no water filters through. Make a hole in the clay with a needle. The water flows through because the hole lets the air out.

Some Chemistry

Air consists of several gases, the most important of which are nitrogen (78%), oxygen (21%), and other gases such as argon, carbon dioxide and water vapor (1%).

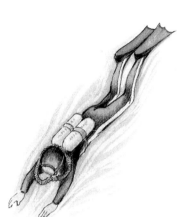

A deep-sea diver's tank of air contains about 400 gallons of compressed air.

Air Is Heavy

A balloon full of air is heavier than a balloon without air.

A quart of air weighs a thirtieth of an ounce. Thus, the weight of the air in an average room of 150 square

Make a notch in the middle of a stick so as to easily attach a thin string to it. Blow up two balloons of the same size and tie them at the ends and at the same distance from the middle of the stick. Hold the string with one hand—the stick remains horizontal. With the other hand, pierce one of the balloons with a needle—the scale tips to the side of the balloon full of air.

feet is about 106 pounds. The weight of the atmosphere (several miles thick) is thus quite important.

To Make Liquid Air

It can be done! By compressing and deep freezing it (at about -190 C or -372 F).

Liquid air is blue. It is stored in thermos bottles.

Why do high altitude mountain climbers use oxygen bottles?

The higher the elevation, the thinner the air. Above 15,000 feet, breathing becomes very difficult. Any physical effort is very tiring.

In planes flying at high altitudes (10,000 feet and more), the air provided for passengers is pressurized.

What is there beyond the atmosphere?

A Vacuum.

Rockets and satellites travel in it.

The bottle is full of water. It is impossible to reduce the volume of water by pressing strongly on the cork. Liquids cannot be compressed.

Air Can Be Compressed

It is possible to reduce the space occupied by air by compressing it. A bottle full of air can be sealed by pushing in a cork. This is not possible with a bottle full to the top with water. Water, like all liquids, cannot be compressed.

Fire

Wild and Violent . . .

Fire occurs naturally in various places on the earth. Roaring torrents of hot, glowing matter rise through the fractures in the earth's crust.

Volcanoes, mouths of fire which remain unpredictable for long periods, often cause great destruction.

Lava consisting of partially molten rocks may reach temperatures above 1,000°C, or 1,832°F.

. . . but Essential for Life

Fire is the greatest discovery made by humans. Some 750,000 years ago, they learned to start and use it. Ever since then, fire has always been present in our lives. With fire we can provide heat, cook food, melt metals, produce light, and burn waste.

Early humans making fire

Metal Casting

What Is Combustion?

It is the transformation into light and heat of the energy stored in fuel. Anything that can burn is said to be *combustible*.

Burning Gas

Escaping Gas

Hot Fuel

Combustibles may be:

solid—plastics, wood, coal
liquid—cooking oil, gasoline, alcohol, petroleum
gaseous—illuminating gas, propane

To burn, a combustible needs the oxygen of the air. When it burns it produces carbon dioxide and water vapor.

Barbecue

Fireplace

Gas Stove

Furnace

Types of Lamps

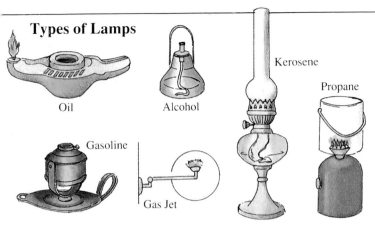

Oil

Alcohol

Gasoline

Gas Jet

Kerosene

Propane

A Ball of Fire That Provides Heat and Light

Although 93 million miles away from the earth, the sun can sometimes burn our skin! Its temperature reaches 10,800 F at its surface; in the center it is between 16 and 20 million degrees! It gets so hot because it is not really a fire—it is a *nuclear reaction*.

All Kinds of Flames

Flames are not all the same. According to the fuel, they have different colors: yellow, yellow and red, red and blue, blue. The bluer the flame, the hotter it is. A yellow flame is less hot. It contains substances which have not burned. These substances may appear in the form of smoke.

Some fuels burn without a flame, like the tobacco in a cigarette.

Fire Hazard!

This sign shows the dangers of fire. Our friend can become our enemy. Indeed, every year large areas of forests are destroyed. Fires in homes or theaters can turn into catastrophes with many victims. Fire-fighting equipment is important and efficient and firefighters are well trained. Fires are often due to negligence.

Fire Prevention

- Do not start a fire in a forest.

- Do not open bottles containing flammable liquids close to a flame (gasoline, ether, for instance).

- Do not restart a fire with a flammable liquid.

- If there is a gas leak, do not make a spark or flame close by.

- Do not run with your clothes on fire because air currents will make them burn faster.

DANGER! FIRE!

Canadair: a plane specially equipped for fighting forest fires.

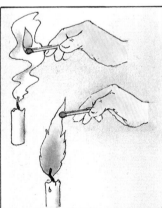

To relight a candle at a distance

When a candle is blown out, flammable paraffin gas keeps coming out of it for a while. By igniting this gas, a candle can be relit at a distance.

Weather Station

What Is a Weather Station?

It is a place where data is collected with the help of very precise measuring instruments for the purpose of weather forecasting.

Today, there are about *10,000 weather stations* in the world.

The accuracy of forecasting has increased in the last ten years from 24 hours to 72 hours. In 15 years, it may be possible to forecast weather 10 days ahead. Besides the data collected on the ground, additional information comes from sounding balloons, marine buoys, planes, and especially satellites that transmit excellent pictures of the upper atmosphere at various places above the earth.

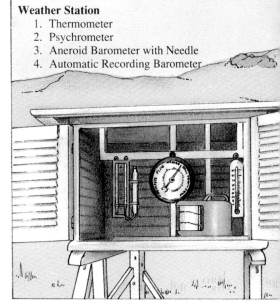

Weather Station
1. Thermometer
2. Psychrometer
3. Aneroid Barometer with Needle
4. Automatic Recording Barometer

The Thermometer

It measures the lowest *temperature* at night and highest during daytime so as to calculate the mean daily temperature. This measure is expressed in degrees and is written ___ °C or ___ °F.

Thermometer measuring maximum and minimum temperature.

The Psychrometer

It measures the humidity of the air by the reading of two thermometers—one dry and the other kept moist with a wet cheesecloth. The wet-bulb thermometer is cooled by the evaporation of water; the drier the air, the faster the water evaporates and the lower the thermometer reads.

The Barometer

This instrument measures the weight of the air, called *atmospheric pressure*. This pressure varies. When it drops, bad weather is approaching. When it rises, weather conditions improve. A barometer is marked off in millimeters (mm) or inches. The average atmospheric pressure is 760 mm, about 30 inches.

A barometer can be made according to the following model:

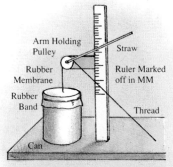

The stretched membrane lowers and rises as the atmospheric pressure changes. This movement is recorded by the straw which indicates the pressure.

Wind Vane

It indicates the direction of the wind.

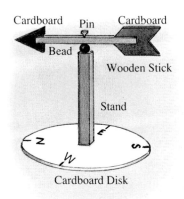

Anemometer

It measures *wind speed*.

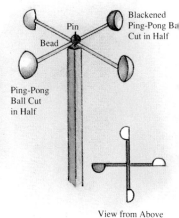

View from Above

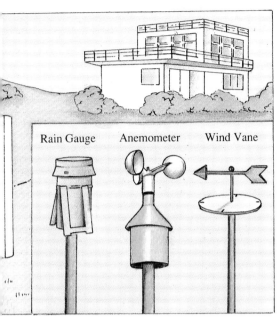

Rain Gauge   Anemometer   Wind Vane

Observation Data Sheets

They show the different recorded data and allow certain weather forecasts.

Here is a model that can be used:

	temperature: maximum minimum	pressure: morning evening	wind: direction speed	hygrometry	rain gauge	description of the sky
Monday						
Tuesday						
Wednesday						
Thursday						
Friday						
Saturday						
Sunday						

Rain Gauge

The *amount of rainfall* during a given time is measured with this instrument.

It is possible to make a rain gauge yourself using materials you have at home.

To make this rain gauge, cut down a plastic soda bottle. Then place a ruler in it.

The amount of rainfall is measured in inches or millimeters.

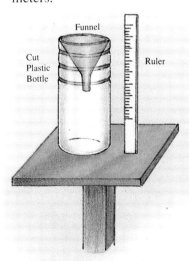

Funnel

Cut Plastic Bottle

Ruler

Hygrometer

It measures the amount of *humidity* in the air. It is marked from 0 to 100. The higher the value, the more water vapor is in the air.

It is possible to make a hygrometer using simple materials you have at home.

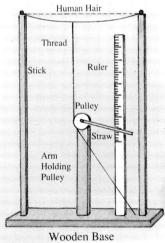

Human Hair

Thread

Stick

Ruler

Pulley

Straw

Arm Holding Pulley

Wooden Base

According to the humidity in the air, hair shortens (air is drier) or lengthens (more humid air), a movement recorded by the straw which moves in front of a ruler marked from 0 to 100.

Where Should a Weather Station Be Located?

Weather vanes and anemometers must be placed in an open space where there are no obstacles to block the wind.

Barometers, thermometers, and hygrometers must be protected from rain and sunshine. They must be placed inside a well-ventilated shelter painted white.

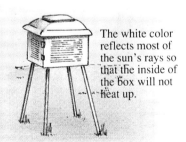

The white color reflects most of the sun's rays so that the inside of the box will not heat up.

Is meteorology a new science?

No, in 350 B.C., the Greek scholar Aristotle wrote a treatise titled *Meteorologica* (Meteorology). However, it was not until the 1600s and 1700s that the first measuring instruments were perfected and "meteorological science" was born.

Electricity

In Which Cases Does a Bulb Light Up?

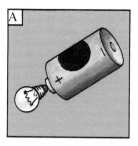

A

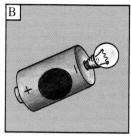

B

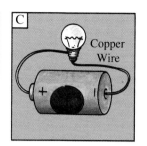

C
Copper Wire

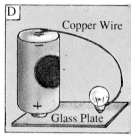

D
Copper Wire
Glass Plate

E

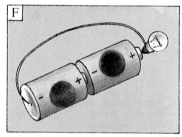

F

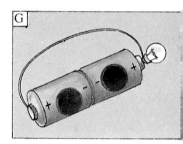

G

Answer: C,E,F.

The Role of the Switch

In any electric installation, the current flows only when the circuit is closed, that is, when the wires that carry the current are connected. A switch opens and closes the electric circuit.

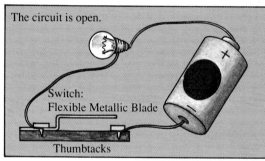

The circuit is open.

Switch:
Flexible Metallic Blade

Thumbtacks

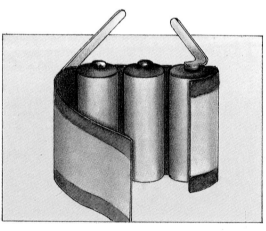

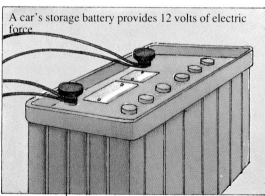

A car's storage battery provides 12 volts of electric force.

The Inside of a Battery

A round battery provides 1.5 volts of electric force.

A flat battery consisting of three round batteries provides 4.5 volts of electric force.

The Car Battery

The storage battery holds electrical energy to start the motor and operate its electrical system when the car is stopped. It is recharged when the motor runs.

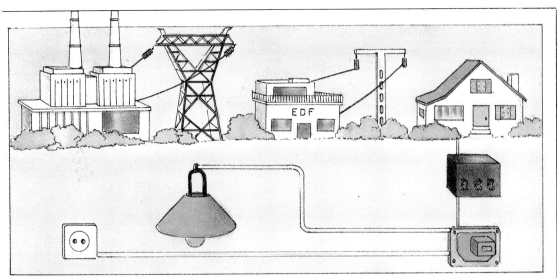

The power station (thermal, hydroelectric, or nuclear) provides the electric current for "domestic" daily use. In the United States, it is supplied at a force of about 115 volts.

Danger!

When the force of electricity is more than 14 volts, it can make a dangerous amount of current flow. In a home such voltage may be fatal. Water and humidity increase the risk of electrocution.

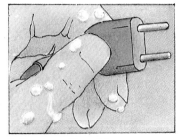

The Bulb Heats Up

The electric current flowing through the filament of the bulb releases heat. If the temperature rises too high, the filament melts. The bulb is said to have "burned out." This release of heat is used in many electrical appliances.

Do Not:

Change a bulb without switching off the lamp.

Use an electric appliance in the bathtub.

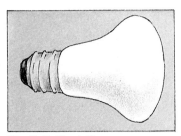

It is *very* dangerous to stick a metal object into a socket.

Touch an electric stove when your feet are wet.

Pull a plug with wet fingers.

Touch an electric wire which has fallen on the ground.

Lightning

Lightning is an electric discharge between a cloud and the ground or between two clouds. Temperature during these giant sparks may be as high as 30,000 C, or 54,032 F. Lightning can kill humans and animals and start serious fires. The lightning rod, invented by Benjamin Franklin in 1752, leads the electric discharge directly into the ground.

Sources of Energy

Whenever something moves or changes in any way, energy is used. Energy occurs in many different forms.

Muscles—the First Source of Energy
Thousands of years ago, human beings knew no energy source except *their muscular force* to move around, to hunt, to lift, to carry. About 10,000 B.C., they learned how to use animals which they domesticated as sources of energy.

Muscular Energy
(Chemical Energy)

Eolian energy (after the name of the god of winds, Aeolus) turns windmills and, since prehistoric times, moves sailboats.

Mechanical Energy
The spring of a wind-up clock and the weights of an old clock provide energy to mechanical parts that in turn produce movement.

Water, Air—Natural Forces
By 100 B.C., *the energy of flowing water* was used to turn the millstones which crushed grains. Today, this form of energy is still used, to produce another kind of energy—electricity (dams, hydroelectric power plants).

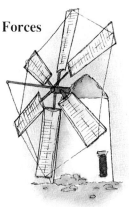

Windmill
(Eolian Energy)

The First Clocks

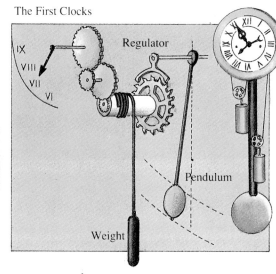

Regulator

Pendulum

Weight

Natural Energy Sources

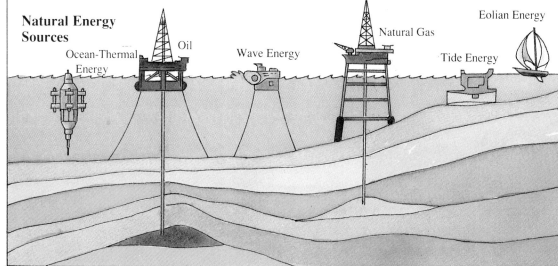

Ocean-Thermal Energy

Oil

Wave Energy

Natural Gas

Eolian Energy

Tide Energy

190

Fuel Energy

Wood and, above all, *coal* were used for the first engines which improved the lives of human beings.

The use of *oil* and *gas* to run engines revolutionized industry. Today, the energy produced during combustion of certain gases propels rockets.

Electrical Energy

Produced and used in great quantities (lightning, heating, to run motors), electric energy is sent through wires quickly and easily.

Electrical Energy

The need for electricity keeps growing; the demand doubles every ten years!

Since fuel resources will not last forever, humans are searching for new sources of energy.

Solar Energy

Captured with mirrors or special panels, the *heat of solar radiation* operates high-temperature furnaces (up to 3,800 C, or 6,872 F), to heat houses, and produce electricity.

Geothermal Energy

At a certain depth in the ground, *aquifers of hot water* are sometimes found. This water can be pumped and used inexpensively for the heating of houses or buildings.

Thus, at the Geysers geothermal energy plant in California, water comes out of the ground at a temperature of 175 C., or 350 F.

Ocean Energy

A plant to use the energy of tides was built in 1934 at Passamaquoddy Bay in Maine, but it did not work well. There is an operating plant in France.

Today, other means are being tested to use the energy of waves and marine currents.

Nuclear Energy

The first nuclear reactor was completed at the University of Chicago in 1942, and hundreds have been built since. Construction of the first American nuclear power-generating plant began in 1964 in Oyster Creek, New Jersey. By 1971, 20 nuclear power plants were operating.

The use of this type of energy is being fully developed.

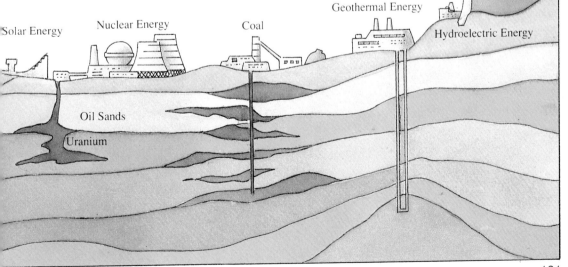

Solar Energy
Nuclear Energy
Coal
Geothermal Energy
Hydroelectric Energy
Oil Sands
Uranium

Nuclear Power—A New Energy

This form of energy is produced with a fuel called uranium. 1 gram of uranium releases the same energy as 2.5 tons of coal!

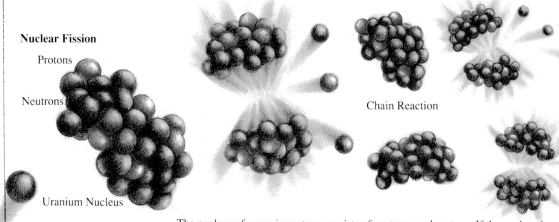

Nuclear Fission

Protons

Neutrons

Chain Reaction

Uranium Nucleus

The nucleus of a uranium atom consists of neutrons and protons. If the nucleus is bombarded with neutrons, it breaks into smaller nuclei and releases a large amount of energy.

How Is Nuclear Energy Produced?

This is done inside a leak-proof container, the *reactor*. When uranium is introduced, a very strong nuclear reaction occurs. Each splitting uranium nucleus releases neutrons that split other uranium nuclei. This "chain reaction" releases an enormous amount of heat.

Where Is Uranium Found?

It is extracted from very large mines in the United States, in Canada, in South Africa, in Australia, and in South America. There are large mines in New Mexico and Wyoming.

Mask and protective suit against radiation.

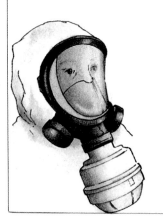

The Atomic Bomb

This is the military use of nuclear energy. With the instant release of energy contained in an atomic bomb, a target is destroyed by the blast of the explosion, by the released heat, and by the spread of deadly radioactive materials.

In August, 1945, two bombs were dropped by the United States on Japan, at *Hiroshima* and *Nagasaki*. Over 170,000 people were killed in a few seconds. This disaster forced Japan to surrender and ended World War II.

Is It Dangerous?

Yes. For that reason nuclear reactors are well protected and continuously monitored. Indeed, the production of nuclear energy releases a great deal of *radioactivity*, radiation which can be fatal to most living things. Very sensitive instruments, kept close to the reactors, measure this radioactivity constantly.

Atomic Explosion.

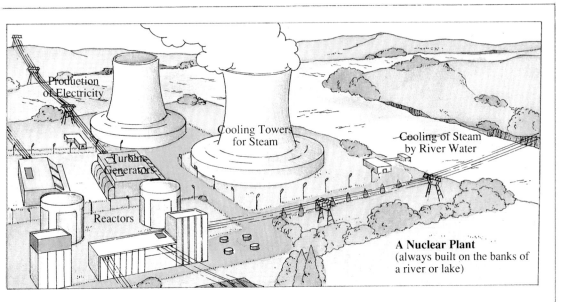

Production of Electricity

Cooling Towers for Steam

Cooling of Steam by River Water

Turbine Generators

Reactors

A Nuclear Plant
(always built on the banks of a river or lake)

Nuclear Plants

In this peaceful use of nuclear energy, the great release of heat can transform water in a boiler into steam under pressure. This steam turns the turbines which produce electricity.

Hundreds of nuclear plants operate today all over the world.

Because of the great risks, these plants are built to resist violent shocks (a plane crash, for instance) or earthquakes.

Protest against a nuclear power plant.

For or Against Nuclear Power

To date, nuclear power plants have been built in 22 countries. However, many people are *opposed* to nuclear power. Because of the dangers involved in radioactivity, they say life is in danger and that even control measures in these plants cannot prevent serious accidents.

Breakdowns and accidents (for instance, the fire in a reactor in April 1986 at the nuclear plant at Chernobyl, in the Soviet Union) have caused fears about the safety of nuclear power. They have raised questions about the future of nuclear power plants. Some communities refuse to allow construction of nuclear plants on their lands. Public protests occur frequently.

Those people who favor the protection of nature (*ecologists*) raise strong protests against nuclear power plants because they produce radioactive wastes. The safe disposal of these wastes is a problem and ecologists are concerned about the means used to dispose of radioactive waste. They are concerned about the possible effect the disposal of radioactive wastes may have on humans, on beaches and on wildlife.

However, *people in favor of* nuclear power stress the extraordinary progress for humankind achieved by the use of this energy which they believe to be clean, less polluting, and less dangerous than certain chemical industries.

193

The World of Sound

Every vibrating object produces a sound (the string on a guitar, our vocal cords, etc.). The air carries sound waves to our ears. In space, on the moon, in places without air, sounds cannot be heard.

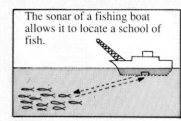

The sonar of a fishing boat allows it to locate a school of fish.

Lightning and Thunder

Why is there often a certain lapse of time between the strike of lightning and the sound of thunder, although both occur at the same time?

This is so because light waves travel faster in the air than sound waves—*186,000 miles per second* for light, *1,100 feet per second* for sound!

Sonar

Certain boats carry this instrument for detecting and locating objects under water. When sound waves emitted by the sonar strike an object, they travel through the water and are reflected toward the ship.

The String Telephone

Material needed: 2 cardboard containers and a few yards of string. This experiment shows that sound also travels through solids. Here, the sound waves follow the string.

Another example (on page 195): the physician's *stethoscope* which allows the doctor to listen to the heartbeat—to breathing. The speed of sound is faster in solids than in the air. In steel, for instance, it is *16,000 feet per second*. In water, about *5,000 feet per second*.

HELLO-O-O

The Echo

Sound waves are reflected by an obstacle and produce an echo—repetition of emitted sounds.

HELLO-O-O

Counting the number of seconds between lightning and thunder, one can tell the distance of the thunderstorm. Every 5 seconds = 1 mile.

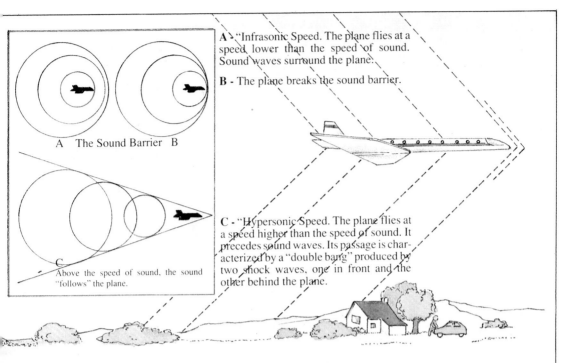

A - "Infrasonic Speed. The plane flies at a speed lower than the speed of sound. Sound waves surround the plane.

B - The plane breaks the sound barrier.

C - "Hypersonic Speed. The plane flies at a speed higher than the speed of sound. It precedes sound waves. Its passage is characterized by a "double bang" produced by two shock waves, one in front and the other behind the plane.

A   The Sound Barrier   B

C   Above the speed of sound, the sound "follows" the plane.

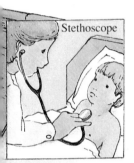

Stethoscope

Faster Than the Speed of Sound

Certain aircraft called *supersonic planes* fly faster than the speed of sound. When their speed reaches about 700 mph, they run into strong resistance called the *sound barrier* or *sonic wall*. If they can overcome this resistance, they break the sound barrier. On the ground this is heard as a tremendous "double bang." The Concorde flies at twice the speed of sound! The first planes that reached this speed fell apart under the effect of vibrations. The sound barrier was broken for the first time on October 14, 1947 by Charles Yeager.

How Many Decibels?

Depending on the vibrating object, sound waves have a greater or lesser intensity, or loudness. This intensity can be measured with certain instruments. The unit of measure is called the *decibel* (dB).

Below is a table indicating the intensity of some sounds at points close to the source:

rustling of leaves: 0-10 dB

quiet conversation: 20-50 dB

loud conversation: 50-65 dB

a train passing by: 65-90 dB

thunder: 90-110 dB

jet plane at takeoff: 110-140 dB

space rocket takeoff: 140-190 dB

Noise becomes painful to the ears starting at 120 decibels.

Are there sounds that we cannot hear?

Yes, our ear does not hear every sound. For instance, ultrasounds are too high pitched and infrasounds too low to be heard by human ears.

Sonars of boats emit ultrasounds that cannot be perceived.

Bats find their way and locate flying insects with the help of ultrasounds which they emit and which return to them as echos. A *dolphin* uses this method in the sea.

To Make a Toy Flute:

Rubber Band

Cigarette Paper

Put your lips here and hum a tune.

Plastic Pipe (inside diameters about ¼ inch, length 4-5 inches).

Magnetism—A Strange Phenomenon

The Lodestone

Discovered more than 2,500 years ago, a rock called *magnetite* has the property to attract iron and steel objects and to give them its power of attraction. Magnetite draws its magnetic property from the largest known magnet—the earth.

A Special Magnet— the Compass

It consists of a magnetic needle mounted upon an axis which rotates freely over a card indicating the cardinal points (N, S, E, W).

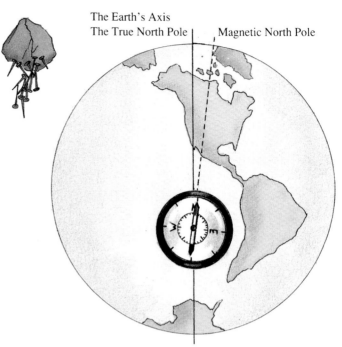

The Earth's Axis
The True North Pole   Magnetic North Pole

Attracted or Not?

Only metals containing iron, steel, or nickel are attracted to magnets. Objects consisting of glass, wood, plastic, copper, or silver are not attracted to magnets.

The needle comes to rest pointing approximately northward.

The Chinese were the first to use the compass. They taught its use to the Arabs who transmitted it to the Western world during the Middle Ages.

Artificial Magnets

Today, magnets no longer consist of a natural rock, magnetite, but are made artificially. They are made in special shapes according to their use.

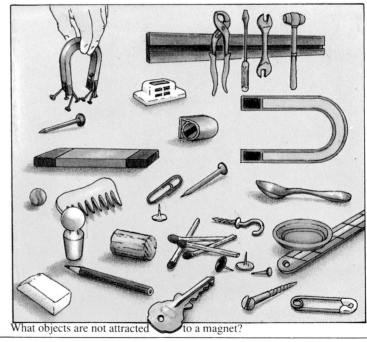

What objects are not attracted to a magnet?

The Poles of a Magnet

There are certain places on the magnet where magnetism is strongest. Bar magnets suspended from a string all line up in the same direction. One end points north (the north-pointing pole) and the other end points south.

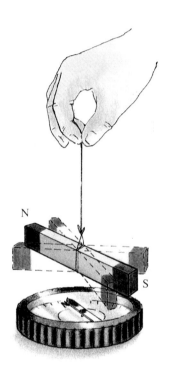

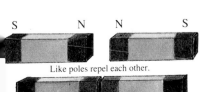

If two bar magnets are brought near each other, we see that poles of the same nature (north, for example) repel each other; they cannot be joined. Poles of different nature (north and south) attract each other.

Like poles repel each other.

Opposite poles attract each other.

To Make Objects Magnetic

Metal objects made of steel and certain alloys can be made magnetic by stroking them with a magnet.

Every magnetic object then immediately has two poles—a north-pointing pole and a south-pointing pole.

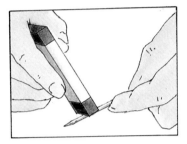

Make a Picture of the Magnetic Field

The magnetic force can be found in the space around the magnet—a magnetic field. To make a picture of the field, cover the magnet with a piece of paper and sprinkle iron filings on the paper.

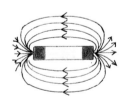

Iron filings around a magnet form loops.

2 different poles. The lines join.

2 identical poles. The lines diverge.

Electricity and Magnets

An electric wire is wrapped around a large nail and the ends of the wire are connected to an electric battery.

When the electric current flows, the nail becomes magnetic. An electromagnet has been made. Some industrial electromagnets can lift great weights.

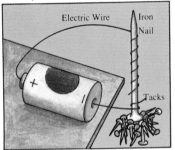

A Simple Electromagnet

Electric Wire   Iron
Nail

Tacks

Can Magnetism Disappear?

Yes, if the magnet is heated, if it is given shocks, or if its poles are not carefully protected. A needle is demagnetized by heating it.

What Instruments Use Electromagnets?

Electric bells, the telegraph, all electric motors, tape recorders.

Tape Recorder

Levers and Balances

Large Force with Little Effort

It is relatively easy to lift and move heavy objects, or to raise water from the bottom of a well with the help of a very simple instrument called a *lever*. The use of levers goes back to very ancient times. The Greek Archimedes (287-212 B.C.) first discovered and studied them.

All Kinds of Levers

Use of a lever in acrobatics

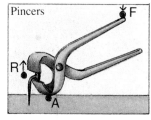

Pincers

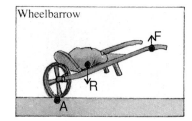

Wheelbarrow

The usefulness of this lever depends on the position of its point of support.

Lifting weight with pulley

Pulley

Some Technical Points

A lever always has three essential points:

• the point of support or fulcrum (**A**)

• the point of resistance (**R**)

• the point where force is applied (**F**)

The longer the distance **AF**, the less force is needed to lift the weight at **R**.

A Practical Use—the Balance

Balances have been known since ancient times. In 2000 B.C., the Egyptians were already using them. The first balances were made of wood.

A balance is a lever in which the fulcrum is usually located exactly halfway between the force (**F**) and the resistance (**R**). The arms of the lever, **AR** and **AF** are therefore equal. When weighing something, you adjust the balance so it is level. Then **F** and **R** are equal.

Common Scale

A Precision Balance

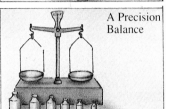
Seesaw

Balances with Equal Arms

The *common scale* was invented in 1670. It is still widely used.

The *precision balance* is used by jewelers and chemists. It is capable of giving accurate readings of very small weights.

The children's *seesaw* works according to the same principle as the common scale and the precision balance. If the children weigh the same, the beam is horizontal.

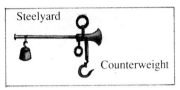
Steelyard
Counterweight

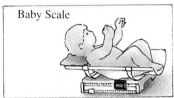
Baby Scale

A Strange Balance

Already known in China by 1000 B.C., the *steelyard* consists of two unequal arms. For weighing, a counterweight is moved on the longer arm, which is marked off in pounds. When equilibrium is reached, the weight can be read directly.

A baby scale is a balance with cursors, a moving slide that can be read.

Everything Is Automatic!

Some balances allow immediate reading of the weight of an object.

For instance, commercial automatic balances or scales such as the postage scale and the household scale.

Some sturdy balances, called *platform weighing machines*, weigh masses up to several tons.

Household Scale

Platform Scale

Postage Scale

Bathroom Scale

Commercial Scale

Automatic Commercial Scale

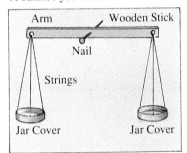
A balance you can make:
Arm — Wooden Stick
Nail
Strings
Jar Cover — Jar Cover

Weight or Mass?

The *mass* of an object is the amount of matter of which it is composed. *It does not vary*. The *weight* is what this mass weighs. *It can vary* according to its location. For instance, on the moon, any object has the same mass as on earth, but it weighs only $\frac{1}{6}$ as much.

The World of Colors

The colors we see are a property of light.

A Little Magic
When a beam of white light (daylight) crosses a glass prism, many different colors appear!

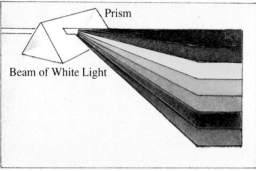

Dispersion of light through Newton's prism.

The white light consists of many colors—red, orange, yellow, green, blue, indigo and violet shade into each other.

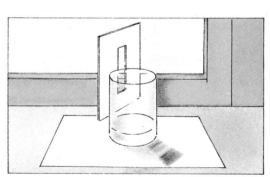

To obtain a solar spectrum

A glass of water on a sheet of white paper.
A small cardboard with a 1/2-inch slit. Put everything in front of a window in the sun.

All these colors represent the *light spectrum*. Three hundred years ago, Isaac Newton explained the composition of light based on the experiment shown above.

Only White Is Visible!
The cardboard disk contains some of the colors of the spectrum. If it is spun rapidly, our

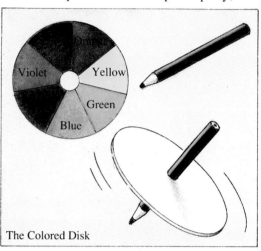

The Colored Disk

eyes can no longer distinguish the separate colors. If the colors are carefully chosen, they will blend together and look white.

Our eyes are most sensitive to the primary colors: red, green, and blue.

The Rainbow
All the colors of the spectrum are displayed in

On a chair, with your back to the sun, you can see a rainbow. It is interrupted by your shadow.

a rainbow. Droplets of water in the atmosphere act like many tiny glass prisms.

Why Do We See a Red Cherry, a Green Apple, and a White Page?

All the objects which surround us absorb certain colors of the spectrum and reflect others. Our eye sees only the reflected colors. Therefore, a cherry appears red because it absorbs all the colors except red, which it reflects. A green apple reflects green and absorbs all other colors. The sheet of paper reflects all the colors of the spectrum and appears white. Eyes are blue because they do not absorb that color.

The cherry appears red because it reflects only the red color.

And Black?

Any object which appears black (coal, fabric, etc.) absorbs all the colors of the spectrum and reflects none. This object can thus be seen only by contrast with surrounding objects. Black is in reality the *absence* of color.

A sheet of paper reflects all the colors and appears white.

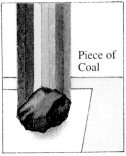

Piece of Coal

Sheet of White Paper

Black absorbs all colors.

From One Color to Another

Additive synthesis: Blue, green, and red are the primary colors of light. When lights of these colors are mixed, all the colors can be obtained including white.

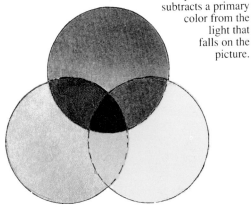

Subtractive synthesis: Cyan (greenish blue), yellow, and magenta (purplish red) are the secondary colors. Each subtracts a primary color from the light that falls on the picture.

Why is the sun red at sunset?

At dusk, the sun's rays cross thousands of miles of the atmosphere at an angle.

Because of this diagonal path, blue and violet rays are scattered by tiny dust particles that act like filters. Consequently, only the red rays reach us.

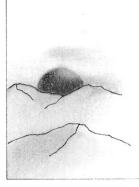

Observing the Sky

Ever since ancient times, humans have observed the sky and tried to understand its mysteries and explain its organization.

Who Was Right?

In the second century A.D., the Greek astronomer *Ptolemy* described a universe of small size, with the earth motionless in the middle. The sun, the planets, and the stars revolved, or turned around, the earth.

In the 16th century, the Polish astronomer *Copernicus* revolutionized this view of the universe. He proposed that the earth and the other planets revolved around the sun, while each rotated around itself.

In the 17th century, the Italian astronomer *Galileo* confirmed Copernicus' discovery. At that time, Galileo was condemned by the Church. Today, we know that he was right.

Do We Know the Dimensions of the Universe?

No, because the universe is huge. Even the most powerful telescopes and satellites cannot see the end of it.

The universe contains *galaxies*. Seen from the earth, millions of them have already been counted.

Each galaxy is formed by stars and planets grouped together into *systems*. There are *billions* of such systems in each galaxy.

Thus, the planet earth belongs to the *solar system* which is included in "our" galaxy—the *Milky Way*.

Star or Planet

A star *produces* light energy whereas a planet is a cold body which *reflects* received light.

A few years ago, it was discovered that celestial bodies also emit radio waves and hence radiotelescopes "with large ears" were built to listen to these celestial bodies.

Uranus

Saturn

Powerful Radiotelescope

Jupiter

Path of a Comet

Pluto

Neptune

Artificial Satellite

What Forms Our Solar System?

A star, the sun, is in the middle and nine main planets with their satellites revolve around it.

Planets	Symbols	Diameter in Miles	Average Distance to Sun in Millions of Miles	Period of Rotation	Period of Revolution Around the Sun
Mercury	☿	3,000	27	59 days	88 days
Venus	♀	7,630	68	243 days	224 days
Earth	⊕	8,000	93	24 hrs.	365.24 days
Mars	♂	4,500	156	24.5 hrs.	687 days
Jupiter	♃	87,500	488	10 hrs.	11 years
Saturn	♄	75,000	875	1 hrs.	30 years
Uranus	♅	30,000	1,810	216 hrs.	84 years
Neptune	♆	31,250	2,800	218 hrs.	165 years
Pluto	♇	3,750	3,700	6.4 days	248 years

What Is a "Light-Year"?

It is a unit of distance used to express the enormous distances in the universe. Light travels at a speed of 186,000 miles per second. A light-year is the distance traveled by light in one year, that is, 5,800 billion miles. At this speed, sunlight reaches us in a little over 8 minutes!

What is a shooting star?

These are *meteoroids* which revolve around the sun and sometimes cross the orbit of the earth. When they enter the atmosphere, they heat and burn up. The light produced by their combustion is a white streak called a meteor.

Is there life on the other planets of the solar system?

It is very unlikely because atmospheric conditions are often very extreme (frozen or burning ground). But there might be life in other systems.

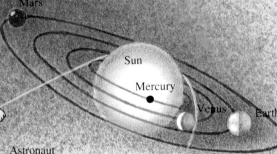

Mars

Sun

Mercury

Venus

Earth

Astronaut

And the Moon?

Located 240,000 miles from the earth, the moon is a satellite of our planet, that is, it revolves around the earth in a little over 29 days. Because of these revolutions, we do not always see the moon in the same way. Sometimes it appears full (full moon), sometimes partly full (the various quarters of the moon). American astronauts landed on the moon in 1969.

At what speed does the earth revolve around the sun?

At the incredible speed of 66,000 mph, or about 19 miles per second!

The Phases of the Moon

Last Quarter

Full Moon

First Quarter

Star Charts

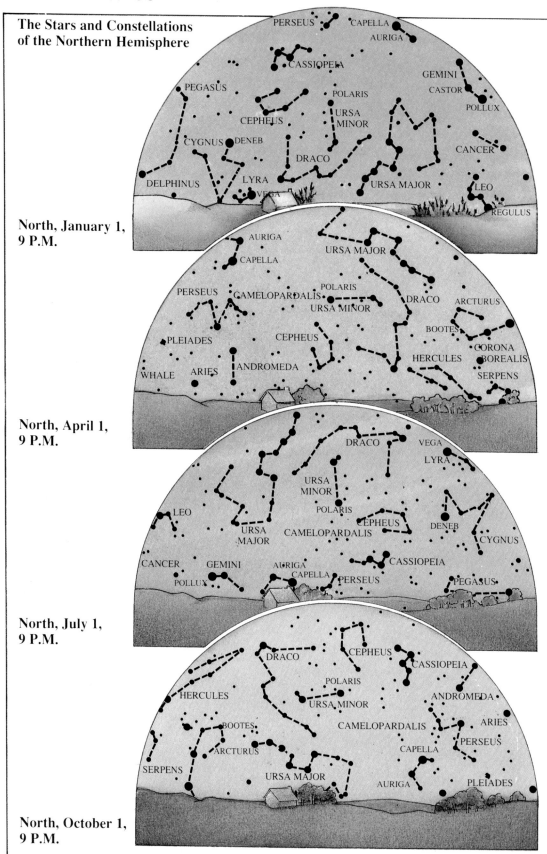

The Stars and Constellations of the Northern Hemisphere

North, January 1, 9 P.M.

North, April 1, 9 P.M.

North, July 1, 9 P.M.

North, October 1, 9 P.M.

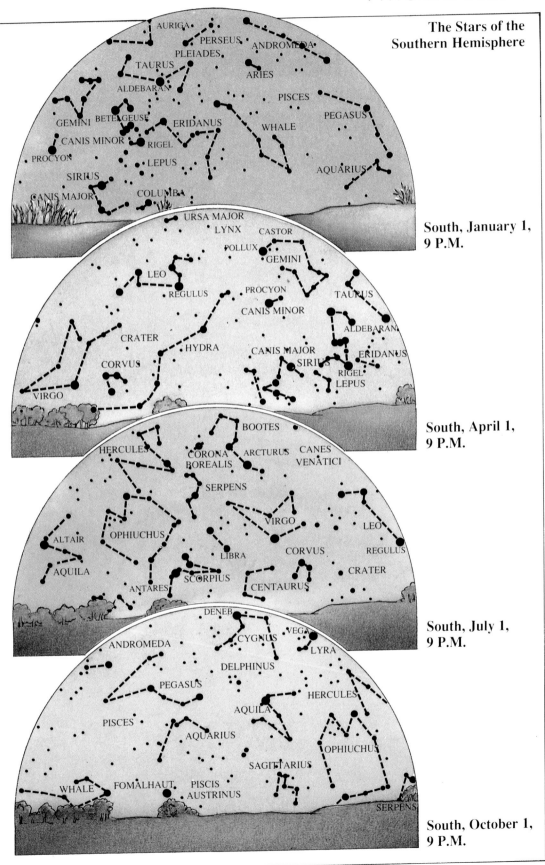

The Stars of the
Southern Hemisphere

South, January 1,
9 P.M.

South, April 1,
9 P.M.

South, July 1,
9 P.M.

South, October 1,
9 P.M.

Measuring Time

There have not always been watches, pendulums, and clocks. Since they did not have such instruments for many thousands of years, humans measured the passing of time by observing natural events—the succession of days and nights, the different positions of the sun in the sky, the phases of the moon, or the tides.

East

West

Sunrise

The Sun at Noon

Sunset

One of the First Instruments—the Sundial

At different times of the day, the length and the direction of the shadow cast by an object placed vertically into the ground was indicated by the *sundial*. These measurements provided an approximate reading of time.

Most ancient civilizations used this instrument. They came into general use in the 13th century.

Sundials were still used in many countries at the beginning of this century.

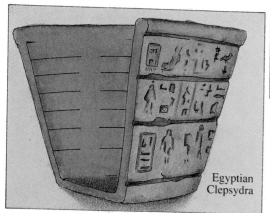

Egyptian Clepsydra

called *clepsydrae*, or water clocks. Used mainly at night, they were easily made but not very precise.

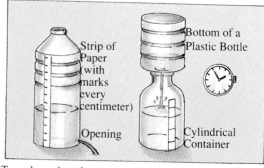

Strip of Paper (with marks every centimeter)

Bottom of a Plastic Bottle

Opening

Cylindrical Container

Clever Egyptians!
In 3500 B.C., the first time-measuring devices appeared in Egypt. These were strange containers with an opening at their base. Time was measured by how long it took for the water to drip through. These devices were

Two clepsydrae that are easy to make. On the right, the watch helps to make the measuring instrument (with a marked off ruler).

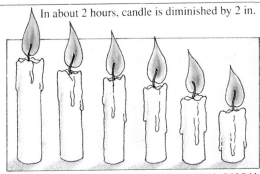

In about 2 hours, candle is diminished by 2 in.

3 P.M.   3:25 P.M.   3:50 P.M.   4:15 P.M.   4:40 P.M.   5:05 P.M.

The "Wax Clock" of the Middle Ages

A burning candle made wax droplets at regular intervals. Thus it was possible to measure time (a quarter of an hour, half an hour, one hour) according to the position of the droplet.

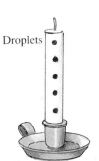

Droplets

The burning of a candle causes the fall of droplets.

Still in Use: the Hourglass

The same principle as the clepsydra, it shows how long it takes for fine sand to flow from the top to the bottom and varies according to the amount of sand and the size of the opening.

Hourglass

Mechanical Clocks

The first clocks appeared in the 14th and 15th centuries. However, they were not very precise. It was not until the 17th century that the use of the *pendulum* provided a regular movement that was more accurate.

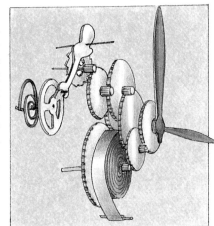

Main parts of a mechanical clock.

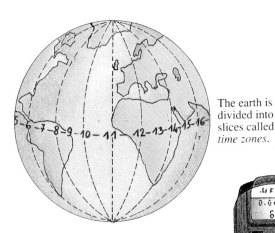

The earth is divided into slices called *time zones.*

Cuckoo Clock

Digital Watch

Chronometer

Calendar

Today

Time is measured today with great precision. Watches with hands, digital watches, and chronometers are all instruments which regulate our daily life.

Switzerland is famous for its watch industry.

To save energy, daylight saving time was introduced. Watches are set *ahead* in the spring when the days become longer and set *back* in the fall.

The earth revolves around the sun in 365.24 days. To account for the odd 0.24 day, one day is added to the month of February every four years; these are the *leap years*

207

Faster and Faster!

Using their legs, human beings were able to cross great distances although speed remained limited to about 10 mph and could not be kept up for too long. Nevertheless, this was the only way humans were able to travel for thousands of years. Little by little, with the help of their imagination, they invented and perfected techniques which enabled them to become masters of the space surrounding them.

Today, we cross great distances with tremendous speed and no effort.

Animals Were the First "Vehicles"
Captured and domesticated, the donkey, the ox, and later, the horse became the first means of transportation.

Roman Chariot

Team of Oxen

The Invention of the Wheel—a Great Step
It was invented about 3500 B.C., most likely in Mesopotamia, and has been used in many different ways over the centuries.

An Original Invention—the Bicycle
The first vehicle with two wheels in line.

1875, a bicycle with pedals, called the "penny-farthing" bicycle, was used for the first time.

1818, the invention of the bicycle.

1770, one of the first steam-powered automobiles by Cugnot.

The Automobile
With its appearance, a new era began. It evolved very rapidly and its role became more and more important, leading to a new way of life and completely changing urban and country landscapes.

1876, the first gasoline cars. Here, an open touring car in 1923.

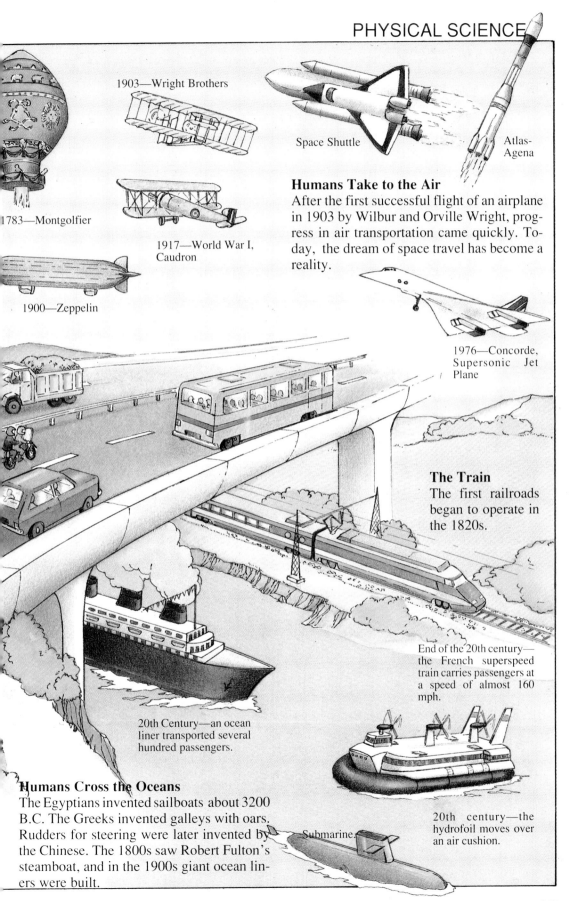

1903—Wright Brothers

Space Shuttle

Atlas-Agena

1783—Montgolfier

1917—World War I, Caudron

1900—Zeppelin

Humans Take to the Air

After the first successful flight of an airplane in 1903 by Wilbur and Orville Wright, progress in air transportation came quickly. Today, the dream of space travel has become a reality.

1976—Concorde, Supersonic Jet Plane

The Train

The first railroads began to operate in the 1820s.

End of the 20th century—the French superspeed train carries passengers at a speed of almost 160 mph.

20th Century—an ocean liner transported several hundred passengers.

20th century—the hydrofoil moves over an air cushion.

Humans Cross the Oceans

The Egyptians invented sailboats about 3200 B.C. The Greeks invented galleys with oars. Rudders for steering were later invented by the Chinese. The 1800s saw Robert Fulton's steamboat, and in the 1900s giant ocean liners were built.

Submarine.

Photography

Some History

Since ancient times, the principle of the "dark room" was used to observe eclipses. In 1826, Nicéphore Niepce of France produced the first photograph in black and white on paper. By 1837, another French inventor, Daguerre, perfected the system. In the 1880s the American George Eastman invented the Kodak camera and gave photography to amateurs.

Daguerre

Eastman

Dark Room

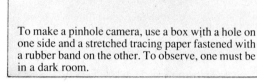

To make a pinhole camera, use a box with a hole on one side and a stretched tracing paper fastened with a rubber band on the other. To observe, one must be in a dark room.

The Ancestor of the Camera—the Dark Room

A tiny hole in a completely dark room allows one to observe the image of what happens outside—*upside down.*

During the 1500s, this method, called the *camera obscura* (dark room) was used to draw objects.

Today

The modern camera has been greatly improved. It is smaller and easy to carry. It has many automatic features, so it is easy to use.

Inside the body of the camera, the image forms on a sheet of plastic with a light-sensitive coating—the film.

One of the first cameras.

The First Cameras

They had an objective, a glass lens which concentrated all light rays. Each camera was a small camera obscura with a lens on one end and a light-sensitive plate on the other. The lens made an image on the plate.

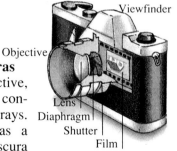
Shutter Release Button
Viewfinder
Objective
Lens
Diaphragm
Shutter
Film

Modern Camera

Some Technical Aspects

The *viewfinder* allows you to frame the picture to be photographed.

The *shutter* regulates the time of the film's exposure to light. It can be adjusted according to the brightness of the light and whether the object to be photographed is moving or still.

When the shutter release button is pressed, the shutter opens and closes in a fraction of a second.

The *diaphragm* regulates the amount of light to which the film is exposed.

An Indispensable Tool

Most sciences and technologies use photography.

It is used in medicine, in scientific research, in analysis and treatment of certain diseases, and in astronomy, for a better understanding of the universe. Aerial photography is used in drawing precise maps.

Through photography, we have been able to learn about the world beneath the sea. Photography is helpful in the study of art works.

It is present in daily life through newspapers, books, advertising, and many other fields.

Development of Film:

Load Film on Spool

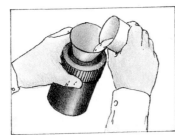
Fill, Develop

Empty

Rinse

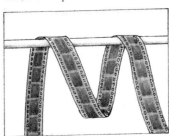
Dry

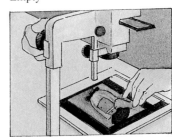
Enlarge

Develop

Fix

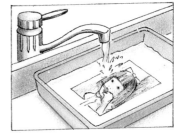
Rinse

Dry

From a Negative to a Positive

When all the film has been exposed, it is treated with chemicals. It is dipped into several trays containing chemical fluids.

The film becomes a negative (blacks and whites reversed). The negative is used to cast an image on light-sensitive paper, which becomes the print.

The Instant Picture

Some cameras (Polaroid) develop the final print instantly.

A Polaroid Camera.

How Life Begins

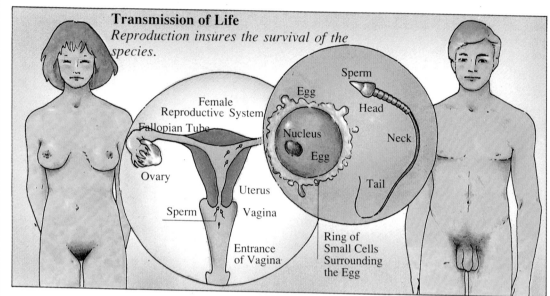

Transmission of Life
Reproduction insures the survival of the species.

Female Reproductive System
Fallopian Tube
Ovary
Uterus
Sperm
Vagina
Entrance of Vagina

Sperm
Egg
Head
Nucleus
Neck
Egg
Tail
Ring of Small Cells Surrounding the Egg

Human beings, as well as most animals, reproduce when a male *sperm* enters a female *egg*. This is the first step in the generation of a new living being. It is called *fertilization*.

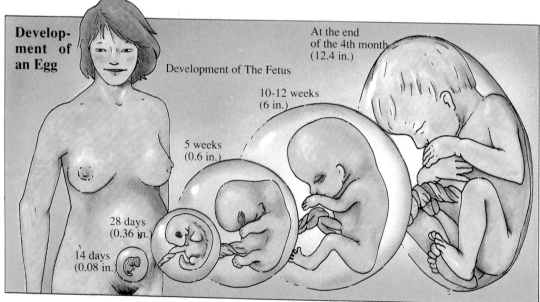

Development of an Egg

Development of The Fetus

At the end of the 4th month (12.4 in.)

10-12 weeks (6 in.)

5 weeks (0.6 in.)

28 days (0.36 in.)

14 days (0.08 in.)

The fertilized egg develops and changes:
- either outside the female body, as in the case of birds, insects, and most fish, that is, animals which lay eggs and often hatch them, or
- inside the body of the mother as is the case of all familiar *mammals*.

The *embryo* develops from the egg during a time which varies according to the species—from a few days to several months. For the development of a living human being, the time is about 270 days (9 months).

A few *comparisons* (days of embryo development):

lark: 12	elephant: 620.
rabbit: 30	hamster: 20
cat, dog: 56/60	lion: 110/116
sheep: 150	monkey: 240
cow: 280	horse: 335

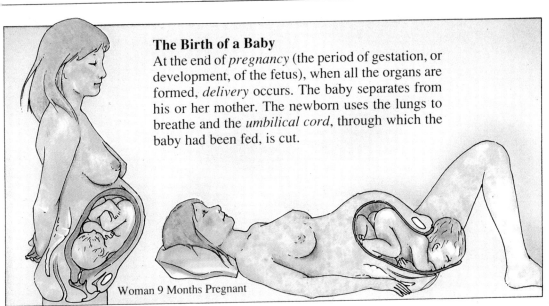

The Birth of a Baby

At the end of *pregnancy* (the period of gestation, or development, of the fetus), when all the organs are formed, *delivery* occurs. The baby separates from his or her mother. The newborn uses the lungs to breathe and the *umbilical cord*, through which the baby had been fed, is cut.

Woman 9 Months Pregnant

Usually, a woman gives birth to only one child. *Twins* (two babies) are born sometimes, but births of *triplets* (three babies) or *quadruplets* (four babies) are rare. Mammals, such as dogs, cats, and rabbits, often have 3, 6, 10, or more offspring at a time.

The Stages in Human Life

After birth, a slow growth continues until approximately the age of 20. *Infancy* is followed by *adolescence* and then *adulthood*. The human being ages and then dies. The average life span is between 70 and 80 years.

A Few Average Life Spans (in animals)

Small Flying Insect = a few hours
Mouse = 3 years
Rabbit = 8 years
Dog = 15 years
Trout = 20 years

Horse = 25 years
Crow = 50 years
Elephant = 70 years
Crocodile = 80 years
Galapagos Turtle = 100-150 years

From Tadpole to Frog

Animals which lay eggs are called *oviparous* (frogs, birds). In its development, a frog goes through a complete *metamorphosis* (change). The egg is laid and fertilized in the water, where it develops into a tadpole. Later, the tadpole grows legs and lungs, loses its gills and tail, and finally turns into a frog.

Viviparous animals are those which bring forth completely formed living young.

And the Plants?

Most plants also reproduce with the help of a male organ, the *stamen*, and a female organ, the *pistil*. Pollen grains produced by the stamen fertilize the ovules of the pistil. The pistil changes into a fruit which contains seeds. A seed contains an embryo plant, developed from the ovule. After germination, these seeds grow into new plants.

There are other means of reproduction in vegetables (asexual reproduction, grafting, budding).

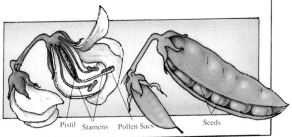

Pistil   Stamens   Pollen Sacs   Seeds

Respiration

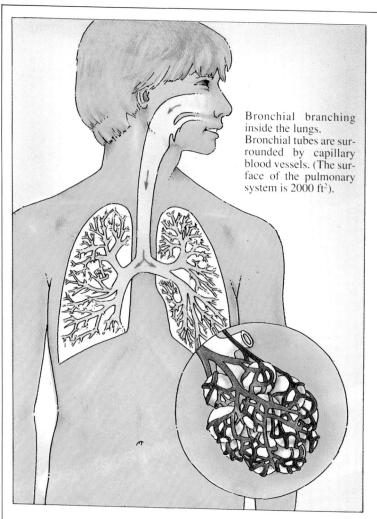

Bronchial branching inside the lungs. Bronchial tubes are surrounded by capillary blood vessels. (The surface of the pulmonary system is 2000 ft²).

An Uninterrupted Circulation

Several times per minute—the number varies according to our physical activity—our chest rises and lowers. We are *breathing*. At first, air enters through the *nose*. It follows the *trachea*, which branches into the *bronchi* and *bronchioles*, and thus circulates in the lungs which expand. This is called *inhalation*.

Thereafter, air is expelled and the lungs decrease in size. This is called *exhalation*.

These two movements are *involuntary* (made without choice).

A Gaseous Exchange

When comparing inhaled and exhaled air, it is found that a certain amount of *oxygen* has disappeared and has been replaced, in almost the

Gaseous exchanges occur with the help of blood.
In blue: blood carrying carbon dioxide.
In red: blood rich in oxygen.

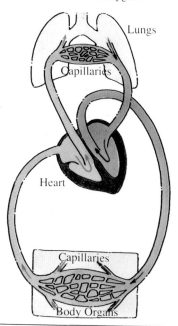

Lungs

Capillaries

Heart

Capillaries

Body Organs

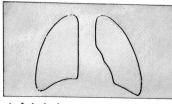

A. Inhalation
The lungs are inflated with inhaled air.

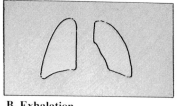

B. Exhalation
Respiratory gases are expelled. 15,000 quarts of air move through our lungs in one day.

Energy Production

All our organs need *energy* to function. Oxygen from the air helps to provide such energy. Collected by the lungs during *inhalation*, oxygen is carried in the bloodstream to all parts of the body. However, when our body organs use energy, they produce a waste product—carbon dioxide—which is dangerous for cells. Carried back to the lungs by the blood, in a direction opposite to the first one, carbon dioxide is released during *exhalation*. The exchange of oxygen and carbon dioxide is called *respiration*.

same proportion, with *carbon dioxide*:
- inhaled air—21% oxygen and 0.04% carbon dioxide
- exhaled air—16% oxygen and 4.5% carbon dioxide

Hence, an exchange between these two gases, respiration, has occurred in our lungs.

Asphyxia (Suffocation)

It is a failure of breathing movements. It can be caused by drowning, by electrocution, by inhaling toxic gases.

A suffocating person is in urgent need of *artificial respiration*, such as mouth-to-mouth resuscitation.

Breathing in Water!

Our lungs do not allow us to breathe in water. Fish have no lungs; they respire with their

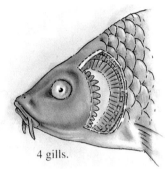

4 gills.

gills. As water passes over the gills, oxygen moves from the water into the fish's blood. Carbon dioxide goes the other way. This is why the water of an aquarium loses oxygen rapidly and must be changed frequently.

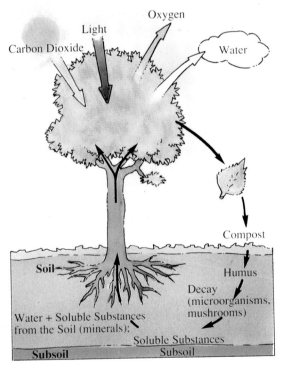

Plants—Source of Oxygen

With the help of light, gaseous exchanges occur in green plants, those which contain a green substance called *chlorophyll*. These plants absorb carbon dioxide and release great quantities of oxygen. Without plants, life would not be possible on our planet.

At night, these same plants absorb small amounts of oxygen and release carbon dioxide. Thus, they respire like animals.

Why Are We Out of Breath after Running?

Muscular efforts produce a lot of carbon dioxide that must be rapidly released and replaced by oxygen. This is why breathing becomes faster.

At rest, we inhale and exhale about 16 times per minute.

This frequency may reach or even go beyond 60 times per minute during a fast run.

Can You Survive without Breathing for a Long Time?

No, it cannot be longer than a few minutes (in the case of divers, for instance). After having been submerged too long, the victim's life can no longer be saved.

Why Do We Have to Eat?

Every living thing must be nourished. Food is needed for our bodies to grow and stay alive.

Food—Source of Energy for Our Bodies

Bread, meat, vegetables, milk, fruit—all contain nutrients (fats, sugars, vitamins) which supply the energy necessary for movement, for the production of heat, and for the continuous functioning of our organs.

Can We Eat Anything?

No, humans need a *well-balanced* diet, especially during their growing years. Too much

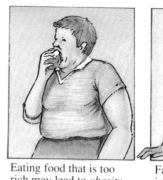 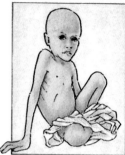

Eating food that is too rich may lead to *obesity*.

Famine, or a diet lacking in vitamins, leads to *malnutrition*.

of certain food items or a lack of others may cause serious diseases.

What Happens During Digestion?

After being chewed in the *mouth* and moistened by *saliva*, food enters the *digestive tract*. It goes through the *esophagus* into the *stomach*. There it undergoes chemical changes and continues on its way into the *small intestine*. This is where the nutrients enter the bloodstream. Waste materials pass through the *large intestine* into the *rectum*, where they are passed from the body.

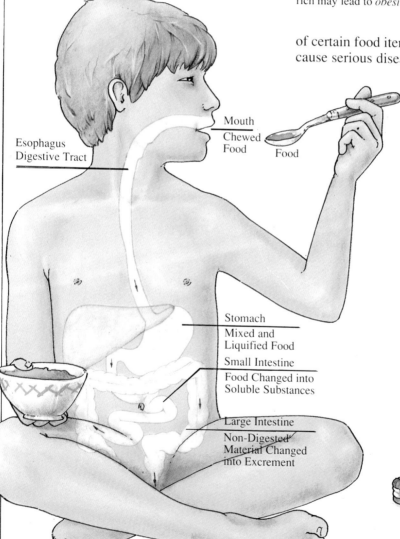

Esophagus
Digestive Tract

Mouth
Chewed Food
Food

Stomach
Mixed and Liquified Food

Small Intestine
Food Changed into Soluble Substances

Large Intestine
Non-Digested Material Changed into Excrement

Are Humans "Omnivores"?
In other words, do they eat both animal and plant foods?

Insectivores

Herbivores

Granivores   Carnivores

Certain animals feed on plants only—they are called *herbivores*. Others eat only meat—they are called *carnivores*. Animals such as rodents that feed on seed or grains are called *granivores*. Those such as moles, shrews and hedgehogs that depend on insects as food are called *insectivores*.

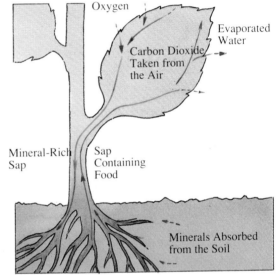

Oxygen

Evaporated Water

Carbon Dioxide Taken from the Air

Mineral-Rich Sap

Sap Containing Food

Minerals Absorbed from the Soil

Plants Also Need Nourishment
The most fragile plants as well as the strongest trees need food to develop and live. Their food is organic matter, made in the green leaves.

The search for the natural way.

HORSE MANURE FINALLY DOMESTICATED

Horse manure is a rich natural fertilizer that is used for growing delicate plants.

The sap, the "blood" of the plant, circulates organic matter produced by sunlight, chlorophyll, water and carbon dioxide, as well as *minerals* absorbed from the soil by the roots (iron, magnesium, phosphorus).

If the soil becomes depleted (loses minerals), plants deteriorate. They wither and die. Gardeners often fertilize the soil.

Fertilizers at Work—Good Crops Ahead!

Natural and chemical fertilizers provide the soil with the nutrients necessary for plant growth. They make it possible to farm in poor soil, and to grow successive crops in the same soil without depleting it.

One should not believe that increased fertilizing ensures better crops. Excessive fertilizing may lead to serious problems. The surplus accumulated in the soil and carried away by rainwater may become toxic if it contaminates aquifers of drinking water.

Vegetarians are persons who do not eat meat.

Good Nutrition

1,095 Meals per Year!

This represents a huge amount of food! We cannot stay healthy by eating whatever we please.

The choice of our meals, both in quality and quantity, is therefore very important.
Good nutrition has to be learned.

A Well-Balanced Meal

Vegetables — Bread — Apple — Cheese — Meat — Water — Grapes — Green Salad — Bread — Olives — Tomatoes

A Poorly Balanced Meal

Potato Chips — Hamburger — Soft Drink (with Sugar) — Cream Puff — Cheese — Rolls — Butter — Bread — Taco — Olives — Cold Cuts

Classification of Food

According to their ingredients, foods are classified into different groups. Water is the only drink necessary for our body. Milk contains water, carbohydrates, proteins, fats, calcium, and vitamins. It is a nearly complete food.

Proteins
Fish, cheese, nuts, milk, poultry, eggs, red meat.

Carbohydrates
Rice, potatoes, peas, pasta, cake, bread, chocolate, sugar.

Fats
Butter, shortening, oil, nuts.

Vitamins
Milk, whole grains, vegetables, fruit.

Energy That Can Be Measured

Every item of food supplies our body with a certain amount of energy replacing that used for our activities.

Food energy is measured in calories.*
Therefore:

- 1 g (.04 oz) of carbohydrates produces 4 calories
- 1 g of proteins produces 4 calories
- 1 g of fats produces 9 calories

The daily energy requirement varies according to age and activity.

For instance, a teenage boy needs an average daily allowance of about 3,000 calories. This is his recommended daily dietary need. *The nutritionist's calorie is what a chemist calls a *kilocalorie*, and is equal to exactly 4,185 joules of energy.

Rules for Good Nutrition

- Eat a variety of food at regular hours.
- Avoid too many fats and sugars.
- Regularly eat green vegetables and raw fruit.
- Eat slowly and chew well.
- Relax after meals.

Well-Balanced Meals

They consist of a variety of foods which supply enough, but not too much, energy-containing nutrients (carbohydrates, proteins, and fats). It is the balance between these nutrients that is very important for our health. They also contain necessary vitamins and minerals.

Below is an example of the "daily dietary allowance" for a teenage boy with about 3,000 calories a day.

Quantities of Food Providing the Same Amount of Energy

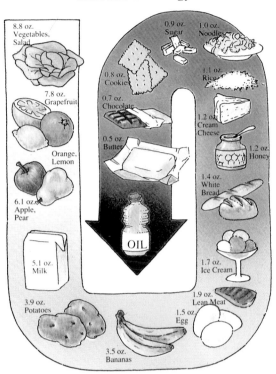

Example of Well-Balanced Meal

Breakfast	Lunch	Dinner
1 cup of whole milk 1 ounce of wheat flakes ½ cup of orange juice 2 slices of toast 1 tablespoon of jelly 1 teaspoon of butter or margarine	Tunafish salad: 3 ounces of tunafish, 1 hard-boiled egg, 1 small stalk of celery, 1 teaspoon of lemon juice, 2 tablespoons of salad dressing, 1 large leaf of lettuce, 2 slices of whole wheat bread 1 teaspoon of butter or margarine 1 large bunch of grapes 1 cup of whole milk	3 ounces of beef pot roast ¼ cup of gravy ⅔ cup of mashed potatoes ½ cup of buttered green peas 2 small enriched rolls 1 teaspoon of butter or margarine fruit cup: ½ orange, ½ apple, ½ banana 2 cookies

Blood—Stream of Life

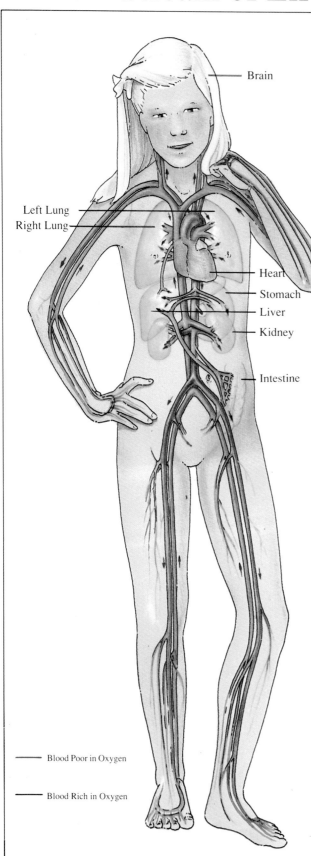

Brain

Left Lung
Right Lung

Heart

Stomach

Liver

Kidney

Intestine

—— Blood Poor in Oxygen

—— Blood Rich in Oxygen

5 Liters (5¼ gallons) of a Most Important Liquid

Blood circulates in all parts of the body.

It supplies the necessary energy (oxygen, digested food) for the functioning of the various parts of the body and removes waste products from them, in particular carbon dioxide, which is carried by the blood to the lungs, where it is exhaled.

Blood consists chiefly of:

- *red blood cells*, which are very numerous and provide the color
- *white blood cells*
- a light-colored liquid medium called *plasma*.

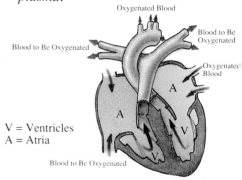

Oxygenated Blood

Blood to Be Oxygenated

Blood to Be Oxygenated

Oxygenated Blood

Oxygenated Blood

A

A

V

V

V = Ventricles
A = Atria

Blood to Be Oxygenated

Blood rich in oxygen is bright red whereas blood containing carbon dioxide is dark red.

A Muscle That Never Sleeps

The heart is a very strong muscle located slightly to the left in the chest cavity. Like a pump, it draws up blood and forces it back, providing a continuous circulation.

The heart consists of two similar parts that are well separated but function together. One receives the blood rich in oxygen, the other receives blood carrying carbon dioxide.

At rest, the heart beats about *70 times per minute*; that is over *100,000 times per day*.

At every heartbeat, blood rich in oxygen leaves the heart going to all our organs; blood carrying carbon dioxide flows toward the lungs to be reoxygenated. Physical effort, high tempera-

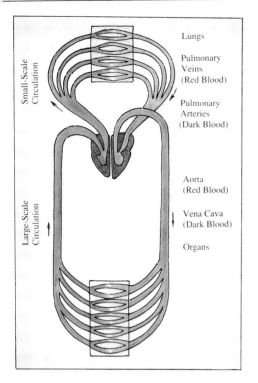

Small-Scale Circulation

Large-Scale Circulation

Lungs

Pulmonary Veins (Red Blood)

Pulmonary Arteries (Dark Blood)

Aorta (Red Blood)

Vena Cava (Dark Blood)

Organs

100,000 miles of Blood Vessels

Blood circulates in a great number of vessels:
- *arteries* carry blood from the heart to the organs
- *veins* return it to the heart
- *capillaries*, as thin as hair, connect arteries to veins. They are the most numerous.

What Is a "Hemorrhage"?

A hemorrhage is a great loss of blood which may be fatal.

When Is a Blood Transfusion Needed?

A blood transfusion is needed after a hemorrhage that is due to an accident during work or on the road, or during long surgery. The lost blood is replaced by that of a donor.

Do We All Have the Same Blood?

Not exactly. There are several blood types. A transfusion can only be made with identical blood. Blood tests are therefore necessary to determine the blood type needed. If the blood types do not match, the patient could suffer a serious reaction.

ture, or fear accelerate heartbeats. They may reach 100 to 180 beats per minute.

Heart disease is one of the leading causes of death throughout the world. Diet, lack of physical exercise, and heredity are all factors leading to heart disease.

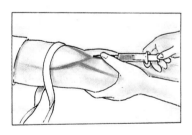

Blood Donor

Between the ages of 18 and 60, people are able to donate blood. This can help to save lives.

Donating blood is not painful and the small quantity of blood taken is rapidly replaced by the body.

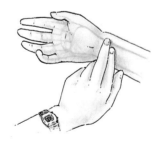

Taking the Pulse

In order to count the number of heartbeats per minute, place two fingers—the index and the middle finger—on the inside of the wrist. This is the site of an artery.

Blood Types

There are four major blood types: **A**, **B**, **AB**, and **O**. They are inherited and transmitted.

What is in 1 mm³ (0.000064 in.³) of blood?

- 5,000,000 red blood cells
- 7,000 white blood cells
- 250,000 platelets (which are the first to stop bleeding).

How long does it take our 5¼ quarts of blood to flow through the entire body?

A little less than a minute!

What is the average heartbeat of animals?

Below are the numbers of heartbeats per minute of four mammals and one bird:

Elephant 18
Dog 100
Cat 180
Mouse 240
Pigeon 300

Seeing

How Do We See?

The image is formed on the retina and is inverted.

The optic nerve sends the message to the brain. At the rear of the eye are visual cells. When we look at an object, these cells transmit the message to the brain. The brain understands the message and gives the meaning of it.

The Eyesight of an Eagle!

Birds have a visual acuity that is much better than ours because their eyes have a larger number of visual cells. With the eyes of an eagle, we could read newspaper headlines from a distance of a quarter of a mile!

The position of the eyes determines the *field of vision*, which is actually 180 degrees.

Barn Owl

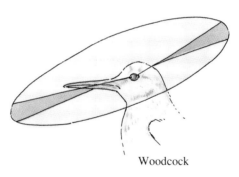

Woodcock

This field can be very much *smaller* or *greater*.

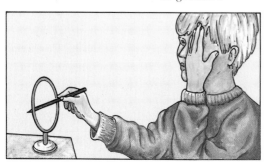

Why Do We Need Two Eyes?

With one eye closed, try to put the pencil through the ring. It is not easy. Now try it with both eyes open.

The binocular vision (with two eyes) makes it possible to estimate distances and to see objects in three dimensions.

To See and to Remember

Every day, our brain records thousands of images. Only a few are selected and stored in our memory (the features of a friend, details of a landscape, or of an object).

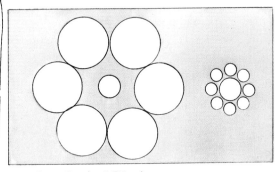

O X P
E X R C

To Have Good Vision

This is a test for sharpness of sight. Place your book at a distance of 20 feet and try to read these letters by closing the right eye and then the left eye.

Visual acuity is measured in twenties—20/20 corresponds to perfect vision.

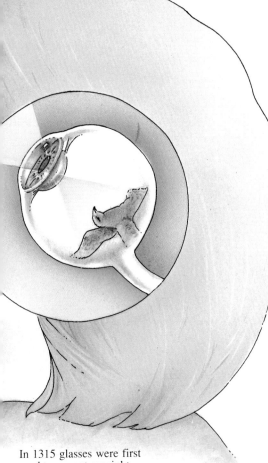

In 1315 glasses were first used to correct eyesight.

Another Optical Illusion

Which one of the two circles located in the middle of the two figures is larger?

Answer: The two circles are equal.

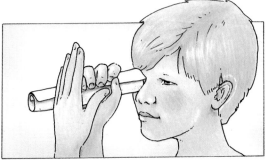

Our Eyes Are Deceiving Us!

The binocular vision in this example gives us the illusion that the hand is pierced by a hole.

A White Rabbit Comes Out of the Hat!

Stare at the eye of the small black rabbit for about one minute. Then look just above the hat. After a few seconds, you will see the white rabbit appear.

Tasting, Smelling, and Hearing

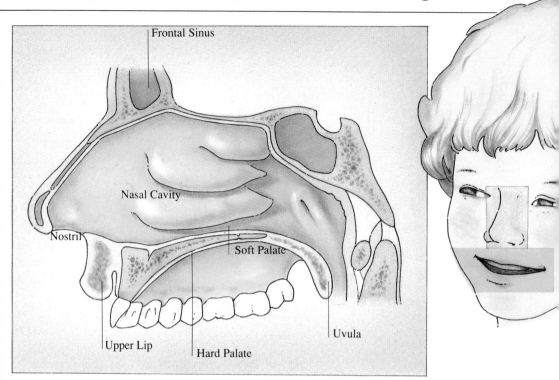

Frontal Sinus

Nasal Cavity

Nostril

Soft Palate

Upper Lip

Hard Palate

Uvula

Sense of Smell

The olfactory system or *sense of smell* is located in the upper part of the nasal cavity. Odorous gases are carried by the air we breathe. Their message is transmitted to the brain by the *olfactory nerve*.

The sense of smell is very acute. It does not play a major role in humans but is highly developed in animals, and humans can make use of theirs. (For example, dogs are often used for detecting explosives or finding persons buried in avalanches.)

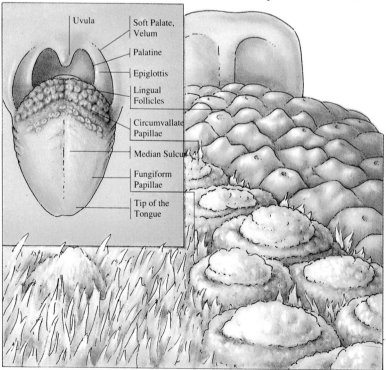

Uvula

Soft Palate, Velum

Palatine

Epiglottis

Lingual Follicles

Circumvallate Papillae

Median Sulcus

Fungiform Papillae

Tip of the Tongue

Sense of Taste

Our tongue is full of *taste buds*, which are organs of taste. Stimulated by food, they transmit four sensations to the brain—salty, sweet, sour, and bitter. All other *gustatory* senses (the "taste" of food) are olfactory, that is, perceived by the nose.

Hearing

The ear is a receptor organ that responds to vibrations of the air—sound waves. These sounds, transformed into nerve impulses, follow the auditory nerve and reach the brain, which interprets them.

The ear is divided into three parts:

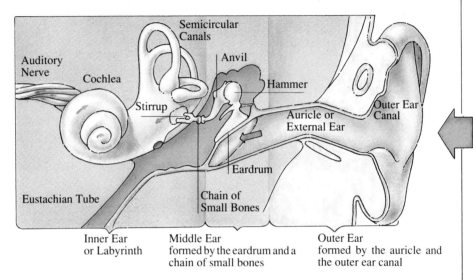

Inner Ear or Labyrinth	Middle Ear formed by the eardrum and a chain of small bones	Outer Ear formed by the auricle and the outer ear canal

A Center of Equilibrium

The semicircular canals of the inner ear give the sense of balance. They tell the brain the position of the head and how it is moving.

Function of the Ear

Sound vibrations, caught by the outer ear, travel down the auditory canal, strike the eardrum and make it vibrate.

The *hammer, anvil, stirrup* start to vibrate and transmit vibrations to the cochlea of the inner ear, where they reach the cilia. These cells produce a message that is sent to the brain by the auditory nerve.

To emit a sound is to emit vibrations. When we talk, air expelled from the lungs passes by the vocal cords, which start to vibrate and produce sounds. The number of vibrations per second (*hertz*) is the frequency of the sound.

The human ear is tuned to frequencies between 16 and 18,000 hertz and hears the sound of a harp or a saxophone as well as the song of a bird. However, the sounds emitted by bats or dolphins are generally not heard by humans because their frequencies are too high.

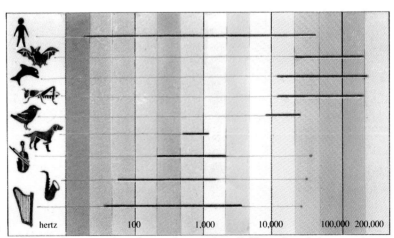

What Do Animals Perceive?

Although animal sense organs are different from ours, they also see, hear, and smell. Very often, their perception of the world is dictated by one especially well-developed sense.

For instance, the *falcon*, whose eyesight is ten times more powerful than ours, can spot his prey from great distances.

The *dolphin* has an extraordinary hearing capacity.

The *fox* has excellent eyesight and a highly developed sense of smell.

The Sense of Touch

A Very Thin but Resistant Covering

Our skin covers and protects our entire body.

The thickness (0.04 to 0.16 in.) of our skin varies according to its location on the body. It is thicker on the palms and soles and thinner on our eyelids and lips.

Skin is very elastic and allows movement. It provides a protective barrier against physical injuries, humidity, cold, and heat.

Skin wears down with repeated rubbing; however, it is constantly being renewed.

The skin surface of an average human being is between 15 and 20 ft.[2]

Hair Shaft (much enlarged)

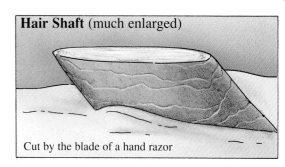

Cut by the blade of a hand razor

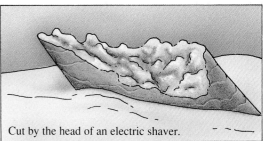

Cut by the head of an electric shaver.

Structure of Human Skin

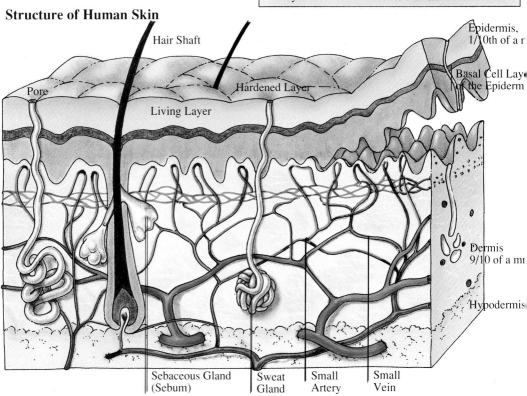

Hair Shaft

Pore

Hardened Layer

Living Layer

Epidermis, 1/10th of a r

Basal Cell Lay of the Epiderm

Dermis 9/10 of a m

Hypodermis

Sebaceous Gland (Sebum) | Sweat Gland | Small Artery | Small Vein

The Organ of Touch

The skin gives us five kinds of sensation: pressure, heat, cold, pain, and touch.
The skin consists of two distinct layers:

- an upper layer called the epidermis
- a lower layer with 5 kinds of nerve terminals through which we perceive the various sensations: the dermis.

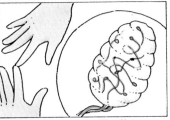
Meissner Corpuscle (Tactile)

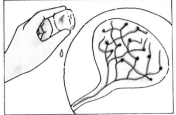
Krause's Corpuscle (Cold)

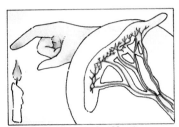
Ruffini's Corpuscle (Heat)

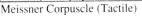
Pacinian Corpuscle (Pressure)

Pain

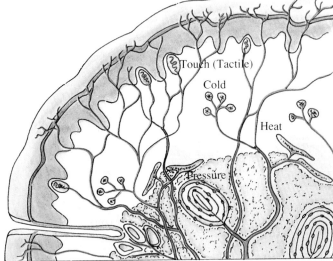
Epidermis and dermis. Various receptor organs of sensations can be observed.

The Sensitive Areas

The nerve terminals transmit sensations to the brain by way of the *spinal cord*.

These terminals are different according to what they transmit (cold, heat, pain) and they are randomly distributed in the skin. Therefore, certain skin zones are more or less sensitive to cold or to pain.

There are *600,000 receptors* which perceive sensation caused by contact of an object with the skin. These receptors are more numerous at the fingertips or on our lips.

There are *200,000 receptors* which perceive sensations of heat and cold.

Over *one million and a half* receptors perceive sensations of pain!

Some parts of the body have no receptors. This is why physicians who practice acupuncture claim to be able to treat certain problems with the help of small needles which they stick into the skin of their patients. The patients do not feel any pain.

What are skin pores?

These are small openings through which wastes are continuously eliminated from our body.

On the average, every day we eliminate one liter (1.057 quarts) of sweat through our skin.

1 cm² of skin has thousands of pores.

Hair and nails are produced by the epidermis.

The skin is a thermostat

Evaporation of sweat allows the skin to act as a thermostat.

Evaporation helps to maintain a constant temperature of the body when the body is heated by a hot outside temperature or by physical exertion.

The Body in Motion

A Precise and Solid Framework

The *skeleton* is formed by *206 bones*. It gives strength and shape to the body.

The bones provide protection (the bones of the skull, the rib cage) and support (the spine).

They are formed by living matter nourished by the blood. Long bones, such as those of the thigh, contain bone *marrow* in which red and white blood cells are formed .

Articulated Joints to Let the Body Move

A *joint* is a place where two bones come together. If the bones can move with respect to one another, the joint is said to be *articulated*. At an articulated joint, the bones are held together by tough cords, called *ligaments*. A pad of *cartilage* between the bones absorbs shocks.

For instance, a hand is particularly flexible because of *26 very small bones* which have articulated joints between them.

Some body parts have no joints. The skull, for example, is formed by eight flat *fused* bones.

The Motors of Movement

There are over *500 muscles* which provide movement to the skeleton.

Muscles are attached to the bones by *tendons*. When a muscle contracts, its tendon pulls on the bone and makes it move.

There are *smooth muscles*, found in the digestive tract, reproductive organs, bladder, arteries, and veins.

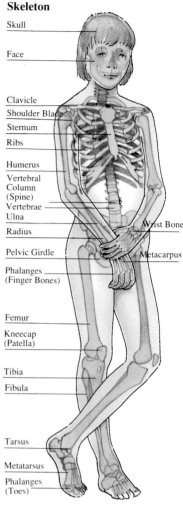

Skeleton

Skull
Face
Clavicle
Shoulder Blade
Sternum
Ribs
Humerus
Vertebral Column (Spine)
Vertebrae
Ulna
Radius
Wrist Bone
Pelvic Girdle
Metacarpus
Phalanges (Finger Bones)
Femur
Kneecap (Patella)
Tibia
Fibula
Tarsus
Metatarsus
Phalanges (Toes)

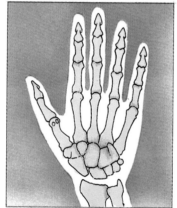

The 26 Articulated Bones of the Hand

There are also *striated muscles*, located in the legs, arms, back, and torso.

Most muscles are controlled by the *brain*. These are the *voluntary* muscles (those of the hand, the arms, the legs).

Other muscles such as the heart, the muscles of the stomach and the thorax work without our intervention.

These are *involuntary* muscles, which are not connected to bones.

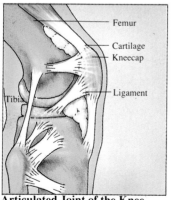

Femur
Cartilage
Kneecap
Ligament
Tibia

Articulated Joint of the Knee

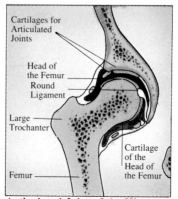

Cartilages for Articulated Joints
Head of the Femur
Round Ligament
Large Trochanter
Cartilage of the Head of the Femur
Femur

Articulated Joint of the Hip (section)

228

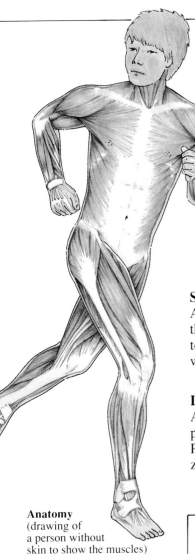

Anatomy
(drawing of
a person without
skin to show the muscles)

Impaired Functioning of Muscles

Violent shocks (bicycle or ski accident) or sudden efforts sometimes cause bone and muscle injuries which may require temporary immobilization.

Fracture

When a bone is broken it is immobilized in a plaster cast while the bony material heals the fracture together.

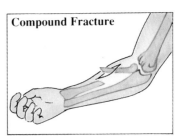

Compound Fracture

Sprain

A sprain occurs frequently at the ankle. It is a stretching or tearing of the ligaments which hold the bone in place.

Laceration

A laceration, or tear, happens to the entire muscle. Pain is severe and immobilization lasts a long time.

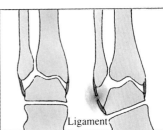

Ligament

Articulated Joint in Place

Sprain
A stretched ligament which may break

Muscle Pull

Sometimes, because of too great an effort, part of a muscle can be torn.

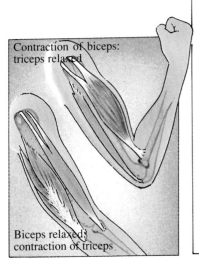

Contraction of biceps: triceps relaxed

Biceps relaxed; contraction of triceps

Which is our smallest bone?

The smallest bone is called the *stirrup.*
It is located in the middle ear and measures between 0.1 and 0.15 in. It weighs between 2 and 4.3 mg.

How many bones are in our face?

There are *14 bones* of which only one is mobile—the lower jaw.

Rickets

Calcium and phosphorus play an important role in the making of bones in children. Vitamin D is necessary to provide calcium. A lack of this vitamin leads to impairment of growth—rickets.

Did you know?

A bone soaked in hydrochloric acid for 24 hours loses two-thirds of its weight and becomes soft.

Are there several kinds of muscles?

Not all muscles are alike. Some are long, short, thin, flat, or in the form of rings.
Actions of muscles can involve *flexion* or *extension.* These muscles are called antagonists because they act in opposite ways.
Extension muscles are most developed in athletes who leap and run.

How many muscles work when walking?

About *one hundred* different muscles are used simply for walking .

What is lactic acid?

When working, a muscle produces a waste product, *lactic acid,* which is eliminated by oxygen during breathing.

The Nervous System

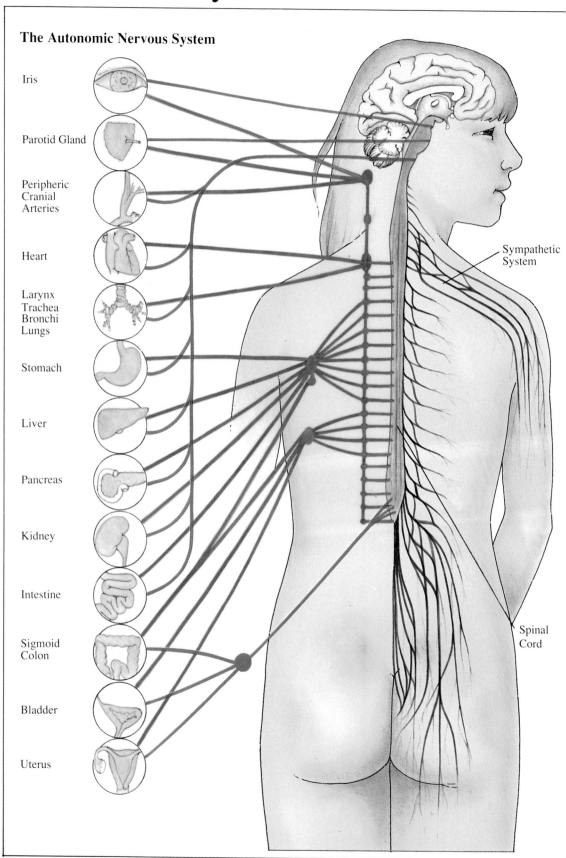

The Autonomic Nervous System

Iris

Parotid Gland

Peripheric Cranial Arteries

Heart

Larynx Trachea Bronchi Lungs

Stomach

Liver

Pancreas

Kidney

Intestine

Sigmoid Colon

Bladder

Uterus

Sympathetic System

Spinal Cord

A Well-Organized and Well-Protected System

The major part of the nervous system, the *cerebrum* or brain, is protected by the skull.

The brain consists of the *cerebrum*, the *cerebellum*, and the *medulla*.

The brain itself is connected to the long *spinal cord*.

The spinal cord is protected by the *spine*.

The brain and spinal cord make up the central nervous system.

Among all the organs, the brain has the greatest complexity and not all the functions of its parts are understood.

The brain weighs about 1/50th of the weight of the human body—about 3 pounds for an adult.

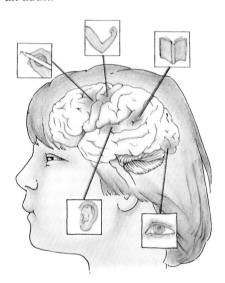

The Control Center

All the nerves of the body are connected to the central nervous system. This is the control center for all sensations, motions and more complex and poorly known phenomena, such as intelligence, feelings, will, and emotions.

Precise Functioning

Sensations are transmitted by nerve cells to one part of the brain where they are interpreted. Orders can then be sent to the muscles by means of *motor* neurons.

This exchange of "reception-emission"

A Communication Network

There are 43 pairs of nerves, 12 of which leave from the brain, and 31 from the spinal cord. These have many branches, which connect the central nervous system with every part of the body.

Two kinds of nerves exist:
- those which transmit information of sensations, the *sensory nerves* (optic nerve, auditory nerve, olfactory nerve)
- those which transmit orders, the *motor nerves* (oculomotor nerve).

Most nerves contain motor and sensory neurons. They are called *mixed nerves*.

The Brain

The brain is a soft organ located in the bony cage of the skull.

It is divided into many parts and every part has a specific function—a center for speech, for writing, etc.

Strangely enough, the right hemisphere of the brain gives orders to the left side of the body and the left hemisphere to the right side.

Among the most important parts of the brain are the cerebrum, the cerebellum, and the medulla.

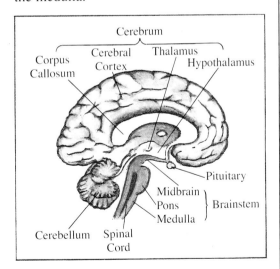

takes place in the thin layer of *gray matter* at the surface of the brain. According to its location, the thickness varies between 1.3 mm to 4.5 mm.

If a nerve section is cut, the corresponding sensation is eliminated.

The Stresses of the Nervous System

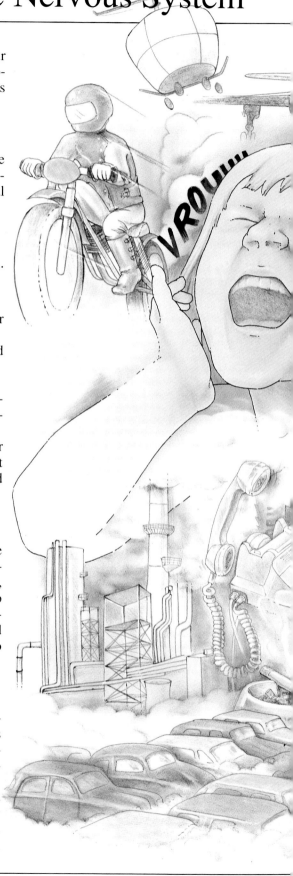

The quality of the environment acts upon our nervous system. Excitement and commotions which are too intense tire our nervous system and create stress.

Noise

To much noise may lead to nervous fatigue with loss of appetite and equilibrium problems. It can sometimes impair our intellectual capacities.

Bright Light

It is also a stimulant for the nervous system.

Alcohol

Even in small amounts, alcohol acts upon our nervous system.

It decreases the speed of our reflexes and causes us to be uncoordinated.

It causes partial loss of memory.

With a large alcohol intake, cells are destroyed and our character can change (laziness, sadness, aggression, violence).

In the United States, alcoholism is by far the most common kind of drug addiction. It causes many deaths from liver damage and automobile accidents.

Tobacco

Abuse of tobacco, smoking, also acts on the nervous system. Nicotine, a very toxic substance in tobacco (1 milligram per cigarette), is highly addictive. It leads progressively to loss of memory, very slow reflexes, an increase in uncoordinated movements, and circulatory disease. Other parts of tobacco smoke produce lung cancer.

Other Drugs

Certain substances (heroin, morphine, cocaine) act directly upon the consciousness and modify behavior, progressively impairing health. Very rapidly, a drug addict becomes entirely dependent upon the drug used. Increase in drug consumption and serious related consequences in our modern society justify the war on drugs. Drug addicts are very sick people who must be helped and

treated; they are a danger to themselves and to all society.

In the United States, many of the crimes committed every day are directly associated with the use of drugs.

Drug abuse treatment centers are available in all areas of the country, but the war on drugs has yet to be won.

Sleep

It is absolutely necessary for the benefit of the nervous system and hence the body's health.

The need for sleep varies according to age. Up to 3 months, a baby sleeps between 22 and 23 hours a day. At 15, a teenager sleeps about 10 hours.

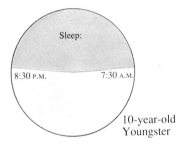

Sleep:
8:30 P.M.   7:30 A.M.

10-year-old Youngster

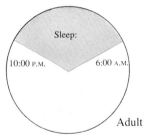

Sleep:
10:00 P.M.   6:00 A.M.

Adult

Need for Sleep from Infancy to Adulthood

Did you know?

In the entire world, 120 million people suffer from serious mental diseases.

There are many types of mental illnesses: schizophrenia, affective, anxiety, and personality disorders.

People with mental illness can be helped by many different therapies.

Viruses and Microbes

What Are Microbes?

Microbes are microscopic living things found everywhere. They live in the air, in the ground, in water, in human and animal bodies, and in plants.

They are not visible with the naked eye.

Their existence was discovered in the 17th century, thanks to the invention of the microscope.

Microbes multiply rapidly. For instance, in a small quantity of fresh milk they increase in a few hours from some thousands to several millions! (The milk curdles.)

1665
Single-Objective Model

Microscope

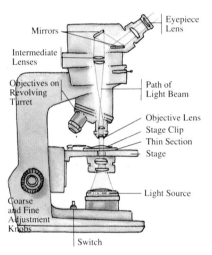

Eyepiece Lens
Mirrors
Intermediate Lenses
Objectives on Revolving Turret
Path of Light Beam
Objective Lens
Stage Clip
Thin Section
Stage
Light Source
Coarse and Fine Adjustment Knobs
Switch

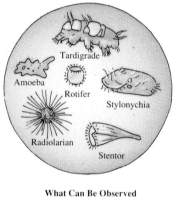

Tardigrade
Amoeba
Rotifer
Stylonychia
Radiolarian
Stentor

What Can Be Observed in a Drop of Water

Some microbes called *viruses* are so small that they cannot be observed with the regular microscope. Their size is of the order of *millimicrons*, that is, a *millionth of a millimeter*! We can see them only with the electron microscope.

Measles Virus

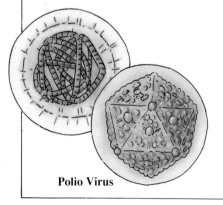

Polio Virus

Electron Microscope

Friends or Enemies?

Microbes are known for causing diseases. Indeed, more than *1,000 infectious diseases* are caused by viruses in humans, animals, and plants.

The common cold, measles, chicken pox, and polio are viral diseases.

Nevertheless, many microbes are useful for humans.

Molds + Bacteria for Dairy Products

Yeast for Bread and Alcohol

Microbes get rid of waste products such as dead leaves, excrement, stagnant water, and refuse of all kinds.

Some microbes are used for *fermentation* (the making of cheese, vinegar, and yeasts).

They also play an important role in the transformation of foods during digestion.

Natural Defense System

The skin provides an efficient barrier against microbes. If this barrier is broken (a wound, for example) there is risk of infection. When microbes enter the body, *white blood cells* try to destroy them. This battle often results in fever.

If the infection continues or becomes more serious, microbes are the victors over white blood cells. Then the organism needs help to defend itself.

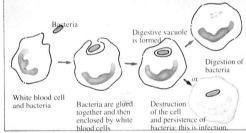

Bacteria

Digestive vacuole is formed

Digestion of bacteria

White blood cell and bacteria

Bacteria are glued together and then enclosed by white blood cells

Destruction of the cell and persistence of bacteria: this is infection.

Artificial Defense

Very hot or cold temperatures kill most of the microbes (water is boiled to render it safe for drinking and food is preserved in a freezer). Certain *medications* help the body to fight against microbial invasion and to stop it. *Antibiotics* such as *penicillin* are very efficient.

What is in a vaccine?

A vaccine contains a very weak dose of the disease against which the body needs protection.

The body responds by making defenses that protect it against a more powerful invasion of the disease.

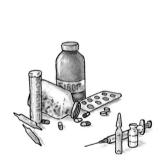

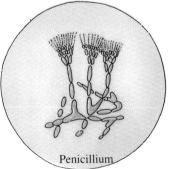

Penicillium

How Does Vaccination Help?

A vaccine is not a medication. It is a means of helping the body to mobilize its defense weapons against serious diseases.

With vaccination, some diseases (diphtheria, whooping cough, and tuberculosis) have almost completely disappeared.

Why is Pasteur famous?

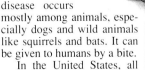

He discovered that microbes cause disease. He also discovered the vaccine against rabies, a viral disease which attacks the brain. The disease occurs mostly among animals, especially dogs and wild animals like squirrels and bats. It can be given to humans by a bite.

In the United States, all dogs and cats must be vaccinated against rabies.

Vertebrates I

Classification

There are many animal species. To distinguish between them, they were first divided into two large groups—*vertebrates* (those with a vertebral, or spinal, column) and *invertebrates* (those without a vertebral column).

These two groups have been subdivided into smaller groups and classified according to their dominant characteristics. These are the groups of vertebrates:

Mammals

Reproduction
They are viviparous. Eggs develop inside the female uterus. They nourish their young with milk.

Protection of the Body
The skin is generally covered with hair.

Environment
They live on the ground and sometimes in water. Some fly.

Respiration
They breathe with lungs. Even those living in water breathe air.

Birds

Reproduction
They lay eggs and incubate them. These eggs, protected by a shell, contain a food supply.

Protection of the Body
The body is covered with feathers.

Environment
They live on land and in the air.

Respiration
They breathe with lungs.

Other Characteristics
They have a beak, two legs covered with scales, two wings.

Reptiles

Reproduction
They lay eggs on the ground but do not incubate them. These eggs are protected by a shell containing food supplies.

Protection of the Body
The body is covered with welded protective scales.

Environment
They live on the ground and/or in water.

Respiration
They breathe with lungs.

Other Characteristics
Some have four legs,

Amphibians

Reproduction
They lay eggs without shells, usually in water. Tadpoles undergo metamorphosis.

Protection of the body
The skin is naked and always wet.

Environment
They live on land and in water.

Respiration
Tadpoles breathe in water with gills. Adults breathe with lungs.

Other Characteristics
They have four legs.

Fish

Reproduction
They lay eggs without shells in water. These eggs are often abandoned.

Protection of the Body
The body is generally covered with scales which can be removed one by one.

Environment
They live in water.

Respiration
They breathe with gills, taking dissolved oxygen out of the water.

Other Characteristics
They have fins.

Vertebrates II

Mammals

Camels

Elephant

Kangaroo

Rhinoceros

Lion

Bat

Zebra

Gorilla

Cow

Sheep

Horse

Dog

Hare

Seal and Baby Seal

Bear

Dolphin

Whale

Swallows

Birds

Pelicans

Vultures

Ostrich

Owl

Goose

Rooster

Turkey

Pheasants

Amphibians

Swan

Newt

Frog

Fish

Pike

Carp

Tuna

Trout

Perch

Shark

Eel

Invertebrates

Numerous animal species belong to this group. They are subdivided into smaller groups and classified according to their characteristics.

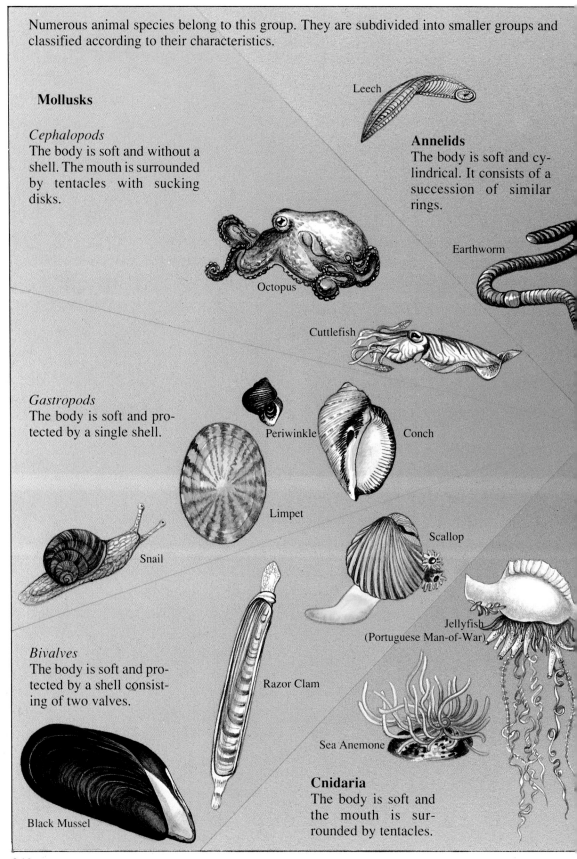

Mollusks

Cephalopods
The body is soft and without a shell. The mouth is surrounded by tentacles with sucking disks.

Octopus

Gastropods
The body is soft and protected by a single shell.

Periwinkle

Conch

Limpet

Snail

Bivalves
The body is soft and protected by a shell consisting of two valves.

Razor Clam

Black Mussel

Leech

Annelids
The body is soft and cylindrical. It consists of a succession of similar rings.

Earthworm

Cuttlefish

Scallop

Jellyfish
(Portuguese Man-of-War)

Sea Anemone

Cnidaria
The body is soft and the mouth is surrounded by tentacles.

Echinoderms
The body is rough and often covered with spines.

Sea Urchin

Insects
They have two antennas, three pairs of articulated legs and two or four wings.

Fly

Brittle Star

Starfish

Pupa

Caterpillar

Swallowtail Butterfly

The class of the insects represents by itself two-thirds of all animal species. More than a million species of insects are known today. The eyesight of insects is highly developed. Some have eyes consisting of many separate parts (sometimes up to 30,000) which allow them to see simultaneously in all directions.

What is "metamorphosis"? From birth to death, many insects, such as butterflies, live in four different forms—egg, caterpillar, pupa, and full-grown insect. The egg is the first life stage of all insects. A large caterpillar (or larva) develops from the egg. When sufficiently fed, the caterpillar changes into a pupa. This metamorphosis occurs in open air or inside a silk cocoon. After some time, the pupa changes into a butterfly.

Spider

Scorpion

Arachnids
They have four pairs of legs. About 40,000 species are known.

Crayfish

Millipede

Crab

Lobster

Myriapods
They have many pairs of legs.

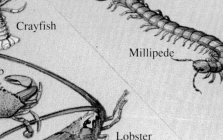

The body of the above types is generally protected by a hard shell. The largest group in the animal kingdom is the Anthropods (insects, arachnids, myriapods, and crustaceans).

Crustaceans
The body is covered by a carapace (shell). They often have five pairs of legs and two pairs of antennas.

Animals in Their Environment

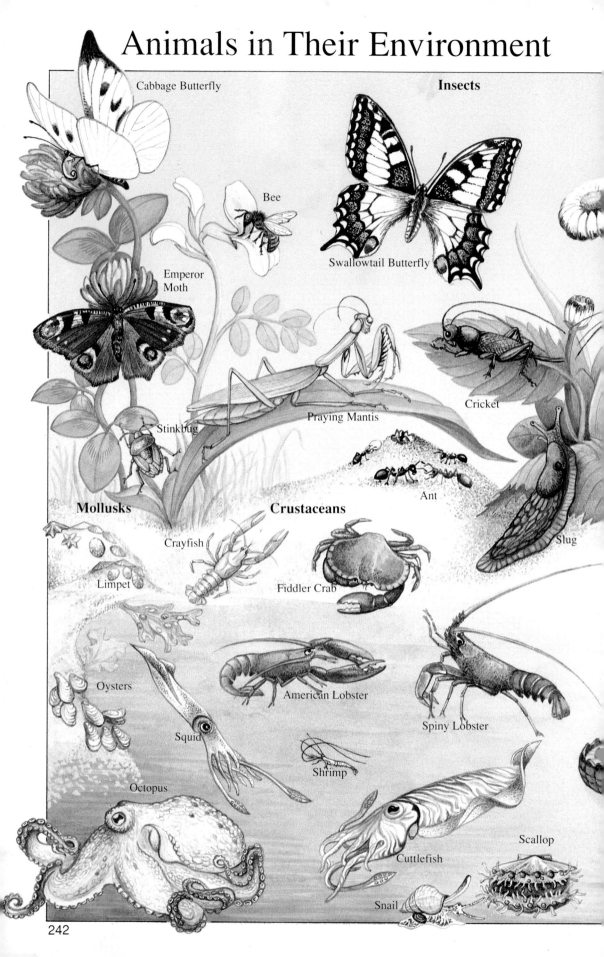

Cabbage Butterfly

Insects

Bee

Swallowtail Butterfly

Emperor
Moth

Cricket

Praying Mantis

Stinkbug

Ant

Slug

Mollusks

Crustaceans

Crayfish

Fiddler Crab

Limpet

Oysters

American Lobster

Spiny Lobster

Squid

Shrimp

Octopus

Cuttlefish

Scallop

Snail

Dragonfly

Fly

Sphinx Moth

Mayfly

Mosquito

Chameleon

Cicada

Maybug

Reptiles

Boa

Python

Cobra

Viper

Crocodile

Iguana

Turtle

The Food Chain

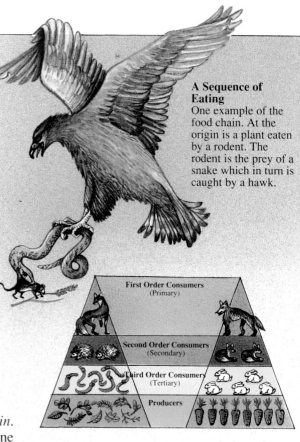

Predators and Prey
In the animal and plant kingdoms there are many series of organisms interrelated in their feeding habits called food chains. Every prey has several predators (those who eat the prey), and every predator in turn has several prey.

A Sequence of Eating
One example of the food chain. At the origin is a plant eaten by a rodent. The rodent is the prey of a snake which in turn is caught by a hawk.

First Order Consumers
(Primary)

Second Order Consumers
(Secondary)

Third Order Consumers
(Tertiary)

Producers

Like the Links of a Chain
This diagram shows a simple *food chain*. Every species is food for the following one and is part of the food chain. There is a transfer of food from one link to the other. *Decomposers* (insects, worms, microbes) transform organic matter (plants and dead animals) into minerals used by green plants, which are at the origin of the food chain.

Some Examples of a Food Chain
The number of links can vary from one chain to the other. The *pyramidal* shape shows that at any level there are more food organisms than eaters. This is the required condition for equilibrium.

What Eats What?
A simplified food chain (river). The arrow goes from the prey to the predator.

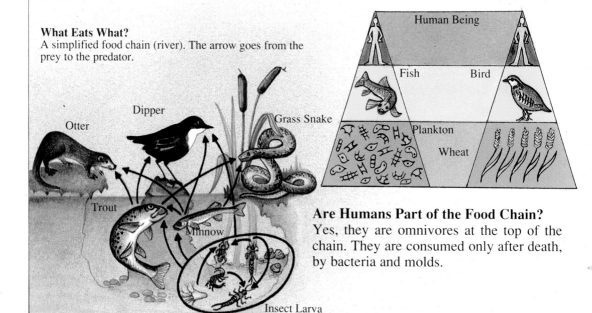

Otter

Dipper

Grass Snake

Trout

Minnow

Insect Larva

Human Being

Fish

Bird

Plankton

Wheat

Are Humans Part of the Food Chain?
Yes, they are omnivores at the top of the chain. They are consumed only after death, by bacteria and molds.

Broken Equilibria

Disorders in a food chain may rapidly lead to the *disappearance* of certain species and, at the same time, cause *proliferation* (increase) in certain other species.

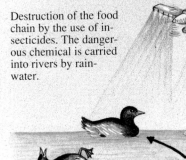

Destruction of the food chain by the use of insecticides. The dangerous chemical is carried into rivers by rainwater.

Humans are sometimes responsible for these imbalances. The killing of many birds of prey has caused proliferation among various rodents.

Killing wolves led to the proliferation of so many deer that much vegetation was destroyed and the deer starved.

Introduction of the Missing Link

To avoid the proliferation of certain species, humans have introduced, sometimes on purpose, certain predators or diseases (the missing link in the chain).

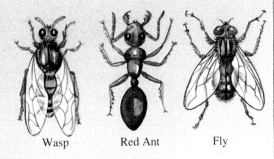

Wasp   Red Ant   Fly

Predators of the "pine caterpillar" introduced by humans.

For example, to exterminate "pine caterpillars," insects that destroyed European forests, humans introduced particular predators in these forests—flies, red ants, and wasps, which eat either eggs, or caterpillars, or harmful butterflies. Care had to be used here to control reproduction of these predators so that they developed less rapidly and less abundantly than their prey.

Three Examples of Devastating Proliferations

1) The setting free of a few rabbits in Australia ended in disaster. Rabbits, who reproduce rapidly, soon became wild and, in about ten years, numbered several hundred million, causing great damage to agriculture.

With an artificially induced contagious disease, *myxomatosis*, the population of wild rabbits was eventually controlled in Australia. However, the disease itself spread over all the continents and attacked domestic rabbits.

2) The mongoose was introduced into some Caribbean islands to control the rats in sugar cane fields. The mongeese became pests because they became too numerous and, also, because they eat chickens.

3) A pair of muskrats was imported from America to destroy large vegetations in swamps in Central Europe. The muskrats proliferated and invaded areas in Germany, Belgium, the Netherlands and France.

Muskrats are animals who dig underground tunnels at the foot of dams causing great damage. They also inhibit the normal development of other species.

Variations in the Plant Kingdom

Animal life is possible only because green plants and algae make food. Plants and algae are the first link in every food chain.

Algae and Fungi

These organisms are stationary, like plants, but they are without roots, without stems, without leaves, and without a vascular system:

Lichens are a combination of algae and fungi. They live and develop in very harsh environments, such as high elevation, deserts, or rocks.

Without Chloro-phyll—Mushrooms and Other Fungi

With Chlorophyll—Algae

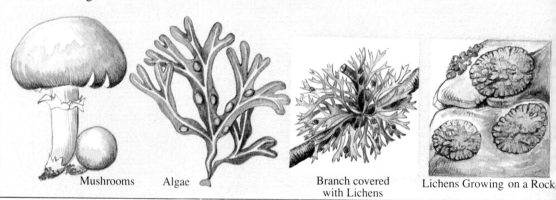

Mushrooms   Algae

Branch covered with Lichens

Lichens Growing on a Rock

Plants That Form Seeds

These plants consist of stems, leaves, roots, a vascular system, and seeds. They are:

Gymnosperms—
The seeds of these plants are exposed. They are not enclosed in an ovary, but are borne in cones (pine, fir, spruce).

Angiosperms—
The seeds of these plants are enclosed in an ovary, which becomes a fruit (pea, bean, buttercup, cherry tree).

Spruce

Scale with Its Two Seeds

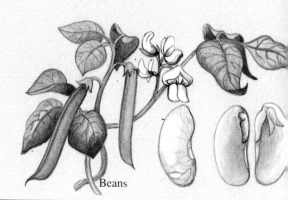

Beans

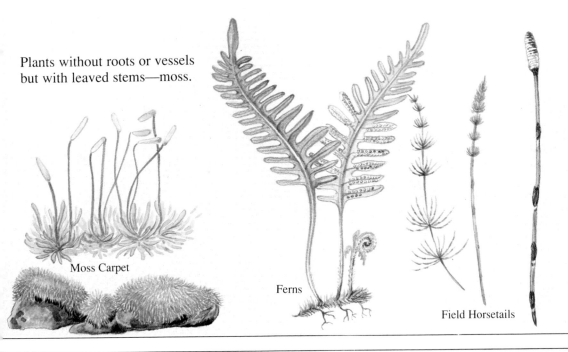

Plants with roots, stems, leaves, and vessels—ferns, horsetails.

Plants without roots or vessels but with leaved stems—moss.

Moss Carpet

Ferns

Field Horsetails

Angisperms are classified into:

Monocots—
• The leaves often have parallel veins.
• The seed has a single cotyledon (wheat, rice, lily of the valley, palm tree, white lily).

Dicots—
• Leaves have branching veins.
• Flowers have either free petals (poppy), welded petals (sage) or no petals (oak, beech).

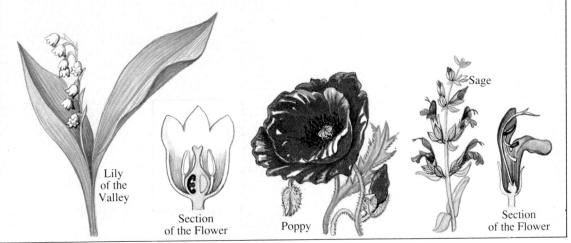

Lily of the Valley

Section of the Flower

Poppy

Sage

Section of the Flower

Discovering the Forest

Some History
The extent of forests has changed through the centuries. Originally, more than half of the United States was covered by forests. However, over the years, many of these forests were cleared for farms, towns, and cities. Today, about one-third of the land is covered by forests, which supply lumber for buildings, pulp for paper, and fibers for products such as rayon. Forests industries are an important part of the American economy.

The tall trees that grow in the Pacific Northwest region are the source of a large part of our nation's forest products. Mills in Oregon and Washington produce plywood, paper, and lumber.

The Different Levels of Vegetation

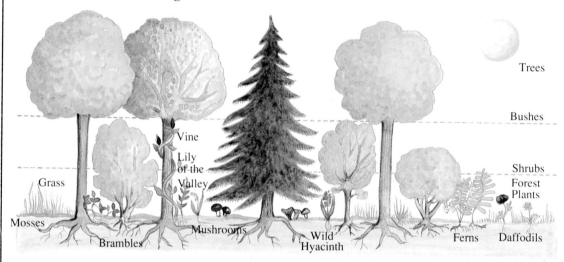

Trees
Bushes
Shrubs
Forest Plants
Vine
Lily of the Valley
Grass
Mosses
Brambles
Mushrooms
Wild Hyacinth
Ferns
Daffodils

A Well-Organized Community
In a forest, each plant occupies a certain level or height. Ferns, shrubs, bushes, and trees are well-arranged in tiers.

In a forest, trees have a different growth pattern than on an isolated patch. Generally, their trunks grow higher because their lower branches, deprived of light, dwindle and die. *Forestry techniques* promote the growth of tall, straight trees suitable for use as lumber.

Life Span of Trees
It varies according to type of tree:

Cluster Pine .... 40/80 years
Scotch Pine .... 60/100 years
Fir .... 120/150 years
Spruce .... 150/180 years
Oak .... 150/225 years

Each Climate Has Its Forest
The New England forest consists of deciduous trees (oaks, birches, beeches).

The Western mountain forests consist of evergreen conifers (pines, firs, spruces).

Tropical rain forests have hundreds of different kinds of trees, some of them deciduous in the dry season.

What Role Does a Forest Play?
It is very important for the equilibrium of the natural environment.

It protects the soil from erosion.
The tree roots hold the ground and sand and prevent soil erosion by rain and wind.

Eroded and gullied soil is no longer fertile and nothing will grow in it.

It purifies the air.
Trees renew the atmosphere through the release of oxygen and thus are necessary for human life.

It affects the climate.
Trees draw from the ground an appreciable amount of water, which they release in the atmosphere as water vapor. The latter contributes to the formation of clouds.

Soil erosion along a freeway.

It shelters a world of animals.
Mammals (rabbits, lynx, deer, birds (thrushes, warblers, horn owls), and many, many insects.

It prevents floods
Its soil holds a great deal of water.

When water overflows a river bank, it can often be absorbed.

A Wealth Worth Protecting
Forests are exploited because they provide a source of revenue. Wood is one of our major riches. It is a raw material suitable for numerous uses (building, furniture, fuel, paper pulp).

However, wood is not an inexhaustible resource. It has to be harvested carefully.

The Enemies of the Forest
Humans
They are responsible for:
• overexploitation
• non-replanting of cut trees
• lack of conservation
• forest fires

Different uses of wood.

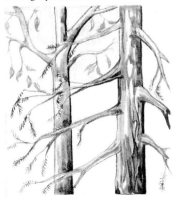
Another enemy: acid rain (water falling through polluted air).

Fire
Forest fires destroy many acres of valuable forest land.
Insects
They often cause considerable damage by chewing leaves or boring into bark. Whole forests can be destroyed by insects.

Wood damaged by insects.

The age of a tree

The age of a cut tree can be found by counting the number of rings visible on a cross section of the trunk —one ring represents one year.

Oxygen and the forest

Each day, 1000 ft^2 of forest produce between 317 and 1,057 quarts of oxygen.

Coniferous and Deciduous Trees

There are two main groups of trees—
coniferous and *deciduous*

The Major Resinous or Coniferous Trees
Their narrow leaves are actually *needles* or *scales*,
which do not shed in winter (with the exception of the
larch).
Their fruits are *cones*, hence the name conifers.
Their sap is called *resin*.

Larch

Fir Tree

Spruce

Cypress

Juniper

Cluster Pine

Scotch Pine

Stone Pine

Yew

Some Deciduous Trees
Their leaves are large or thin blades, which generally fall in winter (*deciduous leaves*). Some broad-leaved trees, like holly or live oak, are not deciduous. Leaves may be *simple* or *compound* (divided into a number of leaflets).

Oak

Horse Chestnut

Chestnut

Birch

Poplar

Elm

Beech

Ash

Plane Tree

Hornbeam

Common Plants and Fruit Trees

Strawberry

White Currant

Raspberry

Blackberry

Fig Tree

Olive Tree

Orange Tree

Lemon Tree

Quince Tree

Apple Tree

Pear Tree

Hazel Tree

Peach Tree

Grapevine

Cherry Tree

Exotic Plants and Trees

Banana Tree

Cacao Tree

Coffee Tree

Palm Trees

There are about 4,000 species. They represent major commercial and agricultural resources for tropical regions. The best known are the coconut palm and the date palm.

Giant Trees

The *eucalyptus* originates in Australia. There are many kinds, and some reach a height of 300 feet.

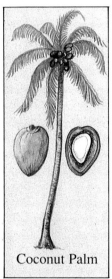

Coconut Palm

Palm Tree

Date Palm

Eucalyptus

Sequoia

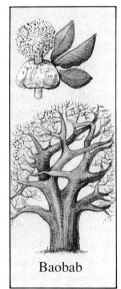

Baobab

The *sequoia* originates in North America. It is one of the largest and oldest living trees in the world (between 1,500 and 2,500 years). It may reach a height of 350 feet. It is a conifer.

The *baobab* grows in equatorial Africa. Its trunk may measure up to 150 feet in circumference.

Mushrooms

They are fungi of various shapes with the characteristics of having neither flowers, nor leaves, nor chlorophyll. Certain species are edible, while others are poisonous, and some species are deadly.

While mushrooms are a favorite type of food, collecting them requires great care. The collector must be able to recognize many species so as to avoid any potential danger by choosing poisonous ones.

Edible Mushrooms

Orange Cup Fungus

Coral Mushroom

Morel

Truffle

Meadow Mushroom

Chanterelle

Black Chanterelle

Milk Cap

Capucin Bolete

King Bolete

The Families of Mushrooms

Agaricaceae (amanita *psalliotis*)

Polyporaceae (polypora) birch polypora

Polyporaceae (of the Woods)

Hydnaceae (hydnum)

Thelephoraceae (craterellus)

Morchellaceae (morel)

Lycoperdaceae (puff ball)

Helvellaceae (helvella)

Clavariaceae (coral mushroom)

Pezizaceae (orange cup fungus)

Tuberaceae (truffle)

Red Clathrus

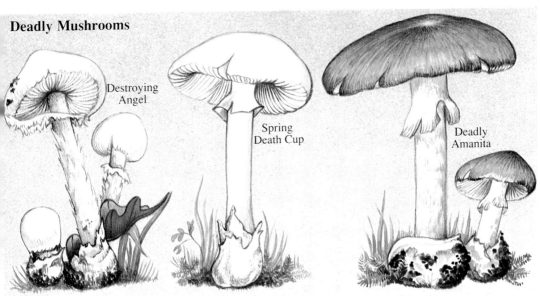

Deadly Mushrooms

Destroying Angel

Spring Death Cup

Deadly Amanita

Poisonous Mushrooms

Rabbit Ear Mushroom

Devil's Bolete

Amanita Aspera

Fly Amanita

Wild Flowers, Garden Flowers I

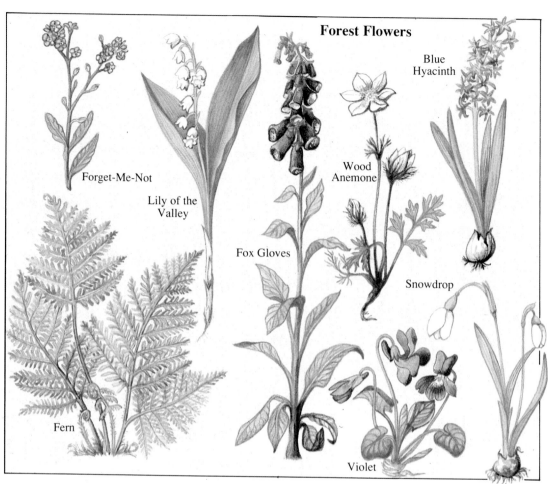

Forest Flowers

Forget-Me-Not

Lily of the Valley

Fox Gloves

Wood Anemone

Blue Hyacinth

Snowdrop

Fern

Violet

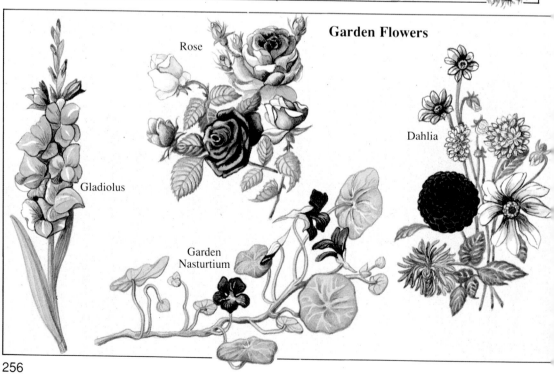

Garden Flowers

Rose

Gladiolus

Garden Nasturtium

Dahlia

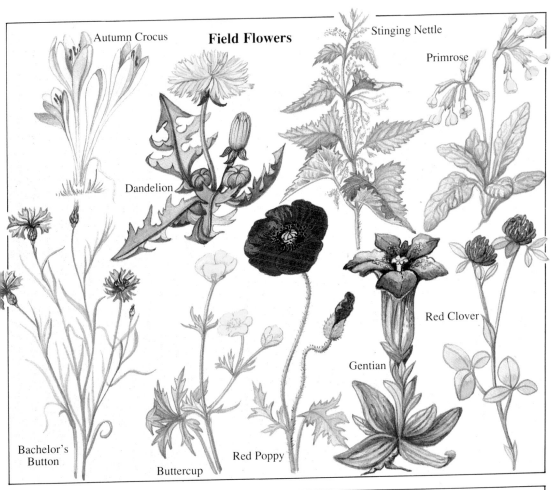

Autumn Crocus

Field Flowers

Stinging Nettle

Primrose

Dandelion

Bachelor's
Button

Buttercup

Red Poppy

Gentian

Red Clover

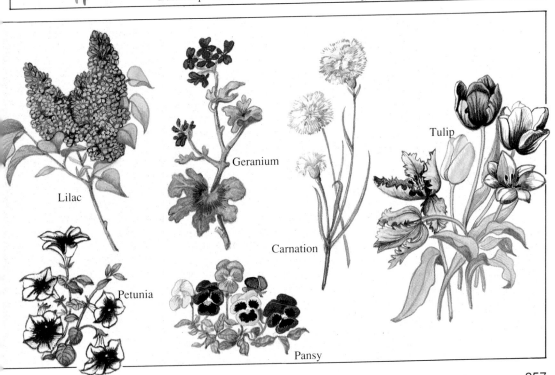

Lilac

Geranium

Petunia

Carnation

Tulip

Pansy

Wild Flowers, Garden Flowers II

Climbing Plants

Virginia Creeper

Morning Glory

English Ivy

They coil around (vine, morning glory) or attach themselves by tendrils (ivy) to various supports.

Aquatic Plants

Water Lily

They are more abundant than land plants and live in rivers and ponds. Some of them are completely submerged (bladderwort) and others only partly (water lily).

Vegetables

Tomatoes

Spinach

Peas

Beans

Carrots

Beets

There are many types of vegetables. Because they are rich in nutrients, we grow them abundantly. The edible parts are either the roots (carrots, radishes, beets), the leaves (lettuce, celery, spinach), the fruits (string beans, tomatoes), or the seeds (peas).

Spice Plants

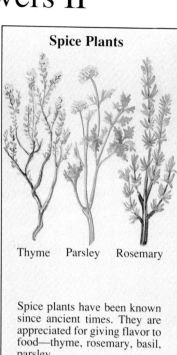

Thyme   Parsley   Rosemary

Spice plants have been known since ancient times. They are appreciated for giving flavor to food—thyme, rosemary, basil, parsley.

Medicinal Plants

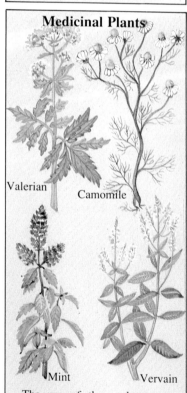

Valerian

Camomile

Mint

Vervain

The use of these plants as "cures" for certain diseases also goes back to ancient practices.

Many of them are still used today in various forms—arnica, valerian, mint, vervain, camomile.

Poisonous Plants

Spurge

Hellebore

Foxglove Autumn Crocus Water Hemlock

Many plants contain toxic substances which are dangerous to humans. For instance, water hemlock, autumn crocus, hellebore, foxglove.

Fiber Plants

Cotton Flax Hemp

These plants provide the raw materials for textile industries. The most important are flax, hemp, and cotton.

Cereals, Fodder Plants

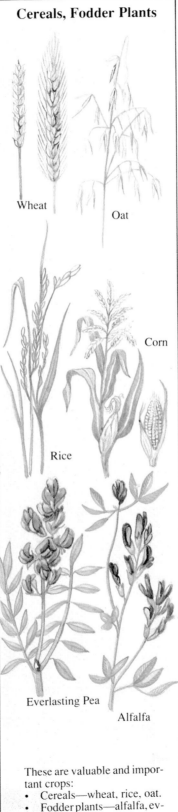

Wheat Oat

Corn

Rice

Everlasting Pea

Alfalfa

These are valuable and important crops:
- Cereals—wheat, rice, oat.
- Fodder plants—alfalfa, everlasting pea.

Succulents

Prickly Pear

Cactus

These plants are the only plants in arid regions. They accumulate water supplies (sometimes up to 90% of their weight) which allows them to survive long droughts—cactus, prickly pear.

Carnivorous Plants

Sundew Venus Flytrap

Among these curiosities of nature are more than 500 species. With the help of special traps, these plants supplement their food intake by capturing and digesting small insects. Some aquatic species feed on small crustaceans.

S.O.S. Pollution!

Nature is threatened. Our environment is in danger. Will we be able to act before it is too late?

Pollution has existed ever since the first cities were founded. With industrial civilization and the increase in world population, pollution has reached an alarming level.

And it gets worse every day. The environment is deteriorating. The survival of humans and numerous animal and plant species is endangered.

Today, many nations are beginning to make use of new and efficient measures to fight the dangers of pollution. However, these measures are expensive and require organization, determination, and cooperation among the nations of the world.

We must be aware, however, that the battle for the environment has just begun.

Air Pollution

Strict laws have been enforced (scrubbers for factory smokestacks, installation of catalysts for car exhausts) in order to reduce production of toxic gases which cause serious diseases, such as chronic bronchitis and asthma, especially in urban environments.

Rainfall contaminated by toxic gases (acid rain) has led to large-scale destruction of vegetation.

Pollution caused by industrial fumes:

In 1 cubic foot of New York air there are :
* in a department store   400,000 microbes
* in Times Square   550 microbes
* in Central Park   75 microbes
* in the Catskills   –5 microbes

Pollution of the Hudson River in New York.

Water treatment plant. Water is "cleaned" before being returned to the river.

Water Pollution

The dumping into rivers of wastes from urban life (sewage) and from industry (toxic chemicals, such as sulphur, chlorine, and mercury) causes dangerous pollution which can become a disaster when amounts are enormous. For example, many rivers in the United States are dying because of pollution. Also, there are nitrates which cause the overgrowth of plants, choking out the oxygen in the water.

Water treatment plants are designed to fight against this pollution. More and more plants are being built.

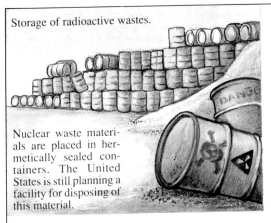

Storage of radioactive wastes.

Nuclear waste materials are placed in hermetically sealed containers. The United States is still planning a facility for disposing of this material.

Spraying crops with insecticides.

Ground Pollution

Garbage

Our cities produce thousands of tons of garbage every day. Some of it is burned in incinerators. Much of it is piled up in landfills, where it decays. People do not like to live near incinerators because they pollute the air, and space for landfills is getting scarce. Proper disposal of garbage can be expensive, and a lot of illegal dumping is done to save money.

Insecticides and Herbicides

Strict laws have been enforced for the control of these chemicals. D.D.T. has already caused the disappearance of certain birds in some areas, and it is now illegal in the United States.

Fighting Noise

One of the major drawbacks of the modern world is noise, which develops and increases at the same rate as technical progress.

Today, it is estimated, for instance, that about 200,000 persons are inconvenienced by the noise caused by Kennedy Airport in New York.

A bird covered with crude oil.

The Protection of Nature

Oceans and seas are also heavily polluted by industrial waste products. Transportation of fuels has caused numerous catastrophes when oil tankers have been wrecked at sea causing massive oil spills. These "black tides" have destroyed marine fauna and flora and polluted beaches.

The black tide caused by the wreckage of the oil tanker "Torrey Canyon" killed more than 100,000 sea birds of various species in 1967.

In 1988, dangerous medical wastes washed ashore in New York and New Jersey, causing the closing of beaches.

To preserve as much natural environment as possible, governments have established nature reserves, and regional and national parks. These projects should be encouraged.

The Mineral Kingdom

Rocks and minerals are components of the earth's crust.
A rock is an aggregate of one or several minerals.

Chalk

Chalk consists of one single mineral—95% is calcite.

Granite

Granite consists of three minerals—*quartz*, *feldspar*, and *mica*.

There are about 2,000 known minerals.

Geometrical Structures

When a grain of salt is crushed, a hand lens reveals that its fragments have the shape of small cubes. Each one of these fragments is a *crystal*.

Most rocks are an assemblage of small crystals. According to the kind of mineral, the crystals have a different geometrical structure.

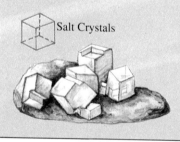

Salt Crystals

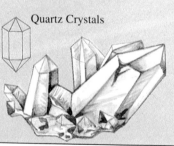

Quartz Crystals

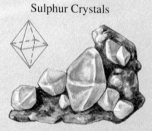

Sulphur Crystals

Igneous Rocks

They form when magma (liquid rock) cools and crystallizes.

The first minerals to crystallize are high in iron, magnesium, and calcium and low in silicon. *Basalt* is a common igneous rock of this composition.

The last minerals to crystallize are potassium feldspar and quartz. Igneous rocks in which these two minerals predominate are referred to as having a *granitic* composition. Granite frequently forms the core of eroded mountains whereas basalt is found in many volcanic eruptions.

Basalt

Sedimentary Rocks

These are rocks formed by debris detached from other rocks (igneous, metamorphic) by mechanical and chemical weathering. Most of these sediments are deposited in lakes, rivers, and seas.

Fossils are remains of former animals and plants found in sedimentary rocks.

The most common sedimentary rocks are *limestones*, *sandstones*, and *shales*.

Oil and *coal* originate from rocks where animal and plant debris accumulated, decomposed, and changed into fossil fuels.

Ammonite

Fossil Ferns
in Sandstone

Spriggina
(segmented worm-like organism)

What Are Ores?

They are rocks which contain economically interesting and exploitable minerals occurring either in a native state or as mixtures (ores of iron, zinc, aluminum).

Valuable Minerals—Gemstones

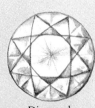

Diamond

Ruby

Sapphire

Aquamarine

Consisting of a single element (carbon), diamond is the hardest mineral. It is also the most valuable.

Emerald

Tourmaline

Because of their rarity, hardness, luster, and transparency, gemstones have a high commercial value.

Sentences

What Is a Sentence?

It is a group of words expressing a complete idea.

- "The bank manager is friendly."—*is* a sentence.

- "A friendly bank manager"—*is not* a sentence.

Four Types of Sentences

Anything we wish to say may be expressed in one of these types.

- "Our goat, Blanche, is happy in the forest."

This sentence is *declarative* because it makes a statement. Declarative sentences end with a period.

- "Is Blanche happy in the forest?"

This is an *interrogative* sentence because it asks a question. Interrogative sentences end with a question mark.

- "What an outstanding animal!"

This is an *exclamatory* sentence because it shows strong emotion. Exclamatory sentences end with an exclamation point.

- "Blanche, come here at once!"

This is an *imperative* sentence. It commands or requests. Some imperative sentences end with a period ("Close the door, please.") while others are more forceful and end with an exclamation point ("Be silent!").

Exercise

Are the following sentences *declarative*, *interrogative*, *exclamatory*, or *imperative*?

1. Has the space shuttle landed yet
2. What a heat wave
3. The World Series takes place in October
4. I'm getting a new bike
5. Come here at once
6. When is your birthday
7. Get ready, get set, go
8. My wallet is gone

Answers

1. interrogative	5. imperative
2. exclamatory	6. interrogative
3. declarative	7. imperative
4. declarative	8. exclamatory

Parts of Speech

Sentences are made up of words, of course. Each of the words we use belongs to a different part of speech: a word is either a *noun*, *pronoun*, *verb*, *adjective*, *adverb*, *preposition*, *conjunction*, or *article*.

Nouns

- There are *common nouns* which name persons (uncle), places (farm), or things (milk).

- Also, there are *proper nouns* which name a particular person (Adele), place (St. Louis), or thing (Coca-Cola).

Pronouns

These words take the place of nouns. Instead of repeating Adele in our sentences, for example, we may wish to use such pronouns as *she*, *her*, *hers*. Instead of always repeating St. Louis or Coca-Cola, we may at times use the pronoun *it*.

- The books were delivered to Adele. (or to *her*)

- I left the message at Adele's house. (or at *her* house)

- Adele is at the restaurant. (or *She* is)

- St. Louis is hot in July. (or *It*)

- I added ice to my Coca-Cola. (or to *it*)

Verbs

These are words that express action, that show what happens. When we say, "My brother *hit* the ball," we are describing the action, telling what the subject of the sentence (brother) did.

Note the verbs (action words) in the following sentences:

- Ellis *left* the airport. (subject is *Ellis*)

- The senator *spoke* to the reporters. (subject is *senator*)

- Light *streamed* through the windows. (subject is *light*)

Some verbs do not show direct action as the ones in italics above. Instead, they tell us what the situation is. *To be* is a good example of such a verb. Some of its forms are:

I *am*
you *are*
he, she, it *is*, *was*

we *were*
they *will be*, *have been*, etc.

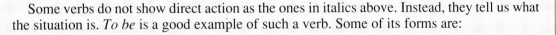

All of the words in italics above are different parts of the important verb, *to be*. So, you see, while most verbs express action, some tell us about the *state of being, what the situation is*.

Parts of Speech

Adjectives

These are words that describe nouns or pronouns. Is it a *new* car, a *red* car, a *flashy* car? Those three adjectives tell about the noun (car); they describe the kind of noun we are talking about.

If we say, He's *generous*, She's *kind*, They are *late*, we are using adjectives to describe pronouns.

In addition to describing *what kind*, adjectives can tell us *how many*.

EXAMPLES
We saw *three* sailors.
Matthew has *two* pairs of sneakers.
Karen broke *six* of them.

Once again, adjectives are being used to describe nouns or pronouns, but in this case they also make the meaning more specific by telling us *how many*.

Words that answer the question *which one* are adjectives.

EXAMPLES
She wants *that* pen. Which one? *That* one.
Sally prefers *these* apples. Mark bought *this* hat.
Take *any* card.

The words in italics are adjectives that are helping to describe nouns.

Adverbs

Adverbs *describe* (modify) verbs. We say that "Marsha sang," but that simple act could be described even further. *When* did she sing? *Where* did she sing?

EXAMPLES
Marsha sang *yesterday*. (adverbs tells *when* she sang)
Marsha sang *beautifully*. (adverb tells *how* she sang)
Marsha sang *here*. (adverb tells *where* she sang)

Adverbs have another function—they modify adjectives.

EXAMPLE
The moon was *very* bright.

Moon is a *noun*. *Bright* is an *adjective* describing (modifying) the moon. *Very* is an *adverb* telling how bright.

EXAMPLES
The dentist is quite skillful. (adverb *quite* modifies adjective *skillful*)
Cynthia is too excitable. (adverb *too* modifies adjective *excitable*)
Arthur was seriously ill. (adverb *seriously* modifies *ill*)

Finally, adverbs also modify other adverbs.

EXAMPLE
The airplane flew too high.

Flew is a *verb*. High is an *adverb* modifying *flew*. *Too* is an *adverb* modifying the adverb *high*. How high? Too high.

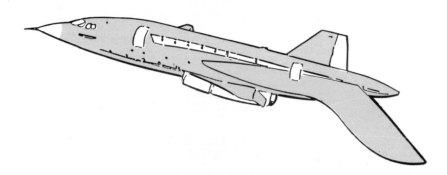

EXAMPLES
Brenda entered the room *very* cautiously. (adverb *very* modifies adverb *cautiously*)
We are *much too* clever for him. (adverb *much* modifies adverb *too*)
Victor did *especially well* on the test. (adverb *especially* modifies adverb *well*)

Prepositions

A preposition is a word that *points*. It shows the relationship between the noun (or pronoun) that follows it and some other word in the sentence. Here are 25 familiar prepositions:

above	between	in	since
about	by	into	to
among	down	of	under
at	except	off	until
before	for	on	up
behind	from	over	with
below			

We need these words to help make our sentences clearer, to show *relationships*.

EXAMPLES
I spoke *to* him.
We live *above* the store.
This milk is *for* you.
The key is *on* the counter.

Notice in the sentences above that the prepositions are followed by nouns or pronouns.

Conjunctions

Conjunctions *join* related words or groups of words. Some of the most familiar conjunctions are:

and	for	or
but	neither	so
either	nor	whether

Parts of Speech

Conjunctions join words:

> ham *and* eggs
> sad *but* true
> new *or* used toys

Conjunctions join *groups* of words:

- I sat down *and* wrote a letter to my parents.

- Be on time *or* you may lose your job.

- My sister had the measles *but* she recovered quickly.

Conjunctions may be used in *pairs*:

- *Neither* Edna nor Betty will be at the picnic.

- I can't say *whether* Sandy or David will be there.

- *Both* the chorus *and* the band will perform.

Articles

In addition to the nouns, pronouns, verbs, adjectives, adverbs, prepositions, and conjunctions, the English language has one other part of speech: *articles*. Articles are easy to identify because there are only three of them: *a, an, the.*

EXAMPLE
I never miss *an* opportunity to make *a* new friend in *the* school.

These three articles always act like adjectives; they modify nouns: *an* opportunity, *a* friend, *the* school.

Identifying Parts of Speech

Study the following sentence to make sure that you understand the part of speech of each word:

ARTICLE	ADVERB	ADJECTIVE	NOUN	VERB	ADVERB	PREPOSITION	ARTICLE	NOUN
The	very	brave	terrier	barked	angrily	at	the	burglar,

PRONOUN	VERB	CONJUNCTION	VERB	PREPOSITION	ARTICLE	NOUN
who	screamed	and	fled	into	the	night.

Tenses of Verbs

Note the verbs in these sentences:

- I *see* Eddie every day.
- I *saw* Eddie yesterday.

In the first sentence, the verb (see) is said to be in the *present* tense. In the second sentence, the past tense (saw) is used to show an action which took place earlier.

Each of our verbs can be used in a present or past form.

Present	Past
Bob *has*	Bob *had*
Bob *walks*	Bob *walked*
Bob *climbs*	Bob *climbed*
Bob *is*	Bob *was*

Exercise

What is the correct form of the verb in each of the following sentences?

(see) 1. Yesterday we _____ Prince in a concert.
(think) 2. I had _____ of that idea last November.
(learn) 3. Beverly is _____ how to skate.
(be) 4. Cary _____ our previous team captain.
(drive) 5. My mother has _____ me to school every day this year.

Answers

1. saw   2. thought   3. learning   4. was   5. driven

Other Tense Forms

In English we can be very precise by using the proper tense of the verb. Knowing all of the verbal tense forms allows you to communicate your meaning effectively. This chart for the verb *to send* introduces you to the future, present perfect, past perfect, and future perfect tenses.

Present Tense	
Singular	*Plural*
I send	we send
you send	you send
he, she, it sends	they send

Past Tense	
Singular	*Plural*
I sent	we sent
you sent	you sent
he, she, it sent	they sent

Tenses of Verbs

Future Tense (*shall* or *will* + the present)	
Singular	*Plural*
I shall send you will send he, she, it will send	we shall send you will send they will send

Present Perfect Tense (*have* or *has* + the past participle)	
Singular	*Plural*
I have sent you have sent he, she, it has sent	we have sent you have sent they have sent

(This tense is used to show action that does not take place at a specific time in the past: "I have often complained about the noise.")

Past Perfect Tense (*had* + the participle)	
Singular	*Plural*
I had sent you had sent he, she, it had sent	we had sent you had sent they had sent

(This tense is used to express an action which was completed in the past *before* some other past action: "We had written to them after they returned from Europe.")

Future Perfect Tense (*shall have* or *will have* + the past participle)	
I shall have sent you will have sent he, she, it will have sent	we shall have sent you will have sent they will have sent

(This tense is used to express an action which will be completed in the future before some other future action: "By the time you receive this letter, we shall have landed in Baltimore.")

Two Other Tense Forms

You should also be familiar with the *present participle* and *past participle* tense forms of verbs.

Present participle examples: writing, living, drawing . Present participles always end in *ing.*

EXAMPLES

Ron *is sending* us an invitation.
Rhonda *is entering* the contest.
Ricky *is dreaming* of a white Christmas.

Part participle examples: walked, wished, rained

EXAMPLES

I *have raced* around this track many times.
Charles *had turned* in his test when I met him.
She *has eaten* in that restaurant every Monday.

(The past participle verb forms are usually used with a helping word—some form of the verb *to have*, such as *has, had, have,* or *having.*)

Regular Verbs

Some verbs are called *regular* verbs. They form their past and past participle by adding **d** or **ed**.

Present	Past	Past Participle
stretch	stretched	(to have) + stretched
breathe	breathed	(to have) + breathed
snow	snowed	(to have) + snowed

Irregular Verbs

Some verbs are called *irregular verbs*. Instead of adding **d** or **ed** as the regular ones do, they form their past and past participle in other ways.

Present	Past	Past Participle
do	did	done
eat	ate	eaten
go	went	gone
see	saw	seen
sing	sang	sung

Plural Forms of Nouns

Regular Plurals

Changing singular nouns to plurals, generally means adding an **s** to the singular:

Singular	Plural
boy	boys
lamp	lamps
table	tables

But nouns which end in **s, sh, ch,** or **x** add **es** to form the plural:

Plural Forms of Nouns

Singular	*Plural*
box	boxes
church	churches
glass	glasses
sash	sashes

Nouns which end in **y** and have a vowel before the **y** form their plural by adding an **s**:

Singular	*Plural*
day	days
donkey	donkeys
toy	toys

When a consonant (a letter other than a vowel) comes before the final **y**, however, we change the **y** to **i** and add **es**:

Singular	*Plural*
baby	babies
diary	diaries
lady	ladies

When a noun ends in **f** or **fe**, an **s** is added to form the plural:

Singular	*Plural*
chief	chiefs
proof	proofs
safe	safes

However, there are some nouns ending in **f** or **fe** that form their plurals by changing the **f** to **v** and then adding **es**:

Singular	*Plural*
half	halves
self	selves
wife	wives

Irregular Plurals

Most nouns form their plurals in a regular way, following the rules explained above. There are other nouns, *irregular* ones, which do not obey those rules. Here are some examples:

Singular	*Plural*
child	children
foot	feet
goose	geese
ox	oxen
tooth	teeth

Exercise:

Do You Know the Plurals of These Words?

1. knife · 2. mouse   3. country   4. woman   5. calf
6. candy   7. valley   8. patch   9. flash   10. fireman

Answers

6. candies   7. valleys   8. patches   9. flashes   10. firemen
1. knives   2. mice   3. countries   4. women   5. calves

Agreement of Subjects and Verbs

If the noun or pronoun which is the subject of the sentence is *singular*, then the verb which agrees with that subject must be *singular* too. In such cases, we say that the subject and verb agree in *number*.

- *She*   *is*   always on time.
  (subject-singular)   (verb-singular)

- *Marty*   *works*   in the laundry.
  (subject-singular)   (verb-singular)

When the subject of the sentence is plural, then the verb which agrees with that subject must be plural too:

- *They*   *were*   at the park.
  (subject-plural)   (verb-plural)

- *Our athletes*   *have to be*   in good condition.
  (subject-plural)   (verb-plural)

Exercise

Pick the correct verb forms to match the subjects in these sentences:

1. Mr. Spencer, the teacher in charge of the buses, (is, are) my cousin.
2. Joshua and Maria (know, knows) how to play chess.
3. We (doesn't, don't) want to surrender.
4. Biologists (study, studies) laboratory animals.
5. They (has, have) no chance to succeed.

Answers

1. is   2. know   3. don't   4. study   5. have

Different Types of Sentences

Simple, Compound, Complex, and Compound-Complex Sentences

Simple Sentences

A group of words can be considered a *simple sentence* if (1) they have a subject and verb, and (2) if the words make a complete thought.

EXAMPLE

Swimming   *is*   great fun.
subj.   verb

Compound Sentences

Two simple sentences can be combined into a *compound sentence* by using a conjunction such as *and*, *but*, *or*.

EXAMPLE

Swimming   *is*   great fun, and   *I*   *recommend* it to you.
subj.   verb   subj.   verb

Complex Sentences

Complex sentences have two or more *clauses* (groups of words containing a subject and verb).

EXAMPLE

Vietnam veterans met in Washington, *where the President spoke to them.*
1st clause   2nd clause

The *main clause* is the first one; the second one is called the *subordinate clause*.

EXAMPLE

We knew that the weather would change *if we remained patient.*
main clause   subordinate clause

Compound-Complex Sentences

Compound-complex sentences have two or more *main clauses* and one or more *subordinate clauses*.

EXAMPLE

Mary went to the movies and *Denise decided to go too*
main clause   main clause

because it was raining.
subordinate clause

Remember

- Simple sentences consist of one clause (subject-verb combination).
- Compound sentences consist of two or more clauses of equal importance joined by a conjunction.
- Complex sentences consist of two or more clauses joined in such a way as to make one clause subordinate to the other.
- Compound-complex sentences consist of two or more clauses of equal importance and one or more subordinate clauses.

Pronoun Usage

In order to really understand English grammar, one must be well informed on the subject of pronoun usage. Pronouns take the place of nouns, and some personal nouns are used as subjects: *I, you, he, she, it, we, they*. Those personal pronouns which serve as subjects are said to be in the *nominative* case.

There is a matching set of personal pronouns which serve as objects and are in the *objective case*: *me, him, her, us, them*.

Basic sentence patterns in English are *subject-verb-object*.

	I	went	home.
	subj.	verb	object

	We	sold	lemonade.
	subj.	verb	object

In speaking or writing, the proper pronouns must be used in sentences. If a sentence requires an object, a nominative pronoun cannot be used. Similarly, the subject of a sentence may not be an objective pronoun.

Right: Harriet sent *me* to the store.
Wrong: Harriet sent *I* to the store.

Right: Lloyd and *I* are old friends.
Wrong: Lloyd and *me* are old friends.

Right: Jane and *I* went to the movies.
Wrong: *Me* and Jane went to the movies.

Study This Chart

Person	*Nominative*	*Objective*
Singular first	I	me
second	you	you
third	he, she, it	him, her, it
Plural first	we	us
second	you	you
third	they	them

Pronoun Usage

Relative Pronouns

Another type of pronoun is the *relative pronoun*. It has five forms: *that*, *which*, *who*, *whom*, *whose*.

In the sentence: "Here is the trophy *that* I won" the word *that* serves two purposes. It replaces trophy as the object of *won*, and it relates the statement *I won the trophy* to *Here is the trophy*.

Important: In using the relative pronouns *who* and *whom*, remember that *who* is in the *nominative case*, to be used when it is the *subject* of your sentence. When an *objective case* relative pronoun is needed, you must use *whom*.

EXAMPLES
Keith is the player *who* made the most points.
(*who* is in the nominative case, the subject of the verb *made*)

Where is the violinist *whom* you told me about?
(*whom* is in the objective case, the object of the verb *told*)

Interrogative Pronouns

The pronouns *who*, *whom*, *whose*, *which*, *what* that introduce questions are *interrogative pronouns*. *Who*, *whom*, and *whose* indicate that the answer will refer to a person; *what* indicates that the answer will refer to a thing; *which* may be used for either persons or things.

EXAMPLES

Who was the singer?	Answer: Mary
What was she carrying?	Answer: A book
Which boy went home?	Answer: Justin.

Exercise

Select the Correct Pronouns

1. The doctor spoke to Barney and (I, me).
2. (We, Us) girls know how to bake a cake.
3. It's Matthew (who, whom) we invited.
4. (They, Them) should know better.
5. (Who, Whom) did you vote for?
6. The principal scolded Vivian and (I, me) for coming late.
7. I'll never forget Marjorie and (she, her).
8. It's you (who, whom) are responsible.
9. The janitor, a man (who, whom) we admire, was fired.
10. Just between you and (I, me) the Lakers will win.

Useful hint: When a pronoun is the object of a verb or the subject of a preposition, it is in the *objective case*.

Answers

1. me 2. We 3. whom 4. They 5. Whom
6. me 7. her 8. who 9. whom 10. me

276

Punctuation

As you read in the section on types of sentences, every sentence ends with some kind of punctuation mark: either a period (.), a question mark (?), or an exclamation point (!).

Periods come at the end of a *declarative* sentence or statement: "We were guests of Mr. and Mrs. Kramer." This sentence not only shows the final period but indicates that periods are also used after abbreviations. In fact, you will find periods after abbreviations of places, titles, academic degrees, and time expressions:

Place	Academic Degree	Month	Title	Time
Boston, Mass.	Ph.D.	Feb.	Dr. R. L. Smith, Jr.	8 P.M. 345 B.C.

Question marks, of course, come at the end of interrogative sentences. "When does the game start?" When we ask a question *directly*, the question mark follows the complete question.

EXAMPLES
"Why did you decide to leave?"
"Why," she asked, "did you decide to leave?"

If the exact words of a question are not used (an *indirect* question, that is), no question mark is needed.

EXAMPLES
She asked him why he decided to leave.
Ellen wanted to know when the show would start.

Exclamation points follow words or statements that express strong feelings or emotions:.

EXAMPLES
Fire!
"Watch out!" Marsha screamed.

Commas must be used properly or your sentences will be incorrect and confusing.

EXAMPLES
The mayor said the governor is a complete fool.
or
"The mayor," said the governor, "is a complete fool."

Commas help to make meanings clear.

EXAMPLE
After shaving Barry went to the party.

We can make better sense out of those words by using a comma which shows that a pause is necessary.

EXAMPLE
After shaving, Barry went to the party.

When to Use Commas
- Between the name of a city and state, and between the day of the month and the year:

EXAMPLES
Seattle, Washington
August 7, 1991

Punctuation

- In an introductory expression:

EXAMPLES
Well, let's go.
Oh no, I'm against it.

- In the salutation of a friendly letter:

EXAMPLES
Dear Marilyn,
My Dear Friends,

- In the close of a letter:

EXAMPLES
Yours truly,
Sincerely yours,

- To separate words in a series:

EXAMPLES
I bought shirts, ties, socks, and gloves.
Beth is bright, modest, loyal, and amusing.

- Before the conjunction *and* when two long sentences are joined together:

EXAMPLE
It was the morning of the test, and I felt that I had not studied enough.

(If two short sentences are joined, use a comma only when it is necessary for clarity)

EXAMPLES
The rains came and we were soaked. (Comma not needed)
Coach sent for Peter, and Bert came along. (Comma needed)

- To separate the name of the person to whom the speaker is talking from the rest of the sentence (*direct address*):

EXAMPLES
"Dad, may I have my allowance?"
"Listen, Laura, this is important for you."
"Is it time to leave, Miss Taylor?"

- To set off interruptions in a sentence:

EXAMPLES
The fireworks, in my opinion, were superb.
It's your turn, however, to make a contribution.

- To set off *appositives* (nouns which are placed next to other nouns to explain or identify them):

EXAMPLES
Bruce, the club's treasurer, gave his report.
The twins, Joanna and Jeremy, came along for the ride.

Summary. Notice how the commas are used in this paragraph:

It was 6:10 P.M., Sunday, July 6, 1975, and about 35,000 people were present when the Kentucky Derby winner, Foolish Pleasure, stepped onto the track in Queens, New York, for the Great Match Race. Joining him was the filly, Ruffian, who was alert, edgy, and eager to run. The winner, certain to be in racing's Hall of Fame, would receive $225,000 with $125,000 going to the loser.

Semicolons. Semicolons (;) indicate a stronger pause than a comma and a weaker pause than a period:

EXAMPLES

Be sure to get there on time; the game starts promptly at 6 P.M.
We sent many protests to the mayor; no answers were received.

A semicolon is used between the clauses of a compound sentence which are joined by adverbs such as *however, furthermore, in addition, moreover, as a result,* etc.

EXAMPLES

All the winners received cash prizes; in addition they were taken to dinner.
Friday's game is an important one; therefore, we must do our best.

(*Note:* Never end a sentence with a semicolon.)

Colons. Colons are used to:

• Introduce lists

EXAMPLE

The president pledged to do the following: reduce taxes, balance the budget, create new jobs, and maintain the peace.

• Introduce explanations

EXAMPLE

The purpose of the experiment was clear: to find a cure for baldness.

• Follow the salutation in a business letter

EXAMPLE

Dear Sirs:
Gentlemen:
Dear Mrs. Camhi:

• Separate the hours and minutes when we express the time

EXAMPLE

8:15 A.M.
10:00 P.M.

• Precede long quotations

EXAMPLE

Winston Churchill wrote: "We shall fight on the beaches, on the land, in the air . . . ."

Punctuation

Apostrophes

Ownership. We show ownership by using certain pronouns:

EXAMPLES
This is *her* dress.
*His nu*mber was called.

There are other ways to show possession, however.

EXAMPLES
This is *Helen's* dress.
The boy's number was called.

Not only is an *s* added to *Helen* and *boy*, but also the punctuation mark called an apostrophe ('). That apostrophe shows ownership, and we use it to indicate possession by one noun:

EXAMPLES
These are *Helen's* dresses.
The boy*'s* numbers were called.

To show possession by *more than one noun*, add an *s* and then add the apostrophe:

EXAMPLES
These are the *girls'* dresses.
The *boys'* numbers were called.

When a plural noun does not end in *s* (such as *men*), we add an apostrophe and an *s* to show ownership (*men's*):

EXAMPLES
children's toys
mice's tails
geese's feathers

(*Note:* When we use a compound expression, the apostrophe belongs with the word nearest to the object which is possessed:

EXAMPLES
Alan and Paul's science project won an award.
Dad and Mom's decision worked out beautifully.

Contractions. Apostrophes are also used to show that letters have been left out in order to form a contraction:

EXAMPLES
is not = isn't
we will = we'll
he had = he'd
she would = she'd

(*Note:* Do not use an apostrophe in the possessive form of personal pronouns such as *ours*, *yours*, *his*, *hers*, *its*, *theirs*. Whenever you write *it's*, for example, *it* must always stand for it *is*.)

Quotation Marks. We use quotation marks before and after someone's exact words:

EXAMPLES

The patriot said, "I regret that I have but one life to give for my country."

Roger asked, "When will dinner be served?"

"You," my brother exclaimed, "are a pain in the neck!"

(*Notes:* • The final punctuation mark of a quotation is placed *inside* the quotation marks.
  • The first word of a quotation is capitalized.
  • Separate the quotation from the rest of the sentence by commas.)

Direct and Indirect Quotations. When we give the speaker's exact words, we are using a *direct quotation*.

But when the speaker's words are changed by whoever is reporting them, we are using an *indirect quotation*; no quotation marks are needed for indirect quotations.

Direct: Eloise said, "I'm going to visit my aunt this weekend."

Indirect: Eloise said that she would be visiting her aunt this weekend.

Quotation Marks in Titles. We use quotation marks around the titles of short forms of writing such as magazine articles, songs, poems, short stories, and book chapters:

EXAMPLES

I love "Stars and Stripes Forever."

We had to memorize "Trees" by Joyce Kilmer.

Poe's "The Tell-Tale Heart" frightened me.

Chapter Four, "Crossing the Road," in *The Grapes of Wrath* is marvelous.

Addition

Concept of the Operation

To add is to join together, to gather, to group elements in order to calculate the *sum*, the *total*.

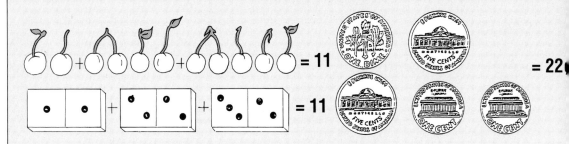

Addition Properties

Addition is *commutative*. The sum of two or more numbers is not affected by reversing their order. Therefore: $8 + 12 = 12 + 8 = 20$

Addition is *associative*:
Therefore:

$$26 + (4 + 10) \quad = \quad (26 + 4) + 10$$
$$26 + 14 \quad = \quad 30 + 10$$
$$40 \quad = \quad 40$$

Addition of Whole Numbers

$4 + 743 + 33 + 5,237 =$
(base 10)

We operate by placing each digit in the appropriate column.

th	h	t	u
5	2	3	7
	7	4	3
		3	3
+			4
6	0	1	7

We read:
six thousand, seventeen.

$101,101 + 1,011 =$
(base 2)

```
   101,101
+    1,011
  ────────
   111,000
```

We read:
one, one, one
zero, zero, zero

Addition of Decimals

$4.234 + 12.316$

```
   4.234
+ 12.316
 ───────
  16.550
```

We add the decimal part and then the whole numbers. The decimal points of numbers and sum are lined up correctly, one beneath the other.

$2.3715 + 23.04$

```
   2.3715
+ 23.04
 ───────
  25.4115
```

Addition of Whole Numbers and Decimals

$34 + 5.25 + 16.153 =$

$$
\begin{array}{r}
34. \\
5.25 \\
+\ 16.153 \\
\hline
55.403
\end{array}
\quad \text{or} \quad
\begin{array}{r}
34.000 \\
5.250 \\
+\ 16.153 \\
\hline
55.403
\end{array}
$$

$0.205 + 153 + 0.030 =$

$$
\begin{array}{r}
0.205 \\
153. \\
+\quad 0.030 \\
\hline
153.235
\end{array}
\quad \text{or} \quad
\begin{array}{r}
0.205 \\
153.000 \\
+\quad 0.030 \\
\hline
153.235
\end{array}
$$

The decimal point is placed between the last digit of the whole number (units) and the first digit of the decimal part (tenths).

At a Glance

Without performing any calculation:
1) *Point out which sums are equal to the given amount.*

54	125	800	46.5
17 + 27	90 + 45	350 + 450	33.25 + 13.25
38 + 16	80 + 45	525 + 275	24. + 12.5
19 + 35	92 + 23	630 + 270	18.5 + 18.
29 + 15	72 + 53	460 + 240	34.5 + 12.

2) *Which one is the correct answer?*

$24.9 + 34.2 =$	78.1	538.1	59.1	58.1
$114.25 + 8.025 =$	1,112.75	122.275	122.75	122.50

The Addition Table

The sum of an addition is found at the *intersection* of the row and column that have the two addends.

0	1	2	3	4	5	6	7	8	9
1	2	3	4	5	6	7	8	9	10
2	3	4	5	6	7	8	9	10	11
3	4	5	6	7	8	9	10	11	12
4	5	6	7	8	9	10	11	12	13
5	6	7	8	9	10	11	12	13	14
6	7	8	9	10	11	12	13	14	15
7	8	9	10	11	12	13	14	15	16
8	9	10	11	12	13	14	15	16	17
9	10	11	12	13	14	15	16	17	18

Find the Missing Digits

$$
\begin{array}{r}
6\text{–}4 \\
+\ \ \text{–}9\text{–} \\
\hline
1,081
\end{array}
\qquad
\begin{array}{r}
2\text{–}4 \\
+\ \ \text{–}61 \\
\hline
1,209
\end{array}
\qquad
\begin{array}{r}
\overline{} \\
6\text{–}.\text{–}8 \\
+\ \ \text{–}3.25 \\
\hline
82.9
\end{array}
$$

Answers

Missing Digits:
$684 + 397 = 1,081$
$74 + 274 + 861 = 1,209$
$69.68 + 13.25 = 82.93$

Correct Answers:
59.1; 122.275

Equal Sums:
to 54:   38 + 16;
         19 + 35
to 125: 80 + 45;
         72 + 53
to 800: 350 + 450;
         525 + 275
to 46.5 33.25 + 13.25;   34.5 + 12

Subtraction

Concept of the Operation

Subtract is to *take away*, *withdraw* a number from another.
Subtraction is the inverse operation of addition.

mark   Sophie
60 in.   50 in.

If a – b = **c**, then b + c = **a**
c is the *difference* that, when added to the smaller number, gives the larger.

$$\begin{array}{r} 60\,in. \\ -\ 50\,in. \\ \hline =\ 10\,in. \end{array}$$

10 in. is the difference between Mark and Sophie's sizes.

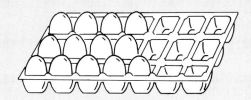

In the box there is room for 8 more eggs. 8 is the *difference* between 21 and 13.
21 – 13 = 8   13 + 8 = 21

Properties of Subtraction

Subtraction is *not commutative*.
   21-13 is different from 13-21

Subtraction is not *associative*.

$$\begin{aligned} 21 - 5 - 3 &= (21 - 5) - 3 \\ &= 16 - 3 = 13 \end{aligned}$$

is different from

$$\begin{aligned} 21 - (5 - 3) \\ = 21 - 2 = 19 \end{aligned}$$

Subtraction of Whole Numbers

2,943 – 1,767 =
(base 10)

th	h	t	u
2	9	4	3
1	7	6	7
1	1	7	6

We operate by placing each digit in the appropriate column.

1,101 – 110 =
(base 2)

$$\begin{array}{r} 1,101 \\ -\ \ \ 110 \\ \hline 111 \end{array}$$

Successive Subtraction Procedure

35 – 12 – 7 =
35 – (12 +7) =
35 – 19   = 16

35 – (12 + 7)
↘ 35 – 19
  ↘ 16 ↗

346 – 25 – 13 – 5 =
346 – (25 + 13 + 5) =
346 – 43   = 303

284

Subtraction of Decimals

14. 286 – 2.479 =

$$\begin{array}{r} 14.286 \\ -\ 2.479 \\ \hline 11.807 \end{array}$$

The numbers are placed in such a way that decimal points are lined up correctly, one beneath the other.

3.049 – 0.79 =

$$\begin{array}{r} 3.049 \\ -\ 0.79 \\ \hline 2.259 \end{array}$$

Subtraction of Whole Numbers and Decimals

216.075 – 183 =

$$\begin{array}{r} 216.075 \\ -\ 183. \\ \hline 33.075 \end{array}$$
or
$$\begin{array}{r} 216.075 \\ -\ 183.000 \\ \hline 33.075 \end{array}$$

243 – 0.075 =

$$\begin{array}{r} 243. \\ -\ \ \ 0.075 \\ \hline 242.925 \end{array}$$
or
$$\begin{array}{r} 243.000 \\ -\ \ \ 0.075 \\ \hline 242.925 \end{array}$$

The decimal point is placed between the last digit of the whole number (units) and the first of the decimal part (tenths).

At a Glance

Without performing any calculation:
1) *Which differences are equal to the given amounts?*

14		105
138 – 124		310 – 205
96 – 72		562 – 467
148 – 114		800 – 695
75 – 61		440 – 315

0.25		1.50
15.5 – 15		15.75 – 14
0.75 – 0.50		105.75 – 104.25
1.50 – 1.25		18 – 16.5
3.25 – 2.00		13.5 – 10.5

2) *Find the missing addends*

0.25	+ ... =	1
0.60	+ ... =	1
9.9	+ ... =	10
34.50	+ ... =	40
45.75	+ ... =	50
99.6	+ ... =	100

3) *Find the missing digits*

$$\begin{array}{r} -,-3- \\ -\ 2,3-5 \\ \hline 1,451 \end{array}$$
$$\begin{array}{r} \underline{\quad}. \\ -\ 17.4 \\ \hline 24.8 \end{array}$$

$$\begin{array}{r} -,-37 \\ -\ 2,3-4 \\ \hline 4,82- \end{array}$$
$$\begin{array}{r} 7.-85 \\ -\ 4.3- \\ \hline -.50- \end{array}$$

Answers

Multiplication

A Substitute for Addition

The calculation of the addition of same numbers can be made through an abridged addition: *multiplication*.

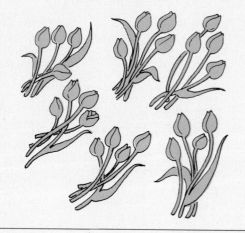

The number of flowers in each of these bunches are:

$$4 + 4 + 4 + 4 + 4 + 4 = 24$$

or

$$4 \quad \times \quad 6 \quad = \quad 24$$

MULTIPLICAND   MULTIPLIER   PRODUCT

Properties of Multiplication

Multiplication is *commutative*

$$4 \times 6 = 6 \times 4 = 24$$

Multiplication is *associative*

$$24 \times 5 = (12 \times 2) \times 5 = 12 \times (2 \times 5) = 12 \times 10 = 120$$

Multiplication is *distributive* over addition

$$5 \times (20 + 4) = (5 \times 20) + (5 \times 4) = 100 + 20 = 120$$

Multiplication of Whole Numbers

$$
\begin{array}{r}
234 \\
\times\, 105 \\
\hline
1{,}170 \\
234\,.\,. \\
\hline
24{,}570
\end{array}
$$

The points correspond to the zeros of the multiplication by 100.

Multiplication by 10, 100, 1,000 . . .

$$45 \times \mathbf{10} = 450 \qquad 45 \times \mathbf{100} = 4{,}500 \qquad 45 \times \mathbf{1{,}000} = 45{,}000 \qquad 45 \times \mathbf{10{,}000} = 450{,}000$$

The product is equal to the number being multiplied followed by as many zeros as there are in the multiplier.

Multiplication of Decimals

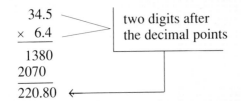

$$34.5 \times 6.4$$ — two digits after the decimal points

```
  34.5
× 6.4
 1380
2070
220.80  ←
```

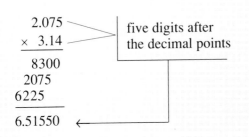

$$2.075 \times 3.14$$ — five digits after the decimal points

```
  2.075
× 3.14
 8300
2075
6225
6.51550  ←
```

The decimal point is moved *to the right* as many places as there are zeros in the multiplier.

24.75 × 10   = 247.5
24.75 × 100   = 2475.
24.75 × 1000 = 24,750.

Pythagoras Table

The product is shown at the intersection of the lines that represent the factors.

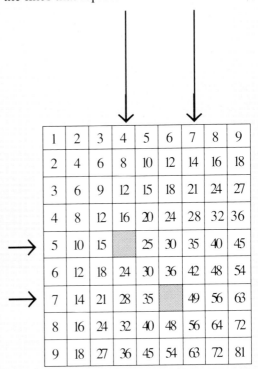

1	2	3	4	5	6	7	8	9
2	4	6	8	10	12	14	16	18
3	6	9	12	15	18	21	24	27
4	8	12	16	20	24	28	32	36
5	10	15		25	30	35	40	45
6	12	18	24	30	36	42	48	54
7	14	21	28	35		49	56	63
8	16	24	32	40	48	56	64	72
9	18	27	36	45	54	63	72	81

Other Ways of Multiplying

You can multiply 28 × 16 by thinking of it as (20 + 8) multiplied by (10 + 6). 28 × 16 = (20 + 8) × (10 + 6). This means that 20 and 8 are *each* multiplied by 10 and 6 and all the products are added:

```
20 × 10 =  200
20 × 6  =  120
8 × 10  =   80
8 × 6   =   48
           448
```

Believe it or not, you can multiply any two numbers together without knowing any multiplication or division except by 2.

Suppose we want 38 × 54. Divide 38 repeatedly by 2, throwing away remainders, until you can't divide any more. Multiply 54 by 2 as many times as you divided 38 by 2:

```
38 × 54
19 × 108
9 × 216
4 × 432
2 × 864
1 × 1,728
```

Now cross out all lines where there is an even number in the 38 column. Add what is left in the 54 column:

```
38 × 54
19 × 108
9 × 216
4 × 432
2 × 864
1 × 1,728
─────────
2,052
```

Division

Concept of the Operation

Division is
- the process of dividing an amount into a number of equal parts in order to determine *the value of one part*.
- looking for *the number of equal parts* contained in a certain amount when the value of a part is known.

28 flowers
- to make 4 bunches $28 \div 4 = 7$
  7 flowers per bunch
- 7 flowers per bunch $28 \div 7$
  4 bunches

Division is the *inverse* operation of multiplication.

$$28 \div 4 = 7 \rightarrow \quad 4 \times 7 = 28$$
$$28 \div 7 = 4 \rightarrow \quad 7 \times 4 = 28$$

Properties of Division

Division is *not commutative*
$28 \div 4$ is different from $4 \div 28$

Division is not *associative*
$(32 \div 8) \div 2 = 2$ is different from $32 \div (8 \div 2) = 8$

Certain calculations may be simplified by breaking them up
$$426 \div 2 = (400 \div 2) + (20 \div 2) + (6 \div 2)$$
$$= 200 + 10 + 3 = 213$$

Dividing Whole Numbers

division with approximate quotient

exact division

```
            16          quotient
divisor   4 | 64        dividend
            4
            24
            24
            0          no remainder
```

```
            21.33       quotient
          3 | 64.00
            6
            4
            3
            10
            9
            10
            9
            1
```

inexact division

```
            15          quotient
divisor   4 | 63        dividend
            4
            23
            20
            3          remainder (always lower than the divisor)
```

The above decimal quotient to the nearest tenth is 21.3; the final 3 in 21.33 is dropped because it is less than 5.

Check:
quotient × divisor + remainder = dividend $(15 \times 4) + 3 = 63$

Division of whole numbers by 10, 100, 1,000 . . .

64 ÷	10	=	6.4
64 ÷	100	=	0.64
64 ÷	1,000	=	0.064
64 ÷	10,000	=	0.0064

The decimal point is moved to the left as many places as there are zeros in the divisor.

Division of decimal numbers by 10, 100, 1,000

64.5 ÷ 10 = 6.45
64.5 ÷ 100 = 0.645
64.5 ÷ 1,000 = 0.0645

Division of Decimal Numbers

64 ÷ 4.5 Convert to whole numbers by multiplying divisor and dividend by 10: 640 ÷ 45.

64.5 ÷ 4.52 Convert to whole numbers by multiplying divisor and dividend by 100: 6,450 ÷ 452

```
    15.8
4 | 63.5
    4
    23
    20
    35
    32
    3
```

```
      14.2
45 | 640.0
     45
     190
     180
     100
      90
      10
```

```
       14.2
452 | 6,450.0
      452
      1930
      1808
      1220
       904
       316
```

Divisibility

It is possible to know whether a number is exactly divisible:

by 2 If it is an even number, ending in **0, 2, 4, 6, 8**.
124, 230, 46,278 are divisible; 231, 1,275 are not.

by 3 If the sum of its digits is *equal* to **3, 6,** or **9.**
210, 4,536, 12,435 are divisible; 125, 12,743, are not.

by 5 If the *ending* digit is **0** or **5.**
1,250, 34,245 are divisible; 342, 624 are not.

by 6 If the number is *divisible*, at the same time, by **2** (even number) and by **3** (the sum of the digits is 3, 6, 9). 108, 2,082, 21,330 are divisible; 453, 4,538 are not.

by 9 If the *sum of its digits is equal* to **9.**
450, 3,231, 26,145 are divisible; 345, 1,270 are not.

At a Glance

Without performing any calculation find out by which numbers (2,3,5,6,9) the following numbers are divisible:

216   540   135

Answers

135 is divisible by 3,5,9.

540 is divisible by 2,3,5,6,9.

216 is divisible by 2,3,6,9.

Fractions

Addition

- *A whole number and a fraction*

$$3 + \frac{2}{3} = \frac{9}{3} + \frac{2}{3} = \frac{11}{3}$$

The whole number is converted to a fraction, with the same denominator as the denominator of the fraction.

- *Two fractions*

If the fractions have the same denominator:

$$\frac{3}{7} + \frac{5}{7} = \frac{8}{7}$$

we add the numerators.

If the fractions have different denominators:

$$\frac{3}{4} + \frac{5}{6} =$$

The fractions are converted to a common denominator by multiplying the terms of each fraction by the denominator of the other.

$$\frac{3 \times 6}{4 \times 6} + \frac{5 \times 4}{6 \times 4} = \frac{18}{24} + \frac{20}{24} = \frac{38}{24} \quad \text{or} \quad \frac{19}{12}$$

The fraction $\frac{38}{24}$ *has been simplified.* Each of its terms has been divided by 2.

$\frac{19}{12}$ is an *irreducible* fraction. It cannot be simplified any more.

- *A decimal number and a fraction*

$$2.3 + \frac{3}{4} =$$

The decimal number is converted to a fraction: $2.3 = \frac{23}{10}$

$$\frac{23}{10} + \frac{3}{4} = \frac{23 \times 4}{10 \times 4} + \frac{3 \times 10}{4 \times 10} = \frac{92}{40} + \frac{30}{40} = \frac{122}{40} = \frac{61}{20}$$

In *decimal notation:* $\frac{61}{20} = 3.05$

Subtraction

- *A whole number and a fraction*

$$9 - \frac{3}{5} = \frac{45}{5} - \frac{3}{5} = \frac{42}{5} = 8\frac{2}{5} \quad \text{or } 8.4$$

We operate as in the addition.

- *Two fractions with a common denominator.*

$$\frac{7}{5} - \frac{4}{5} = \frac{3}{5}$$

We subtract the numerators.

Different Denominators. They are converted to the same denominator.

$$\frac{4}{5} - \frac{2}{3} = \frac{4 \times 3}{5 \times 3} - \frac{2 \times 5}{3 \times 5} = \frac{12}{15} - \frac{10}{15} = \frac{2}{15}$$

- *A decimal number and a fraction*

$$3.2 - \frac{7}{4} = \frac{32}{10} - \frac{7}{4} = \frac{32 \times 4}{10 \times 4} - \frac{7 \times 10}{4 \times 10} = \frac{128}{40} - \frac{70}{40} = \frac{58}{40} = \frac{29}{20} = 1\frac{9}{20} \text{ or } 1.45$$

Multiplication

- *A whole number and a fraction*

$$6 \times \frac{3}{4} = \frac{18}{4} = \frac{9}{2} = 4\frac{1}{2} \text{ or } 4.5$$

We multiply the whole number by the numerator of the fraction.

- *Two fractions* $\quad \frac{3}{5} \times \frac{4}{3} = \frac{12}{15} = \frac{4}{5} \text{ or } 0.8$

We multiply the numerators together and the denominators together.

- *A decimal number and a fraction*

$$2.4 \times \frac{5}{6} = \frac{24}{10} \times \frac{5}{6} = \frac{120}{60} = 2$$

Division

- *A whole number and a fraction*

$$4 \div \frac{3}{5} = 4 \times \frac{5}{3} = \frac{20}{3} = 6\frac{2}{3}$$

We multiply the whole number by the fraction inverted.

$$\frac{3}{4} \div 4 = \frac{3}{4} \div \frac{4}{1} = \frac{3}{4} \times \frac{1}{4} = \frac{3}{16}$$

- *Two fractions*

$$\frac{3}{4} \div \frac{5}{6} = \frac{3}{4} \times \frac{6}{5} = \frac{18}{20} = \frac{9}{10} \text{ or } 0.9$$

- *A decimal number and a fraction*

$$3.6 \div \frac{2}{3} = \frac{36}{10} \times \frac{3}{2} = \frac{108}{20} = \frac{54}{10}$$

$$= 5\frac{2}{5} \text{ or } 5.4$$

Test Your Skills

Which fraction represents the largest amount?
The smallest?

1) $\frac{1}{3}; \frac{1}{5}; \frac{1}{2}; \frac{1}{8}; \frac{1}{4}; \frac{1}{6}$

2) $\frac{2}{3}; \frac{1}{4}; \frac{5}{6}; \frac{3}{4}; \frac{1}{5}; \frac{4}{5}$

Answers

smallest: $\frac{1}{5}$

2) largest: $\frac{5}{6}$

smallest: $\frac{1}{8}$

1) largest: $\frac{1}{2}$

Measuring Time

$$1\ HR \qquad 60\ MIN \qquad 3600\ SEC$$
$$1\ DAY \qquad 24\ HR \qquad 1440\ MIN \qquad 86400\ SEC$$

Sexagesimal System of Numeration

60 sec. = 1 min.   60 min. = 1 hr. = 3,600 sec.

Base 60 is used for measuring time.

Therefore, 75 sec. = 60 sec. + 15 sec.   65 min. = 60 min. + 05 min.
= **1 min. 15 sec.**   = **1 hr. 05 min.**

1 min. 15 sec. and 1 hr. 05 min. are *sexagesimal numbers*.

To Simplify Certain Calculations

Sometimes, time is expressed with the decimal system. An hour is then divided into 100 parts. These are a few equivalents

7 hr. 15 min. = 7.25 hr.   7 hr.30 min. = 7.50 hr.   7 hr. 45 min. =7.75 hr.
(25 hundredths of an hour)   (50 hundredths)   (75 hundredths)

Transformations

A. To find the number of seconds represented by 3 hr. 12 min. 20 sec.:

3 hr. = 3,600 sec. × 3 =   10,800 sec.

12 min. = 60 sec. × 12 =   720 sec.

20 sec. =   20 sec.
$\overline{}$
11,540 sec.

B. To find the number of hours, minutes, and seconds in 7,348 sec.:

```
        122 min.                    2 hr.
1.  60 |7,348           2.  60 |122
        60                          120
       ----                         ----
        134                          2 min.
        120
       ----
        148
        120
       ----
         28 sec.
```

(1) The seconds are divided by 60.

(2) The number of minutes is divided by 60.

7,348 sec. = **2 hr. 02 min. 28 sec.**

Divisions of a Day

A day (**da.**) is divided into 24 hr. 1 **da. = 24 hr.**

= 60 × 24 = 1,440 min.

= 3,600 × 24 = 86,400 sec.

Divisions of a Year

A year has **365** or **366** days. There is 1 additional day in February every 4 years (leap year). 1988 was a leap year.

12 months (2 semesters or 4 trimesters).
52 weeks.

A century lasts 100 years.

A millennium lasts 1,000 years.

Addition of Units of Time

3 hr. 25 min. 38 sec. + 1 hr. 37 min. 43 sec. =

```
    3 hr. 25 min. 38 sec.
  + 1 hr. 37 min. 43 sec.
  ─────────────────────────
    4 hr. 62 min. 81 sec.
```

23 hr. 45 min. 35 sec. + 6 hr. 25 min. 40 sec. =

```
    23 hr. 45 min. 35 sec.
  +  6 hr. 25 min. 40 sec.
  ─────────────────────────
    29 hr. 70 min. 75 sec.
```

```
+           1 min. – 60 sec.
  ─────────────────────────────
  4 hr.   63 min.    21 sec.
```
We take away 60 sec. that we replace by adding 1 to the minutes column.

```
+           1 min. – 60 sec.
  ─────────────────────────────
  29 hr.   71 min.    15 sec.
```

```
+ 1 hr. – 60 min.
  ─────────────────────────────
  5 hr.   03 min.    21 sec.
```
We take away 60 min. that we replace by adding 1 hr. to the hours column.

```
+  1 hr. – 60 min.
  ─────────────────────────────
  30 hr.   11 min.   15 sec.
```

```
+  1 da.  – 24 hr.
  ─────────────────────────────────
  1 da.    6 hr.    11 min.   15 sec.
```

We take away 24 hr. that we replace by adding 1 to the days column

---

Subtraction of Units of Time

3 hr. 25 min. 12 sec. – 1 hr. 48 min. 27 sec. =

```
    3 hr.   25 min.   12 sec.
  – 1 hr.   48 min.   27 sec.
  ──────────────────────────
    1 hr.   36 min.   45 sec.
```
We cannot subtract 27 sec. from 12 sec.;

We take away 1 min. (60 sec.) from 25 min.; we add these 60 sec. to the 12 sec.: 12 sec. + 60 sec. = 72 sec.

or

```
    2 hr.   84 min.   72 sec.
  – 1 hr.   48 min.   27 sec.
  ──────────────────────────
    1 hr.   36 min .  45 sec.
```
We cannot subtract 48 min. from 24 min. We take away 1 hr. (60 min.) from 3 hr.; we add these 60 min. to the given 24 min.; 24 min. + 60 min. = 84 min.

```
  1 da. 12 hr. 15 min.   25 sec.
  –        24 hr. 10 min.   50 sec.
  ──────────────────────────────
```
We cannot subtract 50 sec. from 25 sec.; we take away 1 min. (60 sec.) from the 15 min. We add these 60 min. to the given 25.   25 sec. + 60 sec. = 85 sec.

```
  1 da. 12 hr. 14 min.   85 sec.
  –        24 hr. 10 min.   50 sec.
  ──────────────────────────────
```
We cannot subtract 24 hr. from 12 hr.; consequently we convert one day to hours (24), which we add to the given 12 hr.   12 hr. + 24 hr. = 36 hr.

```
    36 hr. 14 min. 85 sec.
  – 24 hr. 10 min. 50 sec.
  ──────────────────────────
    12hr. 04 min. 35 sec.
```

Using a Calculator

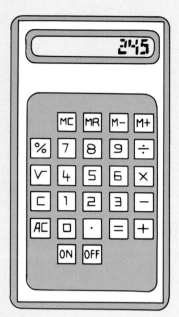

As a general rule a simple minicalculator is able to perform:
a) computations of addition (+)
   subtraction (-)
   multiplication (×)
   division (÷)
b) computation of square root (√)
c) computation of percentages (%)

Besides it has:

- a correction key $\boxed{c}$

- a key $\boxed{M+}$ addition to the number in the memory

- a key $\boxed{M-}$ subtraction from the number in the memory

- a key $\boxed{MR}$ to recall from the memory

- a key $\boxed{MC}$ to erase the memory

- a key $\boxed{AC}$ total erasure

Display capacity: 8 digits.

To Perform Addition

of whole numbers
245 + 431 =
We punch:
245 $\boxed{+}$ 431 $\boxed{=}$ 676

of decimals
136.2 + 282.5 =

We punch:
136$\boxed{.}$2 $\boxed{+}$ 282$\boxed{.}$5 $\boxed{=}$ $\boxed{418.7}$

Use of the correction key
    25 + 14   =

We punch:
25 $\boxed{+}$ 15 $\boxed{C}$ 14 $\boxed{=}$ $\boxed{39}$

To Perform Subtraction

1) 621 – 196 =
2) 196 – 621 =

We punch:
1) 621 $\boxed{-}$ 196 $\boxed{=}$ $\boxed{425}$
2) 196 $\boxed{-}$ 621 $\boxed{=}$ $\boxed{-425}$

Repeated Calculations

To add the same number several times:
35 + 18 + 18 + 18 =

We punch:
35 $\boxed{+}$ 18 $\boxed{=}$ $\boxed{=}$ $\boxed{=}$ $\boxed{89}$

To subtract:
38 – 4 – 4 – 4 =
We punch:
38 $\boxed{-}$ 4 $\boxed{=}$ $\boxed{=}$ $\boxed{=}$ $\boxed{26}$

In other calculators 35 + 18 + 18 + 18 must be performed by punching:

$\boxed{18}$ $\boxed{M+}$ $\boxed{M+}$ $\boxed{M+}$ $\boxed{MR}$ $\boxed{+}$ 38 $\boxed{=}$ $\boxed{89}$

To Perform Multiplication or Division

1) 263.4 × 48 =
2) 624 ÷ 3 =

We punch:

1) 263 $\boxed{.}$ 4 $\boxed{×}$ 48 $\boxed{=}$ 12,643.2
2) 624 $\boxed{÷}$ 3 $\boxed{=}$ $\boxed{208}$

Mixed Calculations

9 + 4 – 4.5 =

We punch:

9 $\boxed{+}$ 4 $\boxed{-}$ 4 $\boxed{.}$ 5 $\boxed{=}$ $\boxed{8.5}$

2 – 9 + 3 =

We punch:

2 $\boxed{-}$ 9 $\boxed{+}$ 3 $\boxed{=}$ $\boxed{-4}$

(8 × 3) ÷ 2 =

We punch:

8 $\boxed{\times}$ 3 $\boxed{\div}$ 2 $\boxed{=}$ $\boxed{12}$

Using the Memory

(30 × 20) + (40 × 25) + (60 × 15) =

We punch:

30 $\boxed{\times}$ 20 $\boxed{M+}$

40 $\boxed{\times}$ 25 $\boxed{M+}$

60 $\boxed{\times}$ 15 $\boxed{M+}$

We punch $\boxed{MR}$ $\boxed{2,500}$

Calculation of the Square Root

5 is the square root of 25, because 5 × 5 = 25.
We write $\sqrt{25}$ = 5 (square root of 25 is 5).

The calculator enables us to find immediately the square root of any number.

We punch the number, then we punch the key
$\boxed{\sqrt{\ }}$

EXAMPLE

224 $\boxed{\sqrt{\ }}$ $\boxed{14.966629}$

152 $\boxed{\sqrt{\ }}$ $\boxed{12.328828}$

Calculation of a Percentage

How much is 25% of 235?
We punch:

235 $\boxed{\times}$ 25 $\boxed{\%}$ $\boxed{58.75}$

How much is 85% of 15?
We punch:

15 $\boxed{\times}$ 85 $\boxed{\%}$ $\boxed{12.75}$

Calculation of an Amount after an Increase

$350 + 20% =

We punch:

350 $\boxed{\times}$ 20 $\boxed{\%}$ $\boxed{+}$ = $\boxed{420}$

Calculation of a Decrease after a Discount

$350 – 20% =

We punch:

350 $\boxed{\times}$ 20 $\boxed{\%}$ $\boxed{-}$ = $\boxed{280}$

Some Tests

1) 1,246.58+ 398.75 =

2) 284.5 – 719.25 =

3) (48 × 24) + (37.5 × 19.3)
   + (172.02 × 91.75) =

4) $\sqrt{288}$ =

5) 35% of 6,948 =

Answers:

3) 17,658.585

2) – 434.75

1) 1,645.33

5) 2,431.8

4) 16.970562

Index

A

Abacus, 145
Abbreviations, 125
Absolute monarchs, 39
Acid rain, 115
Aconcagua, Mount, 88
Acropolis, 22, 23
Addition, 282–283
Adjectives, 266
Adverbs, 266–267
Advertising, 132, 135
Africa: colonization, 59; countries of, 86–87; facts about, 86; independent nations, 66
Air: energy source, 190; facts about, 182–183
Airplane: first flight of, 209
Air pollution, 260
Air travel: early, 209
Alaska, 107
Aldrin, Edwin, 71
Algae, 246–247
Alighieri, Dante, 47
Alphabet, 117
Amazon River, 88
Amenhotep IV, 19
America: Civil War, 57; colonization of, 48–49; Constitution, 52–53; discovery of, 45; sections of, 56–57; westward expansion, 56–57; see also United States
American Revolution: 50–51
Amnesty International, 73
Amphibians: facts about, 237; prehistoric, 11; types of, 239
Anagrams, 126
Ancient civilizations: art, 140; common factors in, 21; main civilizations, 20–29; mathematics, 144–147;

poetry, 128; written language, 117
Ancient history: timeline of, 12–13
Anemometer, 186
Angiosperms, 246
Angles, 32
Animals: eating habits, 217; prehistoric, 10–11; senses of, 225
Annelids, 240
Antarctica, 95
Antibiotics, 70, 235
Antonyms, 123
Apartheid, 72
Apostrophes: usage, 280
Arachnids, 241
Archimedes, 198
Arctic area, 95
Arithmetic, 282–295; see specific arithmetic functions
Armstrong, Neil, 71
Art: famous artists/sculptors, 141; historical view, 140–141; prehistoric times, 14; in Renaissance, 46
Articles: part of speech, 268
Asia: countries of, 90–91; facts about, 90
Asoka, 29
Asphyxia (suffocation), 215
Athens (ancient), 22–23
Atmosphere, 182
Atmospheric pressure, 186
Atomic bomb, 63, 192
Attila the Hun, 32
Australopithecus, 11
Automobile: invention of, 55, 208

B

Balances: facts about,

198–199
Ballet, 143
Barometer, 186
Bases: numbers, 150–151
Bastille Day, 51
Battery, 188
Benenson, Peter, 73
Bible, 30
Bicycle: invention of, 208
Bill of Rights, 52–53
Binary system, 150
Birds: facts about, 236; prehistoric, 10; types of, 239
Black: color, 201
Blood: facts about, 220–221; white blood cells, 235
Boiling point, 181
Bonaparte, Napoleon, 51
Bones: facts about, 228
Braille, 119
Brain: facts about, 231
Brazil: economic crisis, 68
Brontosaurus, 10
Buddha and Buddhism, 29, 31
Burghers, 42
Burgundians, 32
Byzantine Empire, 26–27

C

Caesar, Augustus, 25
Calculator: use of, 294–295
Camera: parts of, 210
Canada, 59, 88; facts about, 108–115
Candle: time keeping, 207
Capet, Hugh, 38
Caravels, 45
Carnivores, 217
Cartier, Jacques, 45
Cartoons, 135
Caste system, 29

F

Factories: first, 54–55
Fascism, 62
Faults in earth, 82
Federalist Papers, 53
Federal system of government, 52–53
Ferdinand, Franz, 60
Ferdinand of Aragon, 39
Fetus: development of, 212
Feudalism, 35–39; beginning of, 35; class system, 36, 37; end of, 38; monks and monasteries, 37; system of, 36–37
Film development, 211
Fire: discovery of, 15, 184; facts about, 184–185
Fire prevention, 185
Fish: facts about, 237; prehistoric times, 10; respiration, 215; types of, 239
Flowers: types of, 256–257
Folk dancing, 143
Food: classification of, 219; food chain, 244–245
Forests, 248–249; destruction of, 249; and environment, 248–249
Fossils, 263
Fractions, 149, 290–291
France: absolute monarchs, 39; French Revolution, 51; middle ages, 38, 39
Franklin, Benjamin, 53
Franks, 32, 34
Frederick the Great, 39
French and Indian War, 50
Frog: metamorphosis, 213
Fruit bearing plants, 252–253
Fuel energy, 191
Fungi, 246–247; mushrooms, 254–255

G

Galaxies, 202
Galileo, 202
Gama, Vasco da, 45
Gandhi, Mahatma, 69
Gases and respiration, 214–215
Gems, 263
Genocide, 59
Geographical coordinates, 74
Geometry: figures, 166–167; measurements, 168–169; solids, 170–171
Geothermal energy, 191
Germanic tribes: invasions of, 32–33
Germany: division of, 64, 65
Global village, 71
Gods and goddesses: Egyptian, 18; Greek, 22, 23; Roman, 25
Grammar: parts of speech, 265–268; plurals, 271–273; pronouns, 275–276; punctuation, 277–281; sentences, 264, 274; verb tenses, 269–271
Granivores, 217
Graphic representations: maps, 173; percentages, 175; plans, 172; scale, 172–173
Greece (ancient), 22–23; mathematics, 145, 146
Greenhouse effect, 66
Greenland, 95
Greenwich Mean Time, 76
Guilds, 43
Gunpowder: invention of, 45
Gutenberg, Johann, 44, 117
Gymnosperms, 246

H

Han rulers, 28
Harvey, William, 47
Hastings, Battle of, 33
Hawaii, 107
Hearing: facts about, 225
Heart, 220–221
Henry VIII, King of England, 39
Herbivores, 217
Hieroglyphics, 19, 117, 146
Highways: Roman, 24
Hinduism, 29
Hiroshima, 63, 192
History: timeline of, 12–13
Hitler, Adolf, 62, 63
Holocaust, 63
Holy Roman Empire, 35, 39
Holy Wars: Crusades, 40–41; Muslims, 31, 33
Homer, 128
Hominids, 11
Homonyms, 122
Hourglass, 207
House of Representatives, 52
Human body: blood, 220–221; digestion, 216; nervous system, 230–233; nutrition, 218–219; respiration, 214–215; senses, 222–227; skeletal system, 228–229
Human life: reproduction, 212–213; stages in, 213
Human rights, 72–73
Hunger in world, 85
Huns, 32
Hygrometer, 187
Hypersonic speed, 195

I

Ice: formation of, 180